Middle Class China

CSC CHINA PERSPECTIVES

Series Editor: David S.G. Goodman, *University of Sydney, Australia*

China is becoming an increasingly important influence on many countries across the globe, so that understanding China's society and culture, its history and development is a central intellectual challenge for the future. This valuable series introduces original studies that provide historical and comparative perspectives on China, as well as analyses of contemporary China under the pressure of economic growth.

The CSC China Perspectives series presents both high-quality monographs and edited collaborations, and is produced by the University of Sydney China Studies Centre (CSC). The CSC aims to harness its existing expertise in a wide range of disciplines to provide a greater understanding of China and its impact on local, regional and global affairs.

Titles in the series include:

China's Peasants and Workers: Changing Class Identities
Edited by Beatriz Carrillo and David S.G. Goodman

Middle Class China
Identity and Behaviour
Edited by Minglu Chen and David S.G. Goodman

Middle Class China

Identity and Behaviour

Edited by

Minglu Chen and David S.G. Goodman

University of Sydney, Australia

CSC CHINA PERSPECTIVES

THE UNIVERSITY OF
SYDNEY
CHINA STUDIES CENTRE

Edward Elgar

Cheltenham, UK • Northampton, MA, USA

Published by
Edward Elgar Publishing Limited
The Lypiatts
15 Lansdown Road
Cheltenham
Glos GL50 2JA
UK

Edward Elgar Publishing, Inc.
William Pratt House
9 Dewey Court
Northampton
Massachusetts 01060
USA

A catalogue record for this book
is available from the British Library

Library of Congress Control Number: 2012948161

This book is available electronically in the ElgarOnline.com Social and Political Science Subject Collection, E-ISBN 978 1 781 571 2

ISBN 978 1 78100 570 5

Typeset by Columns Design XML Ltd, Reading
Printed by MPG PRINTGROUP, UK

Contents

Figures

Tables

Contributors

Carolyn Cartier is Professor of Human Geography and China Studies at the University of Technology, Sydney, Australia. She works on urban and regional change and cultural political economy in China, including the role of the state in urban expansion, the politics of culture in urban redevelopment and the production–consumption transition in everyday urban life.

Minglu Chen is a lecturer in the China Studies Centre and the Department of Politics and International Relations at the University of Sydney, Australia. She works on social and political change in China, particularly at local level. She is currently undertaking research projects on new economic elites and, separately, the role of the Chinese People's Political Consultative Conferences. Her book *Tiger Girls: Women Entrepreneurs in the People's Republic of China* (Routledge) was published in 2011.

Dai Jianzhong is the Deputy Director of the Institute of Sociology, Beijing Academy of Social Science, and the Vice Secretary of the Beijing Sociological Association, China. His research interests are methodology, social stratification and class mobility. He has been the head investigator of the nationwide project 'Survey on Private Enterprises and Entrepreneurs (SPEEC) in China' since the mid-1980s. His works (in Chinese) include: *Employment and Labour Relations in Chinese Private Enterprises, Operation of Private Enterprises and Collective Characteristics of Private Entrepreneurs in China, Social Mobility in China during the Process of Modernization*.

David S.G. Goodman is Academic Director of the China Studies Centre, University of Sydney, Australia, where he is also Professor of Chinese Politics. His research concentrates on social and political change in China since the beginning of the twentieth century, especially at the local level. He is the editor of the *New Rich in China* (Routledge 2008) and the author of *Class and Social Stratification in China* (Polity Press 2012).

Hans Hendrischke is Professor of Chinese Business and Management at the University of Sydney, Australia. His research concentrates on the development of local-level business networks, and the relationships between enterprises and the state.

Li Chunling is Professor of Sociology at the Institute of Sociology of the Chinese Academy of Social Sciences, China. She received a BA and MA in history from Peking University and a PhD in sociology from the Graduate School of the Chinese Academy of Social Sciences. Her academic interests include social stratification and mobility, gender studies and the sociology of education. Her recent research projects concern educational inequality, China's middle class and generation stratification.

Jieyu Liu is a lecturer in China Studies at the University of Leeds, UK, having previously been a lecturer in Sociology at the University of Glasgow. She is the author of *Gender and Work in Urban China: Women Workers of the Unlucky Generation* (Routledge 2007) and the editor of *Social Transformation in China* (Routledge, forthcoming 2013). Since 2011 she has been the principal investigator for a UK Economic and Social Research Council (ESRC) funded project on ageing in rural China, examining the impact of rural–urban migration upon familial support for older people.

Jean-Louis Rocca is Professor at Sciences Po, Centre d'Études et de Recherches Internationales (CERI), Paris, France, and has taught at Tsinghua University (Beijing) from 2005 to 2011. His research concerns social stratification, the emergence of the middle class and social movements in urban China. He is the author of numerous books and articles in French, English and Chinese. He published (with Françoise Mengin) *Politics in China: Moving Frontiers* (Palgrave 2002).

Beibei Tang is a Postdoctoral Fellow at the Centre for Deliberative Democracy and Global Governance at The Australian National University, Canberra, Australia. She is currently working on a research project investigating deliberative governance and citizen participation in contemporary China. She is also working on a book manuscript based on her PhD research, which examines the life chances and upward social mobility mechanisms of middle class community residents in post-reform urban China.

Jonathan Unger, a sociologist, is Professor in the Australian National University's Political and Social Change Department and is Director of the ANU's Contemporary China Centre, Canberra, Australia. He has published more than a dozen books about China, including *Education* *under Mao: Class and Competition in Canton Schools* (Colombia University Press 1982), *The Transformation of Rural China* (M.E. Sharpe 2002) and, as co-author, *Chen Village: Revolution to Globalization* (University of California Press 2009). He co-edited *The China Journal,* one of the two preeminent journals in the field, for 18 years from 1987 to 2005.

Yang Jing is Visiting Research Fellow at the East Asian Institute, National University of Singapore, Kent Ridge, Singapore. She received her BSc in Sociology from The Chinese University of Hong Kong in 2002, MSc and DPhil in Sociology from the University of Oxford in 2008. Her research interests lie in the area of social stratification and class mobility in contemporary China, particularly the rise of the 'new middle class' and the formation and transformation of private entrepreneurs, with reference to those as revealed in most industrial societies and post state-socialist countries.

Preface

Discussion of China's middle class is almost ubiquitous, yet the idea is both poorly conceptualized and for the most part empirically untested. Within China there is a tendency to operationalize the notion of the middle class as though it were a Marxist class concept. Outside China there is a tendency to describe all changes of China's Reform Era as leading to the development of that country's middle class, and with it the inevitability of market capitalism and liberal democracy. Reform has certainly increased the size of China's middle class since 1978. At the same time, there is really no single middle class but a series of middle classes. These different middle classes clearly represent a variety of examples of social stratification with different identities and behavioural characteristics. There is, however, little in their behaviour to suggest a propensity for radical socio-political change, let alone a predisposition to either market capitalism or liberal democracy.

This volume concentrates on the behaviour and identity of different elements of China's middle classes in order to analyse the dynamic processes of socio-political change of which they are part. It follows Chinese practice in including entrepreneurs alongside managers, professionals, administrators, intellectuals and teachers as part of the growing middle class. It also follows the practices of analysis outside China in identifying the middle class as much by its consumption – notably of housing, education and lifestyle – as by its place in the class structure. The picture of China's middle class that emerges is one that is inherently complex, but it is one that places the middle class at the centre of the social and political establishment.

In the organization of any workshop and the production of any edited volume, there are always acknowledgements to be made to those whose names do not appear in the following pages. In this case, we would like to thank all those who attended the workshop on 'Class and Class Consciousness in China' in Sydney in January and February 2011 and gave generously of their time and ideas. We would particularly like to thank our co-organizer Beatriz Carrillo and Suisheng Zhao, both of whom have been unflappable sources of support to this volume. We would also like to thank Zoe Morrison, Nisha Brooks and Megan Barry –

the administrative staff of the China Studies Centre – for their admirable organization.

Minglu Chen and David S.G. Goodman
China Studies Centre
University of Sydney
February 2012

Abbreviations

ACFIC	All-China Federation of Industry and Commerce
CASS	Chinese Academy of Social Sciences
CCA	China Consumer Association
CCP	Chinese Communist Party
CEE	Central and Eastern Europe
CPPCC	Chinese People's Political Consultative Conference
EAMC	East Asian Middle Class project
HPF	Housing Provident Fund
HRS	Household Responsibility System
ICC	Shanghai International Commerce Centre
IELTS	International English Language Testing System
NGO	non-government organization
PRC	People's Republic of China
RMB	Renminbi
S/COE	state and/or collective-owned enterprise
SHKP	Sun Hung Kai Properties
SOE	state-owned enterprise
SPEEC	Survey on Private Enterprises and Entrepreneurs in China
TOEFL	Test of English as a Foreign Language
TVEs	township and village enterprises

Introduction: middle class China – discourse, structure and practice

Minglu Chen and David S.G. Goodman

Three decades of economic growth have dramatically altered China's social structure. There is a widespread understanding both inside and outside the People's Republic of China (PRC) that growth has resulted in an increase in numbers and a higher profile for the middle class (Li, Cheng, 2010a). There could of course be few greater contrasts between the last three decades and the pre-Reform Era in China. In the PRC's first three decades, public discourse was all about soldiers, peasants and workers. Consumption, let alone conspicuous consumption, could lead to political problems as well as social ostracization. Since 1978, however, entrepreneurs, managers and professionals have come to occupy the public limelight, and while consumption still remains a relatively small part of China's GDP there is a considerable trend towards a consumer society in urban China (Davis, 2000; Cartier, 2008).

Ideas about the middle classes were not noticeably part of Marx's analysis of social and political change, and Communist Party-states have historically had little to say about the phenomenon (Inkeles, 1971). In the PRC during the years of Mao-dominated politics (1956–76) the equation of the middle class with the bourgeoisie, and the associations of both with capitalism when capitalism was the focus of official criticism, effectively removed the concept of a middle class from both the political lexicon and the social sciences. The use of the term 'middle class' (*zhongchan jieji*) or 'middle strata' (*zhongchan jieceng*) – the latter somewhat politically more secure – only started to (re)emerge publicly after the Chinese Communist Party (CCP) adjusted its attitude to entrepreneurs in and after 2000 (Zhou, 2005). Previously viewed negatively (Zang, 2008) and banned from CCP membership, entrepreneurs were socially and politically resuscitated when the then President of the PRC and General Secretary of the CCP, Jiang Zemin, announced his theory of the 'Three Represents' which, inter alia, highlighted the positive role of the entrepreneur in national development. Most remarkably the CCP quickly came to embrace the concept, not simply of the possibility of a progressive middle class, but of the desirability of creating a middle class China (Guo, 2008a).

Much is clearly expected from China's growing middle class. The CCP looks to the creation of a substantial middle class not simply for a source of legitimacy bought through economic prosperity, but also as the foundation of social harmony (Guo, 2012). China's urban population sees the development of a middle class that they may emulate as fulfilment of a promise of increasing prosperity (Liang, 2011). The outside world looks to this growing middle class as a driver for greater democracy in China (with which it believes it will feel more comfortable) and the PRC's greater global integration (Santoro, 2009).

There is, however, a paradox in all this excitement about social change in China. The middle class is a powerful and mobilizing idea but it is a relatively weak analytical tool. The idea of the middle class implies a comfortable standard of living, social and political stability and majority politics. On the other hand, the constituent social base of the group identified as the Chinese middle class is far from clear. The middle class may be taken to include a wide range of people engaged in a wide range of activities: entrepreneurs, managers of economic enterprises, professionals, officials, teachers and administrators are all often described as part of the middle class. It would clearly be a mistake to think that there is or could be a single middle class, let alone that there are ready commonalities or shared interests amongst all these different elements. It is extremely possible that there may be conflicting interests within these different elements of the middle classes: professionals and entrepreneurs, or entrepreneurs and their managers, may well, for example, exist in various creative tensions. Disaggregating the focus of analysis would seem like a necessary first step before considering the ways in which the emergence of middle classes may have effected or presaged change.

LOCATING THE MIDDLE CLASS

The middle class has long been an elusive concept. Though clearly related to theories of class, it is not strictly speaking part of the more detailed system of thought developed by Marx and Weber about the material wealth, roles in processes of production, exploitation and social status of various classes (Wright, 2005). Outside the pages of academic analysis the middle class is, more often than not, statistically defined in terms of its wealth, income or consumption rather than in terms of less tangible indicators such as class, status and power. There is a certain logic to a statistical identification of the middle class. From this perspective the behaviour of those occupying the middle percentiles (whatever percentage is adopted) has at least a quantifiable basis that might otherwise not be so readily available (Pizzigati, 2010).

At the same time there are both theoretical and practical problems that attend this otherwise straightforward approach to understanding the political economy. Theoretically, class is not just a matter of wealth, income or consumption. Complex societies have multiple hierarchies of different kinds of power. It is the interaction between these hierarchies that commands attention. In any case, wealth, income and consumption may not always be visible and straightforward in practice. These practical problems are particularly acute in the case of the PRC where much wealth and income may be concealed for a variety of reasons. Income is often taken as a proxy for wealth, but in the PRC many positions have long had benefits of housing and health services included as 'hidden income'.

Almost universally, consumption and lifestyle are regarded as markers of the middle class (Fussell, 1992; Savage et al., 1995). Secluded housing estates, the best schools for their children – including private and restricted-access schools where these are available – and access to privileged and often private health services are obvious characteristics, as is the consumption of relatively expensive clothing, automobiles, personal decoration and holidays. The consumerism and lifestyle aspirations of the middle classes are both mapped and promoted by marketers, and China has been no exception in the trend for ubiquitous advertising of the latest brands and products, especially in the last decade (Hanser, 2008; Lu, 2008; Sun, 2008; Zhang, Li, 2010).

In the PRC during the last decade a wide range of different groups of people have laid claim to middle class identity. These include social categories that have emerged only with the recent period of dramatic economic growth, such as entrepreneurs, lawyers and real estate agents. There are also large numbers of professions that existed before, but have changed their manner of operation and increased dramatically in numbers as a result of the introduction of economic restructuring, such as accountants, enterprise managers and architects. Finally, there are those in service positions that have long existed in the PRC and who might also be considered middle class, such as teachers, welfare workers, administrative staff and minor officials of the Party-state. Some elements of the PRC's middle class may be new, but clearly the PRC has long had a middle class, as one would expect from a modernizing regime (Goodman, 2008b).

The explanation of why there is an exceptionally wide range of identities and an apparent inherent variability in the concept of the middle class is largely historical (Robison and Goodman, 1992). At the beginning of the nineteenth century in North West Europe, the driving force of change was the new bourgeoisie, the entrepreneurs and owners of capital who led the Industrial Revolution. They were regarded as the 'middle' class because they were in between the court and the aristocracy of Europe's *ancien régime* on the one hand, and the burghers and the townspeople on the other (Pilbeam, 1990; Mooers, 1991). With time these captains of industry, though clearly not all entrepreneurs by any stretch of the imagination, became an integral part of the ruling class in many different ways, gaining access not only to public and political leadership, but also (in the case of the United Kingdom) ennoblement.

With time too the state became more dominant both through its role towards the end of the nineteenth century in the later industrializing countries, such as Germany and Japan, and generally through the development of the liberal welfare state (Kurth, 1979). A key result of the developmental history of capitalism was the emergence of new social categories of professionals and managers who served the needs of both economic development and the state. These were middle class because they were between economic and political leadership on the one hand, and 'the masses' on the other. They included accountants, lawyers and managers who serviced and supported economic activities, public servants and other direct state employees who administered the operation of the state and its activities, and doctors, nurses, dentists, teachers and university staff who developed and looked after the individual needs of the population. By the middle of the twentieth century, this manifestation of the middle class had become known as the managerial revolution (Burnham, 1941; Galbraith, 1968).

Clearly it is possible to find echoes of all these different dimensions of middle class identity in the PRC's recent experience. Most obviously there is little problem in identifying China's increasing numbers of professionals and managers with the middle classes of other countries and other periods. From the perspective of North America or Europe in the early twenty-first century, however, it is difficult to regard entrepreneurs as middle class per se. Indeed, in the current development of the PRC it is equally clear that many of the more successful early entrepreneurs are rapidly becoming part of the political as well as the economic establishment (Chen and Dickson, 2010). At the same time, the social and economic function of the entrepreneurial class in the contemporary PRC has certain close resonances with their early nineteenth-century counterparts in North West Europe. While not quite as excluded from the political process as their European precursors, the PRC's entrepreneurs did emerge, to some extent, in a social and political space between the earlier political and (under state socialism, by definition) economic establishment on the one hand, and the then political nation of workers and peasants on the other.

THE IMPACT OF THE MIDDLE CLASS

The parallels between the emergence of the Chinese middle class with the emergence of an entrepreneurial class in nineteenth-century Europe is an obvious place to start any assessment of its impact on social change. There is a ready assumption that the emergence or growth of the middle classes everywhere, including in the PRC, will lead almost automatically to democratic change (Robison and Goodman, 1996). A substantial proportion of the research on the development of the middle class in the PRC during the last three decades, inside as well as outside the country, has been dedicated to investigating the prospects for regime change.

There was some early research – after only the first decade of economic restructuring – which concluded that democratic change would follow from the emergence of new entrepreneurial classes in the PRC (Glassman, 1991). Interestingly, most of the subsequent research on the topic has advised strongly against this possibility, stressing instead the close relationship between the new entrepreneurs and the Party-state, as well as the focus on the maintenance of the political status quo (Pearson, 1997; Goodman, 2001; Dickson, 2003a, 2003b, 2004, 2008). The explanation of this apparent difference lies in the genesis of the new entrepreneurs and the subsequent reactions of the political establishment. In the history of nineteenth-century Europe there is at least the myth that the new entrepreneurs were excluded from political power, and therefore needed to widen the franchise and organize as a class to obtain a place in the establishment. In China, many of the new entrepreneurs did not emerge completely from outside the establishment of the Party-state, and where they did they were rapidly incorporated into it.

Private ownership was not the cornerstone of the PRC model of enterprise development. In the first place there was no property law guaranteeing the ownership rights of private entrepreneurs until 2006. There certainly were some private entrepreneurs who decided to go it alone once economic restructuring away from state socialism started in the mid-1980s. At the same time these entrepreneurs' activities were mainly small scale, and across the country many had to remain so if they wanted to stay private. Private entrepreneurs – owner-operators of businesses – who wanted to grow were essentially often required to surrender equity, though not necessarily managerial control, to local government. Without links to local government they were unable to access the elements of production – land, labour and capital – that they need in order to expand.

As these comments about the development of the private sector suggest, the larger-scale and usually more successful enterprises were hybrid public–private enterprises in a somewhat bewildering array of forms (Naughton, 2010). The township and village enterprises (TVEs) that started to emerge in the early 1980s were the first of the type and characteristic of this approach to enterprise development. Under state socialism rural China was organized into People's Communes and their economic activities were not part of the state but rather part of the collective sector. While their output was part of the State Plan, their inputs were not provided by government, and responsibility for production and income generation rested with the owners of the collective: the local peasants. With the start of the Reform Era many rural collectives, especially those in peri-urban areas, found themselves able to develop small industrial concerns, often under the leadership of entrepreneurial types. The issue of ownership was not so much negotiated as ignored.

The final piece in the enterprise development jigsaw was the restructuring of the former state-owned enterprises (SOEs) of the state-socialist era. Here the initiative came from the top-down and the entrepreneurs in question were state managers volunteering or being pushed into new entrepreneurial positions. Many SOEs have continued to operate but with changes that have rendered them more economically efficient. Under the socialist system, large-scale SOEs not only had a core economic activity but would provide housing, canteens, schools, hospitals and other aspects of social welfare to their staff and their families. Since reform, all these operations have been commercialized, along with non-core economic activities that might be commercialized. For example, a factory's truck workshop might have become a new freight company. The staff would have been provided with the original workshop's equipment and assets, and the former SOE parent company would have retained some equity (often half) as the new enterprise developed. In the same process new entrepreneurial managers emerged to lead what remained of the old SOE.

In sum, the relationship between the new entrepreneurs and the Party-state is close, regardless of whether they are former Party-state managers who became new entrepreneurs in a continuing SOE, those who formed new public–private hybrid companies, or private entrepreneurs who quickly learnt the rules of the new game. While it is reasonable to expect all the former SOE managers to be members of the

CCP, many of the so-called private entrepreneurs were also members even before they became entrepreneurs. Surveys from the late 1990s and early 2000s indicate that about a third of private entrepreneurs were CCP members before establishing their new enterprises (Goodman, 2001; Dickson, 2003a). Many of the new entrepreneurs, then, either came from within the Party-state or were CCP members. For those with no such background, the CCP has gone out of its way to bring the new entrepreneurs into the fold of the Party-state, either as CCP members – which accounts for a further quarter of private entrepreneurs (Goodman, 2001; Dickson, 2008) – or by appointing them to positions in People's Congresses and People's Consultative Conferences.

Under these circumstances it is no surprise that there is little evidence of the entrepreneurial middle classes initiating political change. Nonetheless, it may still be the case that other sections of the expanding middle classes – especially intellectuals and other related professionals – may take the lead in this regard. Here the evidence is more mixed but, even so, it suggests not so much the advocacy of fundamental regime change but a greater concern with effecting adjustments to the existing system, particularly with respect to social concerns such as poverty or the environment, or the protection of individual rights. Water usage and environmental degradation have been topics for mobilization on several occasions (Mertha, 2011). Gender issues and women's rights have also had a fairly high profile in urban China, as well as public health issues (Edwards, 2008; Hood, 2012; Rofel, 2012). However, the concept of a non-government organization (NGO) in a system that does not allow for the possibility of a separate sphere of non-governmental activity leads to some interesting situations, including the need (from the Party-state's point of view) for officially recognized and sanctioned NGOs. All the same there have been active NGOs and specific campaigns led by academics, lawyers, doctors and others, across a range of issues.

Housing is one area where the expanding professional and middle classes have become particularly active in pursuit of individual rights. However, this may not be just a middle class preoccupation since, with the commercialization of urban housing, almost everyone has become mindful of their rights and entitlements. On the other hand the middle classes have demanded, and largely obtained, housing that meets the standards of their newly acquired sensibilities. Often this means gated communities, excellent transport facilities and local schools. Sometimes compromises with local government – such as the supply of a certain proportion of social housing alongside or within new developments – are required in order to ensure the delivery of conditions now considered appropriate (Tomba and Tang, 2008).

UNDERSTANDING THE MIDDLE CLASS

Identifying the social space occupied by the growing middle classes is of course not the same as identifying the social backgrounds, attitudes and propensity to action of the individuals themselves. The purpose of the chapters in this volume is to take the discussion of China's middle classes further in those regards. The aim is not simply to produce a more nuanced understanding of the structure of the middle class in the PRC, but to identify the dynamic elements in their behaviour.

Li Chunling (Chapter 1) is a sociologist in the PRC whose starting point is to question her colleagues' insistence that the emergence of a larger middle class will have significant sociopolitical consequences. In her view they argue too much about whether the middle class is a stabilizing or a destabilizing force in society, and whether it will promote a democratic transition or act to preserve the existing order; as a result they advise Central Government either to control the middle class or to enlarge it. Through an examination of the sociopolitical attitudes of the middle classes as reported in survey data, Li concludes that these views are too simplistic in their explanation of complex processes, and too extreme in their analysis of consequences. The views of middle class professionals, as reflected in survey data, are somewhat contradictory: They are not in favour of state authoritarianism but they are the most satisfied with their current living standards and so wish to avoid sociopolitical change. The new entrepreneurs and the managerial class are the most conservative: accepting of both state authoritarianism and social inequality. Intellectuals and the marginal members of the middle class are, Li finds, the least accepting of social inequality and state authoritarianism.

Carolyn Cartier (Chapter 2) is concerned with the development of a consumer society, with consumption as the defining feature of middle class China. In particular, her chapter is concerned with understanding the development of the middle class urban environment. Beijing is in the process of turning to household consumption to transform the country from a production-led to a consumption-led domestic economy, in which private household consumption – rather than continued state investment – drives annual GDP growth. In the process of this planned transition, consumption is proving to be a key context for debate over diverse issues of social and economic change. Cartier examines several conjunctures between consumption and class formation in urban China, and concludes that the rapidity of urban development and economic restructuring has compressed the trajectory of the production–consumption transition and limited middle class hopes and possibilities.

Housing is the subject of Beibei Tang's analysis of middle class consumerist behaviour in Chapter 3. With commercialization of the housing market, home purchase has become a family's major investment. It is a process that has created new social groups and class subjects who are defined by their capacity for consumption and their pursuit of specific lifestyles and social distinctions. This has been argued as being particularly the case for gated communities, high-status accommodation characterized by its provision of privileged lifestyles, privacy, private property and high-level services, and which keeps other social groups, such as the urban poor and migrant workers, out. Through a study of gated communities in Shenyang, Tang presents a different argument. She accepts that these gated communities have led to the formation of new privileged social groups but defines these as housing status groups that play a different role from, and are not the same as, class. She identifies two different paths to gated community residence, only one of which is wealth. (The other is through allocation from an administrative hierarchy.) While these housing communities may eventually contribute to class formation, at present this is not the case, with class consciousness and housing community consciousness each having its own separate existence and manifestation.

Jieyu Liu in Chapter 4 moves the discussion from considerations of class and consumption in the urban environment into the workplace and considerations of the relationships between gender and class. As she points out, gender is often sidelined by discussions of class, though the two are clearly mutually constitutive. Through an ethnographic study of a specific workplace she demonstrates how gender is a major determinant to career and life chances. In the words of one of her interviewee sales staff: 'We are not white-collar workers; actually we are just blue-collar workers that happen to work in the offices'. Gender is not, however, simply a marker of work difference. As Liu points out, it is a major determinant of class formation.

As Beibei Tang and Jonathan Unger point out in their chapter examining the urban educated middle class (Chapter 5), the numbers of lawyers, IT consultants, teachers and other professionals is now so large that they set the tone and tastes for 'respectable' society. Given that the PRC remains an authoritarian political system, it might be thought most likely that this group would be at the forefront of voices arguing for change. In fact the opposite appears to be the case: the urban educated middle class is solidly behind the maintenance of the status quo. The authors conducted a series of interviews with academics at universities and research institutes in Shenyang and Guangzhou between 2007 and 2009. Those interviewed covered several generations of intellectuals. The chapter reports on the changes in the circumstances of these intellectual professionals as reported through these interviews. In particular they were asked about their material wealth and attitudes towards the regime. Given that in the 1980s there was much resistance to the regime and its policy of economic restructuring from precisely these urban educated intellectuals, one important aim was to see how later policy may have been adapted to ensure greater loyalty from this social category. The authors conclude that the Party-state has certainly succeeded in this regard.

Jean-Louis Rocca (Chapter 6) is also concerned with the potential for the development of a Chinese middle class to lead to political change, and he too is wary of jumping to any such conclusion. Through a study of homeowners' movements, he questions whether the role of the white-collar, managerial and professional middle classes in the democratization process is so clearly established, and whether the political behaviour of the Chinese middle class is indeed comparable to that of its counterparts in Western and East Asian countries. He chooses homeowners as his focus because they are often identified as representing the politically conscious vanguard of the Chinese middle classes. Certainly there have been a growing number of social conflicts that have mobilized homeowners to defend their property rights. He examines the work of scholars and journalists in China on this topic, and draws on research that has been undertaken at Tsinghua University. Rocca has also interviewed homeowners throughout Beijing about conflicts in housing communities, as well as activists in homeowner movements. He concludes that while the homeowning middle classes may be able to mobilize and fight on specific issues, there is neither much thought for or desire to engage in wider attempts at political action, whether liberalization or anything else.

Hans Hendrischke's approach in Chapter 7 to the question of the possible political interaction between the Party-state and the entrepreneurial middle classes bears heavily on the new institutional economics and, like Rocca, he is wary of drawing too close a comparison with European antecedents. Hendrischke carefully disaggregates the environment within which entrepreneurs must now act, and draws a significant distinction between the local Party-state, within which the entrepreneurs are and must be embedded, and the central Party-state, with its control of regime maintenance and which for most is almost another country. There clearly is change and accommodation in both politics and economic management at local level, but regime change is not on the agenda. At the same time, as Hendrischke points out, there is an aspect of economic development to these concerns. Entrepreneurs in the more developed areas of China are more likely in many senses to be politically active, and to be able to positively influence, if not capture the institutions of the local Party-state.

In the book's final chapter, Yang Jing and Dai Jianzhong undertake a social analysis of the PRC's private entrepreneurs, based on surveys undertaken for the Chinese Academy of Social Sciences (CASS) over two decades. This is the largest and most comprehensive survey of entrepreneurs undertaken in the PRC. They are concerned to identify where these new entrepreneurs came from and why they chose to become guinea pigs in economic reform at a time when the future was so uncertain. They seek to establish whether the new entrepreneurs share a series of distinctive features and whether the ways they run their businesses have anything in common. In particular they also want to know if the pattern of enterprise development and the characteristics of enterprise management develop over time. The examination of risk-taking is a large part of their study. Dramatically, they highlight a major change in the emergence of enterprises and the development of enterprise management and managers around the year 2000. Up to that time, more private entrepreneurs were from lower social status families and were greater risk-takers. After 2000, entrepreneurs were more likely to be better educated, and considerably more socially and politically net-worked.

There is a common view that the middle classes are homogeneous, and that this homogeneity is not only true within a particular society, but also globally. Certainly, the assumption of middle class homogeneity and stability links policy-makers in Beijing with policy-makers in other world capitals. The myth of 'people like us' is very powerful. The world is not, however, that simple and there are national and local variations in middle class formation and impact, as this collection demonstrates. There is also, again as this collection demonstrates, considerable debate over the identity and behaviour of China's middle classes. The authors hope that this volume contributes to a more nuanced assessment of China's middle classes, an assessment that may facilitate a more accurate assessment of their very specific concerns, social positioning and aspirations.

1. Sociopolitical attitudes of the middle class and the implications for political transition

Li Chunling

Since the beginning of the twenty-first century, a social group with higher income, higher education and higher occupational prestige than the majority of the largely rural Chinese population has been emerging in Chinese cities. The media refers to this group as the 'middle class'. Even though the definition of the middle class is disputed, there is no doubt that it exists in China and that it is expanding quickly (Li, Chunling, 2010). The middle class is gaining attention from the public, the business sector and from policy-makers alike, as well as from sociologists, economists and political scientists. Sociologists in particular have devoted attention to this group, focusing on its sociopolitical functions. Chinese sociologists are debating questions such as: What are the sociopolitical consequences of the emergence of the middle class? Is the middle class a stable or unstable influence with respect to existing authority? Will the middle class promote a democratic transition or preserve the existing political order?

Social analysts give two opposing answers to these questions. Some argue that the middle class is a social force that promotes democracy and hence constitutes a destabilizing force for the government. They expect the government will take careful measures to control this group. But others consider the middle class to be a stabilizing force that supports the existing political and social order. Hence, they advise the government to act to enlarge it. This chapter attempts to adjudicate between these contrasting perspectives by examining public opinion data on the socio-political attitudes of the Chinese middle class. It concludes that both views are too simple in their explanation of complex processes, and too extreme in their analysis of consequences.

THE SOCIOPOLITICAL FUNCTIONS OF THE MIDDLE CLASS

Since Chinese researchers began to discuss the possibility of an emerging middle class in the 1980s, there has been a lively controversy over the sociopolitical functions of the middle class. In the 1980s, radical intellectuals were expecting a democratic movement propelled by the rising middle class, which they perceived as the 'most active supporters of democratization' (Liu, 1988, pp. 62–3; Han, Hulong, 1989, pp. 27–9). By the 1990s, most sociologists had changed their stance, describing the middle class as a stabilizing force for the political order, supporting the government's policies of economic reform and thus serving as a driving force of economic development (Zhang, 1998; Li, 1999, 2001). However, in recent years, a few sociologists have questioned the view that the middle class is a 'stabilizing force', claiming that the middle class could, in fact, destabilize political authority (Zhang, 2009).

The Middle Class as a Destabilizing Force

Sociopolitical theorists from the West, such as Lipset, Huntington and Glassman, suggest that there is a correlation between the emergence of a middle class and the development of a political democracy (Lipset, 1960; Huntington, 1991; Glassman, 1995, 1997). Lipset developed a wealth theory of democracy, arguing, 'the more well-to-do a nation, the greater the chances that it will sustain democracy' (Lipset, 1960, p. 31). He argues that democracy is related to economic development because, in wealthy countries, there is a diamond-shaped system of social stratification in which the majority of the population is situated in the middle stratum of the social hierarchy, and that this stratum is most likely to support a democratic government. Huntington supports Lipset's argument, suggesting, 'the most active supporters of [the third wave of] democratization came from the urban middle class' (Huntington, 1991, p. 67). Other theorists cite the East Asian and South East Asian countries and regions (South Korea, Taiwan, Philippines, Thailand and so on), where the rising middle classes have brought about democratic movements and a series of sociopolitical turbulences. Many scholars with a Western academic background have followed this view to discuss the sociopolitical function of China's middle class (Johnston, 2004; Chen and Lu, 2006; Goodman, 2008a). Some Chinese sociologists, such as Li Lulu and Zhang Yi, take a similar position, arguing that the middle class will become a potent agent in the sociopolitical transition toward democracy and civil society (Li, Lulu, 2008; Zhang, 2009).

The Middle Class as a Stabilizing Force

On the other hand, the most influential Chinese sociologists argue that the Chinese middle class is a sociopolitical stabilizer because middle class individuals tend to be politically conservative. Li Qian and Zhou Xiaohong suggest the following potential explanations for Chinese middle class conservatism: first, they benefitted the most from the economic reforms and subsequent rapid economic growth; second, they depend heavily on the state, which treats them favourably and protects their interests, and thus they have a propensity for state authoritarianism; and third, they show apolitical attitudes and are materialistic (Li, 2001; Zhou, 2005). Scholars holding this view insist that the middle classes in most societies are stabilizing forces for existing regimes because: first, the middle class as a buffer layer between upper class and underclass may ease the tension between these two classes; second, a middle class with modest attitudes and conservative ideology will be helpful to prevent political radicalism breeding in society; third, the middle class as the most active consumer group will be helpful in stimulating economic growth, which will in turn ensure political stability (Li, 2001, p. 18). Some researchers who study the East Asian middle classes propose an additional explanation. Because of traditional forms of political culture, the East Asian middle classes prefer political conservatism and rely on the state for economic security (Jones and Brown, 1994; Jones, 1998). Members of the Asian middle classes are thus seen to hold contradictory attitudes about politics. On the one hand, they are inclined to support liberalism and democracy. On the other hand, they desire sociopolitical stability and are subservient to the authoritarian state in the interest of economic security (Hsiao, 1999, 2001, 2006). These studies find that the East Asian middle classes usually rise in periods of rapid economic growth, in which authoritarian states implement policies to promote economic growth. The middle classes benefit greatly from these policies and thus support authoritarian states in return for economic security and benefits.

The Government's Query on the Sociopolitical Function of a Rising Middle Class

The controversy about the role of a growing middle class in China extends beyond academic discussion and into politics. For political reasons China's authorities have long disliked the term 'middle class'. The term was almost prohibited in formal publications during the 1990s. This was because the term had acquired political connotations when it was referenced by liberal scholars during the 1980s. At that time, 'middle class' mainly denoted private entrepreneurs, a newly emerging social group in the 1980s, which developed quickly in the 1990s. Liberal intellectuals thought the growth of this social group would bring about political change, such as political democratization. Theorists of the Communist Party in the late 1980s and early 1990s asserted that liberal scholars tried to overthrow the socialist system through creating a middle class. Accordingly, authorities continued to deem the middle class a threat to the existing political system (He, 1987, p. 2, 1988, p. 4, 1990, p. 1).

In the late 1990s a few influential sociologists argued that a large middle class was one of the general characteristics of modern societies and could be a stabilizing force, rather than a destabilizing force, in society (Li, 2001, p. 19; Lu, 2001, p. 62). These sociological arguments have become more prevalent since the late 1990s and seem to have gradually convinced Chinese policy-makers that a rising middle class could be a positive element in maintaining political and social stability. These sociologists especially stressed that the growth of the middle class would help to reduce the income gap, which the state considered to be one of Chinese society's most serious problems, one that could even trigger political unrest.

Although political leaders seemed to partly accept this view, they have remained politically distrustful of the middle class. Undoubtedly, the rising middle class will be conducive to economic development. This is especially evidenced in the consumer market, where the middle class has been showing increasing spending power. Even during the financial crisis of 2009, China's middle class retained its strong spending power. However, the authorities remain uncertain about the political influence of the middle class, and the government continues to prefer the term 'middle-income stratum' to the term 'middle class'. In November 2002 Jiang Zemin, then secretary general of the Chinese Communist Party (CCP), stated in his report to the Sixteenth National Party Congress that 'expanding the middle-level-income group' was one of the policy targets of the government. Some analysts considered this statement to be a signal that the government would make an effort to develop the middle class, or middle stratum. Since then 'cultivating' and 'expanding' the middle stratum as an income or consumer group, but not a social group, has been one of the social development goals that the Chinese government has pursued. However, the government has not yet determined whether it should develop a true middle class and whether it would be a good or bad thing for its political rule. The current top priority of the Chinese government is to preserve social and political stability. As such it has become a critical issue for the government to make the political function of the rising middle class clear.

Research Framework and Measurement Method

How can the sociopolitical function of the middle class be clarified? Is the middle class a stabilizing force or a destabilizing force? Chinese sociologists try to answer these questions by examining attitudes of the middle class. They build a link between the sociopolitical function and sociopolitical attitudes of middle class. The middle class, they argue, is a stabilizing force if its members take conservative attitudes. On the other hand, the middle class becomes a destabilizing force if the middle class holds liberal or radical attitudes. Following this logic, a few researchers have tried to examine the sociopolitical attitudes of China's middle class in order to gauge their function (Chen and Lu, 2006; Zhang, 2009). However, such research has reached conclusions based on simple measurements of several scattered items obtained through opinion questions, but not through a systematic measurement of sociopolitical attitudes. The result has been vague and weak evidence in support of conclusions. In addition, it remains unclear whether the middle class is conservative or liberal in its sociopolitical attitudes. It is impossible to reach a convincing conclusion without a clear distinction between conservative and liberal attitudes. This chapter tries to construct an ideal dichotomy of conservative and liberal sociopolitical attitudes, to measure related attitudes of the middle class and other classes based on this dichotomous framework, and to answer the question about the sociopolitical function of the middle class.

CONSERVATISM AND LIBERALISM

In order to construct a comparative framework, we need to clarify the distinct differences between conservative and liberal sociopolitical attitudes toward certain issues, and then find a specific measurement tool to test them.

Conservatism and liberalism as two major political ideologies have had a long history and have been deemed as opposing ideologies in the political fields of many countries. However, the specific meanings of conservatism and liberalism differ partly in different periods and countries (and in different fields: political conservatism and liberalism is very different from economic conservatism and liberalism). Here we choose several major features of conservative and liberal sociopolitical attitudes generally identified by political scientists, and which are relevant to the specific situation of China. The most notable distinction between conservatism and liberalism is the attitude toward sociopolitical change or evolution. Conservatism is inclined to a sceptical attitude towards change and enjoys the status quo, while liberalism prefers social evolution and is dissatisfied with the current situation. If change is inevitable, conservatism likes gradualism but liberalism favours radicalism. The second difference between conservatism and liberalism is related to attitudes towards the state or authority. Conservatism distrusts democracy and prefers authoritative leadership or a strong state while liberalism proclaims the freedom of the individual and advocates political democracy. The third disparity between these two ideologies involves social justice or egalitarianism. Conservatism pays more attention to the defence of property than to justice and equality, while liberalism stresses equality before property rights (Nisbet, 1986; Eccleshall, 1994; Leach, 2002).

Based on these features of conservative and liberal attitudes, we may propose three criteria for classifying these attitudes toward certain issues. These three criteria are all related to the hypotheses of 'stabilizing force' and 'destabilizing force' that theorists debate as the sociopolitical function of the middle class. The first criterion is *satisfaction*, which tests individuals' feelings toward the status quo. High satisfaction implies less expectation of change (conservatism) while less satisfaction hints at more expectation of change (liberalism). The second criterion is *authoritarianism*, which examines individuals' attitudes toward the state and government. Approval of the existing government and preference for state authoritarianism indicates a desire to keep political stability (conservatism) but disapproval of the existing government and preference for a political democracy denotes a wish to promote political change (liberalism). The third criterion is *egalitarianism*, which tests individuals' values with regard to social justice. Less egalitarianism signifies a wish to retain the existing institutions and social order (conservatism) and more egalitarianism represents a willingness to change the current institutions and social order (liberalism) (Table 1.1).

Table 1.1   *Ideal dichotomy of sociopolitical attitudes of conservatism and liberalism*

Criteria	Conservatism	Liberalism	Index of Measurement
Satisfaction: basic feeling toward the status quo	Feeling satisfied and disliking change	Feeling dissatisfied and hoping for some change	1 Satisfaction with individual lifestyle (life-satisfaction index) 2 Satisfaction with social situation (social-satisfaction index)
Authoritarianism: basic attitudes toward the state and government	High confidence in government; preference for authoritarian state	Low confidence in government; preference for political democracy	3 Confidence in government (government-confidence index) 4 Acceptance of state authoritarianism (authoritativeness index)
Egalitarianism: basic value placed on social justice	High acceptance of inequality; concealing interest conflict between groups	Low acceptance of inequality; sympathy for disadvantaged groups and low class	5 Tolerance of social inequality (inequality-perception index) 6 Perception of social conflict (conflict-consciousness index)

Issues of Measurement

In order to test these three criteria through a measurement of attitudes in a public opinion survey, six multi-item indices have been designed to represent the criteria, two indices for each criterion. *Satisfaction* is represented by a life-satisfaction index and social-satisfaction index; *authoritarianism* is represented by a government-confidence index and an authoritativeness index; and *egalitarianism* is represented by an inequality-perception index and a conflict-consciousness index (see Table 1.1). The values of indices are calculated by the scores of two or more questions the respondents answer in the survey. The scores of the questions are calculated based on a Likert scale. Table 1.2 lists these questions and the scores of answers. The measuring items (questions) of each index are selected through use of Cronbach's Alpha and factor analysis.

Table 1.2 Measurement of indices

Index	Question	Score
Life-satisfaction	1 Compared with five years ago, your current living condition is:	Much better = 2 Better = 1
	2 You think your living condition after five years will be:	No change = 0 Worse = −1 Much worse = −2
Social-satisfaction	3 What do you think about the current situation of social stability in our country?	Very stable = 2 Stable = 1 I don't know = 0 Unstable = −1 Very unstable = −2
	4 How do you feel about the current situation of our society in general?	Very harmonious = 2 Harmonious = 1 I don't know = 0 Disharmonious = −1 Very disharmonious = −2
Government-confidence	5 Do you trust the following governmental organizations or functions? A Central government B Local government C Government media D Statistics released by the government E Petition institutions F Judges and policemen	Strongly trust = 2 Trust = 1 I am not sure = 0 Distrust = −1 Strongly distrust = −2

Table 1.2 Continued

Index	Question	Score
Authoritativeness	6 Do you agree with the statements below: A Democracy means the government rule B Government is responsible for managing important affairs of our country, so people should not care about these affairs C People should comply with the government, just like subordinates should comply with their superiors D The government and Party have capabilities to manage our country E People should move out of their houses if the government wants to build public constructions in the location of their houses F People pay tax and the government may decide how to spend it without taking people's viewpoint into account	Strongly agree = 2 Agree = 1 I am not sure = 0 Disagree = −1 Strongly disagree = −2

Table 1.2 Continued

Index	Question	Score
Inequality-perception	7 Do you think the below aspects of our society are fair or unfair? A Wealth and income distribution B Public finance and tax policies C Job and employment opportunities D Opportunities for individual development E The college entrance examination system F Promotion of the government's officials G Public health care H Compulsory education I Political rights J The judicatory and administrative system K Welfare in different regions and industries L Welfare in urban and rural areas M Social security N The general situation of social fairness	Very fair = −2 Fair = −1 I am not sure = 0 Unfair = 1 Very unfair = 2
Conflict-consciousness	8 Do you think there is conflict of interest among social groups in our society?	No conflict = 1 I don't know = 2 A little conflict = 3 Many conflicts = 4 Very much conflict = 5
	9 Do you think it is possible the conflict of interest among social groups will intensify?	Definitely impossible = 1 Impossible = 2 I don't know = 3 Maybe possible = 4 Definitely possible = 5

THE DEFINITION OF THE 'MIDDLE CLASS'

Before analysing the responses to these various questions, it is necessary to define the middle class. While I recognize that there exist many classification schemes, the various ways of classifying the middle class are not the focus of this chapter. Rather, this chapter employs the classification developed by the East Asian Middle Class (EAMC) project (Hsiao, 1999, 2001, 2006). The EAMC project is directed by researchers from Asian countries such as South Korea, Japan, Hong Kong and Taiwan, who are conducting comparative research on the Asian middle classes. The EAMC proposes the following classification system (Table 1.3), based on John Goldthorpe's class scheme (Goldthorpe, 1987).

Table 1.3   Goldthorpe and EAMC project's class scheme

Goldthorpe's Class Scheme	EAMC Project's Scheme
I Higher-grade professionals II Lower-grade professionals	1 Capitalists (employers who hire 20 or more employees) 2 New middle class
IVa Small employers with employees IVb Small employers without employees	3 Old middle class
IIIa Routine non-manual employees IIIb Personal service workers	4 Marginal middle class
V Technicians and supervisors VIa Skilled workers VIIa Semi-/non-skilled workers	5 Working class
IVc Farmers VIIb Agricultural workers	6 Farmers/farm labourers

Among the six classes in the EAMC scheme, three are middle class (new middle class, old middle class and marginal middle class). The new middle class consists of professionals, managers and government officials. The new middle class is usually deemed to be a key part of the middle class. The old middle class is composed of small employers, small owner-operators and self-employed people. The marginal middle class includes low white-collar workers or routine workers. Sometimes the marginal middle class is considered as a marginal group between the middle class and the working class. This implies that the definition of the middle class is plural, namely that there are middle classes rather than a single middle class. The further supposition proposed by the EAMC project is that among the middle classes there is intra-class diversity in attitudes. Different groups of the middle classes have different socio-political attitudes. The capitalist class is generally believed to be an upper class above the middle class while the working class and farmers are a lower class or underclass beneath the middle class.

A small revision to this scheme is required when using the EAMC classification system to define the Chinese middle class. There is a capitalist class in this classification, which is not part of the middle class according to the EAMC scheme. However, at present, the capitalist class, as defined by Western literature, does not really exist in China. It is widely recognized that there is a private entrepreneur class in the country. A few of them are owners of large-sized enterprises and may be considered to be part of the upper class. These large-scale owners usually have close links with the state or governmental officials. But most private entrepreneurs are owners of small or medium-sized enterprises that are regarded by the public as a key part of the Chinese middle class. That is partly because the private entrepreneur class is a new class whose rise has changed the original class structure. As a new element in the social structure, private entrepreneurs might be expected to become a social force to promote social progress just like the new middle class already do.

Chinese private entrepreneurs certainly differ in sociopolitical status from their counterparts in Western societies, where they enjoy privileged status. In China, by contrast, the private entrepreneur class is not the most dominant or advantaged social group. Even though they possess a large amount of economic capital, there is a limit to their social and political influence. The most dominant and advantaged groups in China are high-ranking government officials and CEOs of state-owned enter-prises. They have great power and control over many socioeconomic resources that capitalists do not. Because of this idiosyncrasy, private entrepreneurs are defined as a part of the middle class in China. The group is named as the 'entrepreneur class' in the revised classification, replacing the 'capitalist class' in the EAMC scheme.

An advantage of this classification is that it not only permits examin-ation of the difference in sociopolitical attitudes between the middle class and the working class but also allows investigation of the differences between subgroups of the middle class. Such a framework that acknow-ledges the heterogeneous composition of the middle class is helpful in understanding the true situation of China's middle class and clarifying its sociopolitical attitudes. Many Chinese sociologists have discovered that the different subgroups of the middle class experience different economic conditions, and have different living standards and sociopolitical attitudes. Some sociologists prefer the use of the term 'middle classes' to the simpler 'middle class'. They argue that distinguishing different groups among the middle classes is as important as distinguishing the middle class from the working class or the middle class from the upper class. The four subgroups of the middle class already noted have disparities in their socioeconomic and political status that are readily observable in their sociopolitical attitudes and related functions.

The new middle class is generally considered to be the key part of the middle class, dominating the mainstream because the members of the new middle class occupy important positions in social, political and economic fields. They have institutionalized paths through which to influence policy-makers and elite groups. The entrepreneur class, usually referred to as 'private entrepreneurs' in China, is an active force in economic fields and might be a political actor in the future. This group has been increasing its influence on the policies of local governments, but their influence has been restrained in the process of Central Government policy-making, largely because the top leaders of the Chinese Communist Party remain suspicious of their political loyalty. The other two groups, the old middle class and the marginal middle class, have a socioeconomic status apparently lower than that of the new middle class and the entrepreneur class. Sometimes sociologists deem them to be marginal groups between the working class and the more mainstream middle class. However, some members of these two groups will probably join the queue to enter the new middle class and the entrepreneur class in the future. The old middle class is usually omitted from consideration of the middle class in most Western societies because of its small size but it absolutely cannot be ignored in China where the old middle class is a much larger proportion of China's middle class, especially in small cities and towns.

The major part of the group that comprises the marginal middle class is considered to be a younger generation of the middle class, with higher education, more democratic consciousness and more capacity for political participation. The marginal middle class has been becoming more and more active in the domains of the media, mass culture and especially the internet community. For example, they have been the most active participants in recent social movements. Younger members of the marginal middle class are believed to be much more politically liberal than other members of the middle class. Some analysts imply that the mainstream of relatively conservative political consciousness among China's middle class would change when these young people enter the new middle class (Wu, 2006; Fu, 2010; Dong, 2011).

Based on this analysis we may expect differences in sociopolitical attitudes not only between the middle class and the working class but also within the middle classes. Because this research is based on national sample survey data that did not include cases from the elite groups, the following analysis cannot examine the difference between the middle class and the elite group or upper class.

DATA, VARIABLES AND METHODS

The data used for the research presented in this chapter is national sample survey data on social stability collected in 2006 by the Institute of Sociology at the Chinese Academy of Social Sciences. The sample size is 7061. Because most members of the Chinese middle class reside in cities, only respondents living in urban areas have been included in this analysis, reducing the sample size to 2894.

Six OLS linear regression models were used for examining the sociopolitical attitudes of members of the middle classes. One model was run for each attitude index. The indices are the dependent variables, and the five classes – the entrepreneur class, the new middle class, the old middle class, the marginal middle class and the working class – are the independent variables. Control variables include sex, age and education. Table 1.4 contains the descriptive statistics of each of the variables in the regression analysis.

RESULTS AND INTERPRETATION

Table 1.5 shows the average scores for the five classes across six indices, which indicate roughly the differences in attitudes and feelings towards life-satisfaction, social-satisfaction, government-confidence, authoritativeness, inequality-perception and conflict-consciousness. Table 1.6 lists the results of regression models that further examine the differences among classes by controlling for gender, age and education.

Life-satisfaction

Average scores and regression coefficients display similar results. There are significant differences in life-satisfaction among classes. The higher

Middle class China

Table 1.4   Descriptive statistics of variables (N = 2894)

Variable	Minimum	Maximum	Average	Standard Error
Age	18	69	39.8	13.0
Schooling years	0	20	9.7	4.1
Scores of LS (life-satisfaction) index	−4	4	0.7786	1.6146
Scores of SS (social-satisfaction) index	−4	4	1.1399	1.6596
Scores of GC (government-confidence) index	−12	12	3.7487	4.0239
Scores of AT (authoritativeness) index	−12	12	0.1703	4.0923
Scores of IP (inequality-perception) index	−28	28	−0.2880	8.8481
Scores of CG (conflict-consciousness) index	2	10	6.2458	1.8043
Ratio				
Sex (male)				45.1
Entrepreneur class				0.3
New middle class				19.0
Old middle class				19.8
Marginal middle class				25.2
Working class				35.7

the class status in the social hierarchy, the higher the score in life-satisfaction. The entrepreneur class and the new middle class have the two highest scores for life-satisfaction, followed by the old middle class and the marginal middle class. The working class has the lowest score. Since the number of entrepreneurs in the survey data is limited, the coefficient for the entrepreneur class is not significant in the regression model. The other three coefficients for sections of the middle class are all significant. That means there is a difference in the degree of life-satisfaction between the working class and each of the three (middle

Table 1.5   Average scores of five classes in six indices

Class	Life-satisfaction Index	Social-satisfaction Index	Government-confidence Index	Authoritativeness Index	Inequality-perception Index	Conflict-consciousness Index
Entrepreneur class	1.2708	1.7208	4.4877	0.5825	–6.0967	5.8448
New middle class	1.4845	1.2581	3.5607	–1.5608	–0.2890	6.7455
Old middle class	1.0383	1.2957	3.7236	0.7055	–1.5397	6.0649
Marginal middle class	1.0218	1.0647	3.6022	–0.8535	–0.0533	6.6232
Working class	0.7479	1.0830	3.7317	0.5009	–0.3740	6.2349
Total	1.0160	1.1555	3.6668	0.2662	–0.5225	6.3953

class, the old middle class and the marginal middle class). In addition, these coefficients are positive figures and the coefficient of the new middle class is the largest. That means that the three middle classes have a higher degree of life-satisfaction than the working class. The new middle class has the highest degree of life-satisfaction among the middle classes. The gender coefficient and education coefficient indicate that there is no gender difference and no difference among different educated groups in the degree of life-satisfaction. However, the age coefficient is significant and negative. That means there is a difference among different age groups. Older people have a lower degree of life-satisfaction than younger persons.

Social-satisfaction

Average scores and regression coefficients for social-satisfaction also show differences among classes, with the more advantaged classes having higher social-satisfaction than others. At the same time all the middle classes have higher social-satisfaction than the working class. The entrepreneur class has the highest score, and the new middle class and the old middle class have significantly higher scores than the working class, although the marginal middle class has a score slightly lower than that of the working class. All coefficients of social-satisfaction in Table 1.6 are not significant except the coefficient for the new middle class, which is a positive figure. This means the new middle class has significantly higher social-satisfaction than both the other middle classes and the working class. The coefficients for the entrepreneur class and the old middle class are larger positive figures but are not significant. The marginal middle class has the same level of social-satisfaction as the working class. There is no gender difference, no age difference and no educational difference.

Government-confidence

Average scores for government-confidence seem to be very similar for all categories except the entrepreneur class. The score for the entrepreneur class is much higher. All coefficients for government-confidence in Table 1.6 are not significant except age. That means there is no difference in government-confidence by class, controlling for gender and education. The coefficient for the entrepreneur class is larger than for other classes but is not statistically significant because there are so few cases. It is probably the case that the entrepreneur class has higher confidence in the government than other classes. At the same time, there is no gender difference and no educational difference in government-confidence, but older people still have a higher confidence than young people.

Authoritativeness

Average scores and regression coefficients for authoritativeness display a salient division inside the middle classes. The scores for the new middle class are much higher than other groups of the middle classes and the working class. The coefficients in Table 1.6 indicate that there are significant and large differences among classes, age groups and educational groups. The new middle class and the marginal middle class have negative coefficients, which means that the new middle class and the marginal middle class are less likely to support an authoritarian state than the working class, the old middle class and the entrepreneur class. In other words, the new middle class and the marginal middle class have more democratic consciousness. In addition, the higher educated have

Table 1.6   Unstandardized OLS coefficients for the linear regression of attitude indices on classes

Dependent Variable/Independent Variable	Life-Satisfaction Index	Social-satisfaction Index	Government-confidence Index	Authoritativeness Index	Inequality-perception Index	Conflict-consciousness Index
Class (reference group: working class)						
Entrepreneur class	0.542 (0.768)	0.706 (0.812)	1.031 (1.966)	1.543 (1.903)	−6.339 (4.329)	−0.844 (0.857)
New middle class	0.787** (0.105)	0.231* (0.111)	0.072 (0.268)	−0.806** (0.260)	−0.415 (0.591)	0.104 (0.117)
Old middle class	0.424** (0.095)	0.188 (0.100)	−0.020 (0.243)	0.222 (0.235)	−1.378** (0.534)	−0.054 (0.106)
Marginal middle class	0.326** (0.089)	0.002 (0.094)	0.039 (0.228)	−0.577** (0.221)	−0.033 (0.502)	0.211* (0.099)
Sex (male)	−0.002 (0.059)	0.007 (0.063)	−0.106 (0.152)	0.004 (0.147)	−0.401 (0.335)	0.109 (0.066)
Age	−0.017** (0.002)	0.000 (0.003)	0.017** (0.006)	0.031** (0.006)	0.006 (0.014)	0.001 (0.003)
Schooling years	0.008 (0.009)	−0.015 (0.009)	−0.039 (0.022)	−0.222** (0.021)	0.062 (0.030)	0.098** (0.010)
Constant	1.179** (0.153)	1.231** (0.161)	3.475** (0.390)	1.226** (0.378)	−0.730 (0.860)	5.170** (0.170)
Adjusted R^2	0.056	0.001	0.004	0.098	0.002	0.058
N	2894	2894	2894	2894	2894	2894

Note: Standard error shown in parentheses; ** = $p < 0.01$; * = $p < 0.05$.

more democratic consciousness and tolerate less state authoritarianism than the less educated. Older people approve of more state authoritarianism than younger people.

Inequality-perception

Average scores and regression coefficients for inequality-perception again manifest a salient division inside the middle classes. The scores for the entrepreneur class and the old middle class are much bigger negative figures than those for the new middle class and the marginal middle class. All coefficients of inequality-perception in Table 1.6 are not significant except the coefficient of the old middle class. The coefficient of the old middle class is a negative and quite large figure. This means the old middle class has much lower inequality-perception than other classes. In addition, the coefficient for the entrepreneur class, even though it is not statistically significant because of so few cases, is a very large negative figure. That seems to imply that the middle classes with economic capital (such as the entrepreneur class and the old middle class) have a higher tolerance of social inequality or lower expectation of social justice. There are no differences by gender, age and education groups in inequality perception.

Conflict-consciousness

Average scores for conflict-consciousness do not display large differences among classes although the new middle class and the marginal middle class has a slightly higher score than the working class and the working class has a slightly higher score than the entrepreneur class and the old middle class. Among the coefficients of conflict-consciousness in Table 1.6, only two coefficients for the marginal middle class and education are significant. That means the marginal middle class has more conflict-consciousness than other classes and that the higher educated group has more conflict-consciousness than the less educated.

SUMMARY AND CONCLUSION

The middle classes show significantly higher levels of satisfaction with their standard of living than the working class. The new middle class shows the highest level of satisfaction, with 71.8 per cent indicating that their standard of living has improved in the past five years and 68.6 per cent indicating that they expect their standard of living to improve in the next five years. These findings suggest that members of the middle classes, especially the new middle class, will likely hold conservative attitudes and be resistant to sociopolitical change, as they do not want their standard of living to be negatively affected.

The new middle class has a higher degree of satisfaction with social circumstances in China than the working class and the old and marginal middle classes. Of the new middle class 80.1 per cent responded that the social circumstances in China are 'stable' and 76.6 per cent indicated that the social situation is 'harmonious'. Stability, in this context, refers to social order, whereas harmony refers to the relationships between people or social groups. These findings imply that the new middle class is the most likely to want to maintain the existing social order and to object to changes that might bring about any social turbulence. The further implication is that the new middle class may have a more conservative attitude in this respect.

There is no significant difference between classes in the degree of confidence they have in the government. All classes view the government in a relatively positive light, but there are some differences evident in terms of particular issues. For example, all classes show a high degree of confidence in the Central Government, but express a lower degree of confidence in official statistics. 94.1 per cent of the new middle class, 94.8 per cent of the old middle class, 95.4 per cent of the marginal middle class, 94.2 per cent of the working class and 89.9 per cent of the entrepreneur class indicate that they somewhat believe or very much believe in the Central Government. These findings suggest that the middle classes have a high degree of confidence in the government and thus are likely to want to preserve the existing political order.

The new middle class and the marginal middle class view state authoritarianism less favourably than the working class and the old middle class. The new middle class is the least likely to support an authoritarian state. However, while they prefer a less authoritarian (i.e., more democratic) government, this analysis suggests that they do not want change that will bring about sociopolitical turbulence.

The entrepreneur and old middle classes are much more accepting of social inequality than the new and marginal middle classes and the working class. These findings suggest that there is diversity between the middle classes on their attitudes about social inequality. More specifically, the middle classes with economic capital are less concerned with social equality than the middle class with cultural capital, implying that the entrepreneur and old middle classes are more likely to have conservative attitudes, while the new middle class are more likely to have liberal attitudes.

The marginal middle class perceives there to be significantly more conflict of interest in Chinese society than do the entrepreneur and old middle classes. Echoing the findings on social inequality, these results suggest that the middle classes with economic capital are more likely to hold conservative views, while the marginal middle class (the lower strata of the middle class) is more likely to hold liberal views and be more sympathetic towards disadvantaged groups and lower classes.

There are striking differences in sociopolitical attitudes between classes, particularly between the new middle class and the working class. However, we cannot conclude that the middle class is simply more conservative or liberal than the working class. In some respects, such as in perceptions of social circumstances in Chinese society, the middle class is more conservative than the working class. In other respects, such as preferences regarding state authoritarianism, members of the middle class are more liberal than their working class counterparts.

More importantly, there are internal differences between the middle classes in sociopolitical attitudes. The new middle class, that is, the middle class with high cultural capital, hold a contradictory sociopolitical attitude. On one hand, they view state authoritarianism unfavourably, preferring a more democratic state; on the other hand, they display the highest levels of satisfaction with their current living standards and thus want to avoid sociopolitical change. The entrepreneur class and the old middle class, that is, the middle class with high economic capital, holds relatively conservative political views. They are more likely to support state authoritarianism and are more accepting of social inequality. The marginal middle class, that is, the lower strata of the middle class, holds the most liberal views. They are the least accepting of social inequality and state authoritarianism, and are the most sympathetic to the lower class.

Regression analyses suggest that age and education have partial effects on sociopolitical attitudes as well. Education is positively correlated with liberalism, especially with having a preference for a more democratic government. As the middle class becomes more educated, liberal democratic attitudes may become more common in the future. It is worth noting that younger people also prefer a less authoritarian state and have less confidence in the government, further implying that liberalism and support for democracy may be on the rise among the middle class as more young people enter it in the future.

Within the Chinese middle classes, there is a diverse set of sociopolitical attitudes, ranging from conservative to liberal. Members of the middle classes are largely satisfied with the current sociopolitical situation and have a high degree of confidence in the government. However, a portion of the middle classes also has high expectations for political democracy and social justice. Such contradictory attitudes imply that the Chinese middle classes may be inclined to choose the Third Road, a gradual sociopolitical transition. In that case, the Chinese middle classes are presently serving as a sociopolitical stabilizer. However, there is also some potential for them to become a destabilizing force on the sociopolitical order in years to come.

2. Class, consumption and the economic restructuring of consumer space

Carolyn Cartier

From the national economy to the local level of the household, consumption has become a major subject for defining the new Chinese middle class. The Central Government is relying on household consumption to transform the country from a production-led to a consumption-led domestic economy, in which private household consumption – rather than continued state investment – drives annual GDP growth. In the process of this planned transition, consumption is proving to be a key context for debate over diverse issues of social and economic change. This chapter examines several conjunctures between consumption and class formation in urban China, where the rapidity of urban development and economic restructuring has compressed the trajectory of the production–consumption transition and limited middle class hopes and possibilities.

The rapidity of urban growth and transformation in contemporary China complicates understandings of production–consumption and class relations because values and priorities in urban society have been subject to multiple extraordinary upheavals. Indeed, across the twentieth century Chinese cities have been the geographical focus of political-ideological debates over production and consumption. In the Republican period, cities were sites of state-promoted consumer campaigns in favour of China-made goods (Gerth, 2003). After the Chinese Communist Party established leadership in 1949, the Party-state sought to transform 'consumer cities' into 'producer cities' (Murphey, 1980), which halted commercial development. When Shanghai and the other 13 coastal port cities opened under reform in 1984, pre-war facades characterized their urban-built environments. Under reform, wholesale reconstruction of new urban commercial districts has created vast new landscapes for citizen-consumer experience.

This chapter begins by evaluating existing understandings of the middle class in China in relation to ideals about consumption and consumer possibilities. In contrast with historic understandings of class formation, new definitions of middle class are increasingly expressed in terms of income groups and their characteristics in new consumer citizenship. Next, the discussion turns to the landscape of the new Chinese city for expressions of class formation and consumption, and debates over income inequality and housing affordability. The chapter culminates in a discussion of the urban restructuring of consumer landscapes in Beijing and Shanghai, where transnational urban developments are replacing historic markets, leaving middle class consumers with more window-shopping opportunities and fewer destinations for daily necessities in the city centre.

CLASS AND CONSUMPTION

Examining consumption in relation to meanings of class is complicated by different understandings about contemporary meanings of 'middle class' in China, and the changing significations of class under reform. The official replacement of the language of class, *jieji*, with the less politically resonant language of stratum, *jiecang*, indicates how the contemporary Party-state has repositioned its interests: 'the embourgeoisement of cadres' (So, 2003, p. 367) under reform, through the reorganization and diversion of state assets, must be represented in relatively neutral and 'harmonious' language. Chinese Academy of Social Sciences (CASS) research discusses the problems of definition, and rejects the use of 'class' for its 'negative connotations' (He, 2006, p. 71). Officially, the defining of class in contemporary China has abandoned the socialist language of production and capital relations.

Whereas CASS surveys develop a triangulated analysis based on income, occupation and consumption, statistical data produced by the National Bureau of Statistics use income classes, typically broken down by decile and quintile (cf. Zhou, 2004, 2005; Guo, 2008b, 2009). The consumption portion indexes durable goods based on owning an array of home appliances and a car. Car ownership yields 12 points in CASS surveys, whereas pianos and motorcycles, for example, are worth only four points per item and washing machines, having become relatively common household appliances, count for only one point (Guo, 2009, p. 48). This suggests that big-ticket items weigh disproportionately in defining and symbolizing membership in the new Chinese middle class (see Table 2.1). Since the formation of a new middle class and class mobility are also being constrained by the resurgence of historic elites in China and renewed elite networks (Goodman, 2008b), class dynamics will disproportionately concern representational meanings through consumption practices.

The portrayal of the middle class by government statistics presents a broad middle income group across the second, third and fourth quintiles of the income spectrum, in the descriptive categories 'lower-middle', 'middle' and 'upper-middle' incomes. This income-based definitional standard echoes international comparative norms: the idea of a broad middle class based on income and shared 'culture' has formed the societal core of American nationalism since the industrial era, destabilized only at the end of the twentieth century by the neoliberalization of the US economy. It may also be telling that the national imaginary of American middle class life includes democratic access to wage labour and skilled and professional employment, since Party-state ideology encompasses a democratic ideal. It is characteristic of Chinese economic planning to define economic futures before they materialize. Thus, the degree to which Chinese citizens may experience social mobility and whether they can afford a home is centrally at stake in the debate over the shift to a consumption-led economy. If the current economy limits material progress and brackets consumption, then middle class status may become an ideal limited to a didactic arena of discursive reproduction for state ideology of social harmony.

Statistics on the consumption of 'durable goods' – things that are purchased only once in three or more years and not consumed to completion – demonstrate some predictable and interesting patterns (Table 2.1). In 2009, while over 10 per cent of upper-middle-income households owned a car, overall fewer than 10 per cent of middle-income households claimed automobile ownership. By contrast, the highest income decile demonstrates automobile ownership at a rate nearly double that of the high-income group. Ownership of a motorcycle decreases with increasing income, demonstrating the predictable pattern seen in developing countries, and suggesting that car ownership is a widespread aspirational condition for the middle class. Indeed, in 2009 automobile sales in China overtook sales in the US for the first time and the trend continues. In 2011, US auto sales totalled 11.6 million cars by comparison to 19 million in China (Leggett, 2011). The statistics also show near-universal adoption of mobile telephones and that consumption of mobile phones has likely replaced the demand for cameras, which is otherwise inexplicably low as a single category. Government statistics also include the piano as a distinct item of consumer demand, which identifies it as an indicator of known aspirational interests and places its

Table 2.1 *Ownership of durable goods per 100 households by level of income, 2009*

Income Item	1st Decile	2nd Decile	2nd Quintile	3rd Quintile	4th Quintile	9th Decile	10th Decile
	Lowest	Low	Lower-middle	Middle	Upper-middle	High	Highest
Motorcycle	18.8	23.4	26.4	24.2	22.5	19.24	15.4
Automobile	1.2	2.2	4.2	7.4	13.6	20.2	38.1
Washing machine	85.5	91.6	94.8	97.1	98.8	100	102.4
Refrigerator	75.4	86.8	94.0	97.3	100.4	103.4	106.4
Colour television	111.3	120.9	125.9	133.5	143.4	155	168.6
Computer	25.6	41.8	54.5	66.2	78.2	89.4	109.8
Stereo system	12.8	19.1	23.4	27.1	32.8	38.5	48.3
Video camera	0.7	2.1	3.4	6.4	10.4	14.3	22.2
Camera	10.7	18.7	28.8	39	53.1	66.9	85.8
Piano	0.2	0.4	1.2	1.9	3.3	4.6	7.5
Microwave oven	23.2	36.5	47.8	59.2	70.6	77.0	85.4
Air conditioner	35.6	60.0	79.3	101.6	130.3	159.0	206.0
Water heater/ shower	52.5	68.1	77.2	86.3	92.6	98.9	106.4
Dishwasher	0.3	0.5	0.5	0.7	0.8	1.2	2.3
Exercise equipment	0.5	1.4	1.8	2.8	5.3	8.5	12.3
Fixed telephone	66.9	74.0	78.0	82.2	87.1	90.6	94.8
Mobile telephone	129.5	157.8	174.8	184.5	194.5	205.5	216.4

Source: *China Statistical Yearbook* (2010, p. 351).

ownership among urban households as a relatively high-level consumer practice of cultural-educational-leisure pursuits.

In comparison with the evolution of consumer society in industrialized countries, the difference of consumption in China under reform is the collision of didacticism – experiential realities of people learning to consume (again) – with extreme income inequality in the consumer marketplace. For the middle class, real estate dominates consumer possibilities and spotlights the contrasts between classes. Number one of the two 'big items', the home (whether flat, duplex, townhouse or free-standing house), is the focus of household investment allocation. New housing in China is regularly sold with unfinished interiors, giving rise to an enormous market for interior finishing and design services. On the one hand, if a middle class household has purchased a flat, then household income will be allotted to finish and furnish the home. On the other hand, middle class homeownership – a cornerstone of social stability in industrialized countries – is rapidly becoming a myth in many cities because middle class households, as defined by income (rather than occupation), are being distanced from entering the housing market. People want answers to skyrocketing real estate prices: just who can afford to buy a flat?

One calculus around the blogosphere has it that a farmer working an average plot of land would need to have toiled since the Tang dynasty – over 1000 years – in order to afford a 100 m^2 apartment in central Beijing at 2010 prices, about 3 million RMB (US$450 000). In 2009 the common contemporary statistical standard of housing affordability, a ratio of median house price divided by gross annual median household income, stood at 25 for Beijing ('Beijing residents ...', 2010), compared, in 2010, with 11 for Hong Kong, seven for major Australian cities, led by Sydney, and seven for the most expensive US cities, New York and San Francisco (Demographia, 2011). That Hong Kong has the highest Gini coefficient (measuring income inequality) among industrialized economies under-scores the severity of the inequality in mainland Chinese cities.

Concerns about lack of housing affordability and unreliability of official statistics are spurring local and national public interest in China. In 2010, the online media company Sina.com[1] initiated a public survey to assess the extent of unoccupied investment property. Consider the con-texts generating such national interest: day after day, urban homeowners return to their buildings and look up to realize repeatedly that, in about half the units, literally no one is home – disproportionate numbers of flats are dark week after week and month after month. Results of the survey found that about 65 per cent of flats that had been sold in apartment buildings were visually vacant in Beijing over a six-month period, compared with about 50 per cent in Shanghai ('Netizens hone ...', 2010). The estimate for total unoccupied and unsold flats nationwide is 64 million, enough to house approximately 200 million people (Xie, 2010) – two-thirds of the total population of the United States. Empty flats demonstrate not only the extent of property speculation but also how individuals or households with investment income have no need to generate rental income: re-selling or 'flipping' a flat is easier if it is kept in new condition. With no property tax in China, and relatively simple transactions for cash sales, spurred by considerable 'grey' or unreported income fuelling cash transactions, real estate is the prime site in which to place investment capital.

Whether or not families own their own home, representations of middle class homeownership ideals bombard the consumer marketplace. From advertisements to real estate fairs and on-site show flats, consumer citizens are faced with a vast array of information on the values and styles of homeownership.[2] The significance of residential property devel-opment in the contemporary Chinese city and its marketing to consumer citizens draws on aspirational representations of values and lifestyle, literally constructing notions of upward mobility and mapping them onto new housing developments. This conjuncture of the rise of the new middle class with the rebuilding of the contemporary city makes the middle class 'about segregation of social strata in a new mapping of urban space' (Anagnost, 2008, p. 499). The distinctively close relational meanings between property, social strata, class formation and consumer-ism are effectively 're-branding class as propertizing culture' (Skeggs, 2005, p. 46).[3]

Conjunctures between urban restructuring, new class formation and processes of globalization intersect international and transnational mean-ings of class – meanings that complicate and extend the definition of class by the conventions of nation-state geography. Where globalizing capital intersects China's production–consumption transition, the trans-national capitalist class is especially interested in understanding class in China on the basis of household income and consumption. The trans-national capitalist class is the mobile, international formation of mutually interested corporate executives, high-level government officials, leading technical professionals and the merchants and media interests who furnish, entertain and represent them (Sklair, 2001). Formed under late capitalism and coextensive with the rise of China under reform, the transnational capitalist class includes China's economic, political and cultural elites, who shape the future of China's economy and its major cities.

The consumer arena of the transnational capitalist class is highly specialized and differentiated by branded goods and services, including informational services and sources. The service base of the transnational capitalist class increasingly produces its own information through in-house research groups of the major consulting, finance and investment firms. Among these firms, whose publications challenge and supplement both official sources and published peer-reviewed academic information, reports published by the McKinsey Global Institute circulate widely. The report, 'A Consumer Paradigm for China' forecasts China's production–consumption dynamics (Devan et al., 2009); 'From "Made in China" to "Sold in China"' charts the rise of a Chinese middle class based on future income and purchasing power (Farrell et al., 2006b). Figure 2.1 draws on selected data from 'A Consumer Paradigm for China'. Its data show how China's private domestic consumption as a percentage of GDP is comparatively low in relation to both industrialized economies and those of its frequently co-named 'BRIC' members, namely Brazil, Russia and India.

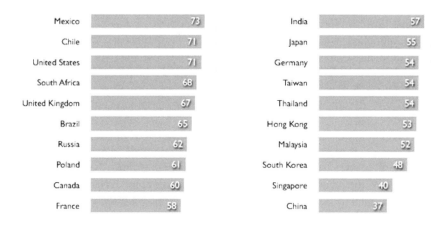

Source: Devan et al. (2009).

Figure 2.1   Private domestic consumption as a percentage of GDP, 2008

Figures 2.2 and 2.3 draw on the McKinsey report, 'The Value of China's Emerging Middle Class' (Farrell et al., 2006a), which divides the middle class into two income bands and projects up to 2025 when the 'upper-middle class' is predicted to reach its spending potential. Thus, not unlike

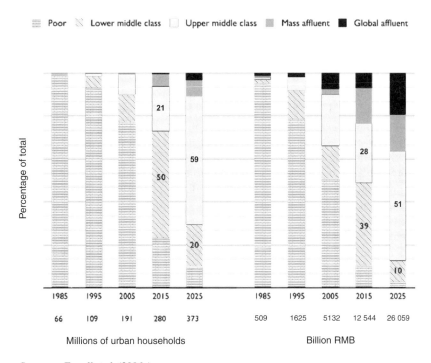

Poor   Lower middle class   Upper middle class   Mass affluent   Global affluent

Source: Farrell et al. (2006a).

Figure 2.2 Chinese urban households   *Figure 2.3 Urban disposable income*

China's official government sources, the world economy of international brands defines class by household income but with particular emphasis on predicting what the Chinese consumer will spend. Such forecasts guide product development targeted at middle-income and affluent consumers, who differ demographically in contrast with populations of industrialized countries because they are and will continue to be relatively young, ranging in age from late 20s to early 40s. These forecasts do not include the contribution to total spending of 'grey income' and illegal income.

Past official estimates allowed that in 2008 grey income amounted to up to 15 per cent of GDP. While widely circulating non-government studies on grey income conclude that disposable income of urban households is significantly higher than the official figure (Credit Suisse, 2010); these studies were funded by the multinational financial services company Credit Suisse and conducted by Wang Xiaolu, Deputy Director of the National Economic Research Institute, China Reform Foundation. Based on over 4000 samples taken in 64 cities in 19 provinces in 2008, the data show that nearly two-thirds of grey income accrued to the wealthiest 10 per cent of households, tripling actual income over official figures. High-income households of the ninth decile had income twice as high as reported figures. Together the top two income groups gained 80 per cent of total informal income (ibid., pp. 3–4). Grey income is so common that it grew faster than GDP during 2005–08 and '[T]he facts show that grey income has its origins in the misuse of power and is closely connected to corruption' (ibid., p. 32). To return to housing affordability, the inclusion of shadow income would bring down the Beijing housing affordability ratio by a factor of three for Beijing elites, making the housing market in China's capital more comparable to expensive housing markets in Australia and the US. However, this condition further peripheralizes the possibilities for middle class home-ownership, in both financial and geographical terms, to relatively distant suburbs.

URBAN RESTRUCTURING AND NEW CONSUMER LANDSCAPES

Developing in an era of rapid global change, China's new urban modernity draws on unprecedented international access to information and knowledge, investment capital, technical expertise and cultural forms. In the past 30 years under reform, many cities in the coastal region, including Guangzhou, Hangzhou and Shenzhen, have redeveloped old city centres and developed iconic new city centres in an international style on lands peripheral to the historic urban area (for example, see Cartier, 2002). These rounds of redevelopment have restructured the urban economy and the urban landscape, transforming cities from places of manufacturing into places of international business services. New urban landscapes present the Chinese city as a mix of sleek spaces for transnational elites and boutique destinations for urban trendsetters, yet also as virtual dreamlands for those who are marginalized by the redevelopment process.

The redevelopment and expansion of existing cities and the construction of hundreds of new ones in China under reform has been driving industrial growth. The new Chinese city has re-instantiated capitalist commercial development in urban cores by replacing socialist era housing and factories of the Maoist producer-city with landscapes of urban

modernity: gated housing compounds, outsized commercial developments, luxury high-rise housing and architectural icons with spectacular
rooflines vying for recognition along ever-changing skylines. In the
aftermath of the 2008 Summer Olympics in Beijing and the 2010
Shanghai Expo, the special positions enjoyed by Beijing and Shanghai in
national development planning continue to resonate across their contemporary urban landscapes in triumphal event architecture. Their built
environments are the material evidence of the production process fuelling
urban growth, offering in turn vast new landscapes for private consumption.

The urban landscape of new consumerism in China has often been
associated with cities of the south, especially Guangzhou, Shenzhen and
Hong Kong, where export-oriented economic reform kicked off in the
1980s. In the 1990s, after the Chinese government allowed citizens to
begin to travel overseas for leisure vacations, Hong Kong became the
typical first choice for an 'overseas' shopping trip (Cartier, 2008, 2009).
Yet the side story missed in the widespread coverage of the Beijing
Olympics and the Shanghai Expo was the simultaneous development of
extensive commercial and retail space (Figure 2.4). Data on commercial
floor space show that Shanghai and Beijing have led the country in the
redevelopment of commercial space, commonly for service-industry
offices and retail, since 2003. Moreover, contrary to expectations that
Shanghai would lead the way in new commercial development – enjoying
a return to its status as the historic centre of fashion, style and
commercial culture in China – Beijing substantially outpaced Shanghai in
commercial development from 2004.

Rapid urban redevelopment and modernization of the built environment regularly results in gentrification – the process of new real estate
development that pushes out historic residents and businesses in favour of
elites and high-value enterprises better able to pay the higher rents. But
the concept of gentrification is seldom directly discussed in analysis of
Asian urbanization. Across Asia, government norms of post-war redevelopment have stressed goals of urban renewal and modernization as core
elements of nation-building, in which beleaguered urban residents play
their part by lining up for housing compensation and packing up for
housing reassignments. In Beijing, the rapid development of commercial
space in the mid-2000s directly reflects the highly documented loss of
historic courtyard houses in the central city during the run up to the
Olympics.

Historic centres of consumption in China, especially markets, have also
been widely lost. The first major case in Beijing was the controversial
redevelopment of the dynasty era Dong An Market in the Wangfujing

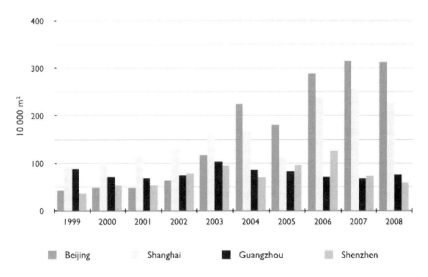

Source: *China Real Estate Statistics Yearbook* (1999, 2001, 2004, 2007, 2009).

Figure 2.4   Commercial floor space completed, 1999–2008

district. The city closed the historic market for redevelopment in 1993. The site was redeveloped in the run up to the Beijing Olympics into a shopping mall and office towers, named Xin Dong An Plaza, built under a 50–50 joint venture between the state-owned Beijing Dong An Group and Sun Hung Kai Properties (SHKP), one of the three big property firms of Hong Kong. The market demolition 'signified the first phase of Wangfujing's redevelopment and the imminent eviction of hundreds of people from their neighbourhood. For this reason, many Beijingers resented Xin Dong An's appropriation of the famous market's old name' (Broudehoux, 2004, p. 115). The rapidity of urban growth and transform-ation in contemporary China complicates understandings of class form-ation through the production–consumption transition because many people question the new priorities and values being thrust upon them. After opening, the B1 level of Xin Dong An Plaza offered rental space to some stallholders from the original market at vastly higher rents in a faux 'Old Beijing Street' setting.

Demonstrating the speed and style of urban change, and paralleling transformations under way around central Beijing, SHKP announced in 2007 that it would re-brand Xin Dong An Plaza 'Beijing apm' to target young consumers aged 19 to 35 (SHKP, 2007). A contrivance of am–pm, 'apm' is a brand that SHKP conceived for a shopping mall in the Kwun

Tong district of Hong Kong to attract young consumers to the marginal location with the promise of 'late night shopping'. An industrial area of the Kowloon Peninsula, Kwun Tong is a Hong Kong 'new town', one of several established by the British colonial government to provide post-war public housing. After China opened to the world economy, Hong Kong industry moved into the Pearl River Delta and new towns became targeted for high-rise and commercial redevelopment. Taking the 'apm' brand to Beijing instantiates SHKP's youth consumer strategy for Hong Kong, featuring 'trendsetting international brand retailers, some ... opening in China for the very first time' (ibid.), in the heart of China's historic marketing landscape. The project demonstrates how commercial property development targets and develops China's developing social mobility. It also demonstrates the calculus of planned gentrification: the renovation, according to SHKP, 'will lift annual rental income ... by 30 percent to 50 percent ... per square foot ... making rents at the top end of the range in the capital' ('SHKP lands ... ', 2007).

Historically the centre of Chinese modernity, Shanghai has also emerged from two decades of redevelopment under reform as a city socially and economically restructured. According to a popular maxim, the centre of Shanghai is now for elites and foreigners, the next ring is for professional newcomers and the outer ring is for locals. Costs of living in the city centre have skyrocketed with the redevelopment and replacement of old central city residential areas with new commercial spaces and mixed-use commercial-residential real estates. Housing costs in the centre are now associated with upper-middle and high-income groups, whereas costs are lowest in the outer ring, where many middle- and lower-income households and retired state workers relocated to after being compelled to move out of central city locations. Households that were forced to relocate often received compensation at levels lower than the cost of new housing in the same location (Hsing, 2009), thereby potentially leading to a lower standard of living. The process of state-led gentrification reshuffles who lives where, with the outcome that the primary beneficiaries of accumulation are government, private property developers and the recipients of grey income.

The spatial process of change also demonstrates the effects of class formation in the commercial and mixed-use residential spaces of new transnational-style buildings in urban cores. Especially in new commercial districts, each better-designed commercial-residential building becomes a site for reworking the production–consumption dynamic. In the spare, high-modernist landscapes of China's new financial districts, mixed-use design is contained vertically within the building: retail services at the bottom, office space in the middle range and hotels and private condominiums at the top. This arrangement of mixed-used verticality is common in contemporary skyscraper design, placing the transnational capitalist class in its social position at the symbolic top of the global economy. Entering by car and living in spaces from which they view the city from great heights, residents of such buildings have little need to encounter the semi-public space of the street – where real life inequality may play out with discomforting unpredictability. The 21st Century Tower in the Lujiazui financial district of Pudong is an outstanding example of a project developed for the transnational capitalist class (Figure 2.5). Such state-planned projects in China wholly subsume historic places and people as a collateral process of producing the newly built environment, as if Pudong was a vast greenfield site when it was named Shanghai's special economic zone in 1990.

On the Puxi side of the city, Shanghai transformed part of its internationally renowned commercial street, Nanjing Road (in the Hankou district, perpendicular to the renewed historic Bund) into a pedestrian shopping area. It offers a mix of local, national and international brand shops and has become a primary destination for domestic and international tourists. However, to position themselves as having discriminating taste, local Shanghai people regularly proclaim that they do not shop there, distancing themselves from the tourist masses. They prefer instead local neighbourhoods and the department stores of Huaihai Middle Road, the artery of the historic French Concession, which has re-emerged as Shanghai's leading place of consumer distinction under reform. Several fashion department stores punctuate Huaihai Middle Road and a few side streets maintain historic consumer character, including South Maoming Road where women's clothing businesses continue to specialize in the *qipao*, a form-fitting sheath dress that provoked a national debate and launched an international style.

Huaihai Middle Road crosses the Puxi side of Shanghai through Luwan and Xuhui districts, which have been significantly spared the wholesale raze-and-redevelopment treatment. Many streets in these districts are lined with plane trees, fronting blocks of historic low- and medium-density housing. Dozens of historic houses from the Concession era are now under government conservation, suggesting how Shanghai's historic elite populations have managed to maintain the district through the upheavals of the twentieth century. Luwan district[4] is also the site of China's nationally outstanding culture-led urban redevelopment, Xintiandi, a heritage conservation retail and entertainment district, and Tianzifang, a gentrified concentration of boutique shops on Taikang Road that grew out of artists' studio spaces and creative industry flats in a former state-socialist era factory

Note: 21st Century Tower is a mixed-use, 50-storey building in the Pudong district of Shanghai, a dynamic international business centre. The first 21 floors will be Class-A office space, followed by an 11-floor Four Seasons Hotel, and 12 floors of condominiums managed by the Four Seasons. The office lobby and residential entrance will be at the base of the tower, with the hotel's reception and amenities areas located in the adjacent podium. The project is located on Century Avenue, the main East-West Pudong thoroughfare.

Source: Reproduced with permission of Gensler Design, © 2011.

Figure 2.5   21st Century Tower, Shanghai

compound. Economically and aesthetically successful, Xintiandi introduced the paradigm of cultural heritage redevelopment to China (Luo and
Sha, 2002; Xue, 2010). In 2006, Tianzifang was named the best creative
industry zone in China, in addition to receiving numerous municipal awards
(Zhu, 2009).

Xintiandi and Tianzifang are emblematic of creative industry developments and boutique consumer destinations in world cities, and the
Shanghai government has designated dozens of creative industry zones.
Tianzifang especially represents the current popularization of art in
consumer culture and the crossover between shopping and art in the
gallery shop of new urban design. It is one among several gentrified art
studio districts in China on the international map of cultural consumerism, including the Moganshan Road/Suzhou Creek area in Shanghai and
'798' in the Chaoyang district of Beijing. The concept behind Xintiandi
is different, deriving from an earlier version of 'urban renaissance'
redevelopment, first realized at Faneuil Hall in Boston and later adopted
in the revitalization of Covent Garden, London, and other post-industrial
landscapes. Architects characterize Xintiandi as China's version of the
'festival marketplace' (Xue, 2006, 2008), reinterpreted for Shanghai by a
US architecture firm and another Hong Kong property developer, Shui
On Land.

In each case, the cultural political economy represented by their
commercialization foregrounds the cultural-knowledge economy's basis
in design aesthetics, intellectual property rights and associated brands.
The small, mostly independent retail businesses of Tianzifang present
things in artisanal style, while Xintiandi emphasizes a combination of
international chain stores, boutiques and high-end regional chains selling
'Chineseness' in an all out environment of sophisticated display, which
works on the semi-rational principle that people will pay more for a
distinctively presented product. Local reception of Xintiandi and Tianzifang in Shanghai is predictably mixed, and both have become associated
with transnational lifestyle interests and cosmopolitan tourists in search
of 'hip' Shanghai. Yet, however transnational in appearance, the consum-
erscapes of Xintiandi and Tianzifang are not architecturally elite spaces
globally and, among places like 'festival marketplaces' and gentrified
artists' districts, are emblematic of new middle class leisure destinations
patronized by urban professionals. As China's middle-income households
grow in number, places like Xintiandi – copied by cities across China –
will become normalized within the consumer landscape.

In contrast to these well-known consumer sites of the new urban
cultural economy, the most popular consumer destination on Huaihai
Middle Road was further west, at the juncture of Xiangyang Road in

Xuhui district. The Xiangyang Road Fashion and Gifts Market was
Shanghai's famous market for fabric, fashion and 'fakes'. Drawing
millions of domestic and international consumers each year to over 800
shops in an area of 24 000 m², the market reportedly served 50 000
customers a day and 100 000 people on holidays ('Curtain call …', 2006)
(Figure 2.6). In the space of the contemporary city, the scale of the
low-rise Xiangyang blends with the surrounding housing of the historic
Concession. But like markets in other cities, it became a site of targeted
redevelopment. The market operated normally, regularly paying its
municipal taxes, until the Shanghai government gave it notice for closure
on 30 June 2006.

Source: 新华网 (Xinhua Net) (1 July 2006).

*Figure 2.6   Xiangyang Road Market, Xuhui district, Shanghai, 30 June
2006*

Covered widely in the media in the run up to its closure, the Xiangyang
Market became the focus of public discussion over intellectual property
rights (IPR) and intellectual property law enforcement ('Government

cramps …', 2006). The closure of the market was timed to coincide with the 2006 Ministry of Commerce national 'Action Plan on IPR Protection in China' and in recognition of multiple legal actions on IPR infringement brought by international luxury brand companies in Shanghai, which had begun to win large legal settlements ('Shanghai suppresses …', 2006). Since Luwan district is engaged in economic planning to form a 'brand corridor' on Huaihai Middle Road, transforming its commercial occupants from local shops to famous national and international brands, these forces converged to close the market. Yet as a reporter for the *Liberation Daily* observed, 'Xiangyang Market also has originality', because the majority of retailers at Xiangyang were selling common Chinese brands ('Xiangyang market …', 2006).

The Shanghai government targeted the Xiangyang Market site for mixed-use commercial residential development, and like the Dong An Market site, SHKP was the property developer for the project, named the Shanghai International Commerce Centre (ICC). The name Shanghai ICC also transfers a name from an existing SHKP Hong Kong property to a major mainland city – the ICC in Kowloon is the tallest building in Hong Kong. The project for the Shanghai ICC is not a skyscraper but rather a set of mid-rise office buildings and residential towers with a multiple-storey shopping mall, called the 'International apm'. In the run up to the opening of the 2010 Shanghai Expo – with its symbolic ideological platform to present Shanghai to the world as a consummately 'better city', achieving higher standards on all fronts – the closure of the Xiangyang Market and development of the Shanghai ICC was arguably a symbolic statement about the nature of the production–consumption shift in the city. Like other consumer redevelopments, the Shanghai ICC replaced a historic low-cost market with a destination for international branded goods targeting high-middle and high-income groups and urban elites. The Shanghai ICC has won several design awards, and the *China Daily* characterized the project as 'green, elegant and efficient' ('New Shanghai ICC …', 2010).

In substantially different ways, the problem of destroying the 'fake' in order to clear the ground for new consumer futures also implicates the work of the China Consumers' Association (CCA) (CCA, 1997). In 1997, the CCA rolled out its first annual campaign, 'Good faith no fraud' in conjunction with '3-15', International Consumer Rights Day. Since then, its annual themes track national government policy (Table 2.2). Working in the interests of low- and middle-income consumers, the CCA is guiding the development and consciousness of the consumer citizen. It operates in rural and urban places, issuing warnings about scams and low-quality products, and didactic materials on the selection of quality products. In response to rising social problems associated with youth consumerism, it develops programming to quell the youth consumer luxury trend (China Consumers' Association, 2008, 2010). But in the rapidity of China's contemporary transformation, in which production, consumption and industrial and post-industrial cultures collide, meanings and symbols of branded goods serve the need for differentiation among a vast array of consumer possibilities and choices. As some local media commentators observed at the close of the Xiangyang Market, what is the market problem with 'fakes' if there is a huge demand for copies?

Table 2.2   China Consumers' Association – campaign themes

Year	Campaign	
1997	Good faith no fraud	讲诚信反欺诈
1998	For rural consumers	为了农村消费者
1999	Safe and healthy consumption	安全健康消费
2000	Knowledgeable consumption	明明白白消费
2001	Green consumption	录色消费
2002	Scientific consumption	斗学消费
2003	Build a reliable consumer environment	造放心消费环境
2004	Credibility and rights protection	戊信维权
2005	Health and rights protection	艮康维权
2006	Consumption and the environment	肖费与环境
2007	Consumer harmony	肖费和谐
2008	Consumption and responsibility	肖费与责任
2009	Consumption and development	肖费与发展
2010	Consumption and service	肖费与服务

Source: China Consumers' Association, annual reports.

CONCLUSIONS

Contested definitions of class point to the nature of changing values in society as well as to tensions over the emergence of the new middle class. On the one hand, urban professionals expect higher incomes and higher standards of living with rising economic development. Yet the idea of middle class as consumers who 'vote in the marketplace' also serves as the context for the construction of a discursive middle class, through which the high-income groups, as political and economic elites, may also seek to represent themselves in order to disassociate themselves from the taint of grey income. If elites seek to converge with the idea of a Chinese middle class, and 'middle classness' becomes an element of nationalism, then consumption and 'consumerability' will shape emergent class relations in the domestic marketplace, intersecting with globalizing consumer citizenship. The marketplace – the mall – will be the reliable place of class mixing if the sorting of the housing market, based on extreme income inequality, continues to define class as 'propertizing culture'.

China's urbanization in the contemporary era of globalization intersects myriad consumer cultural forms, and the new urban cultural economy in the Chinese city draws on these resources to develop its new retail economies for increasingly sophisticated consumer interests. Urban China's highly aestheticized spaces of consumption are seductive in new ways, providing surfaces of elite-styled spaces for both elite and public consumer experience. Yet aesthetic minimalism in the contemporary consumer environment is also the new spectacle, masking how this latest round of urban and economic restructuring contributes to increased social inequality. The cultural-knowledge economy leads growth in the world economy, while its entry into China intersects with the intensification of intellectual property rights enforcement and the opportunities it engenders for international and luxury brands.

Consumer activity is expanding in urban China and is experienced across income brackets and in diverse contexts. Supported by the Chinese Consumers' Association, consumption is turning into knowledgeable activity in the simultaneous interest of both the household and the state. The design of new urban landscapes beckons consumer interaction and guides consumer experience. New transnational shopping malls are built on sites of significant historic markets, drawing associated meanings from past places in a process not unlike that of the construction of colonial Christian churches on sites of native worship. Housing affordability for the middle class may be partly resolved by increased automobile consumption in order to access suburban housing. Even access to the city in China is being redefined through consumption, less by dependable opportunities to participate in the consumer economy than by property investment, allied with municipal governments, projecting lifestyle futures.

NOTES

1. Sina owns Weibo.com, the leading microblogging service.
2. In Shanghai, I visited a show flat in a multiple-building 'gated community' in which the closet of the master bedroom was made from clear lucite panels suspended from the 3 m high ceiling and hovering above the floor, lending the room an appearance of spaciousness and rendering the designer clothing it contained as galleried aesthetic objects.
3. These conditions explain the proliferation of studies on Chinese 'gated communities' in China, which focus on the manifestations of urban residential redevelopment rather than the overall process of urban restructuring and socioeconomic change.
4. With some controversy, the Shanghai municipal government merged Luwan district into Huangpu district, the district fronting the Huangpu River, in 2011.

3. Urban housing-status-groups: consumption, lifestyles and identity

Beibei Tang

In the past three decades, commensurate with China's high-speed economic development, the centre of domestic consumption has switched from food in the 1980s, to electronic goods in the early 1990s, to apartments, houses, automobiles and new leisure activities in the mid-1990s (Davis, 2000; Croll, 2006, pp. 32–57). To maintain the powerful engine of China's economic growth, the state created a group of consumers who had the ability to carry out the consumption 'revolution' that has been taking place since the 1980s (Zhang, X.Q., 2002; Zhang and Yap, 2002). As in other developed countries, the purchase of a new house constitutes the highest-cost and longest-term purchase a household is ever likely to make. With the gradual maturation of the housing market in China, home purchase has become more than a mere consumption good; it has also become an investment for urban residents. Nationwide, annual investment in commercial housing has tripled from 422 billion RMB in 2001 to 1364 billion RMB in 2006, and the area sold for commercial housing has increased from 199 million m² in 2001 to 554 million m² in 2006 (*China Real Estate Statistics Yearbook*, 2007, pp. 4–6, 2009, p. 3). National statistics reveal that the urban homeownership rate for the nation as a whole reached 80 per cent in 2004 (Hou, 2005).

In addition to its economic significance, the transformation of China's urban housing sector is also a process that has created new social groups and class subjects who are defined by their capacity for consumption and their pursuit of a 'comfortable life' and social distinction (Pow, 2009, Zhang, L., 2010). In particular, gated communities characterized by their unique feature of spatial enclosure also enjoy high-level services that forge symbols of 'high status', in that they provide privileged lifestyles, privacy, private property and an enclosure to keep out other social groups such as the urban poor and migrant workers (Tomba, 2004; Wu, 2005; Pow, 2009; Zhang, L., 2010). As a result, this process has transformed urban housing in China from a publicly owned good into a private commodity, and has also led to the formation of new privileged social groups – which I define as China's urban 'housing-status-groups'.

In contrast to the economically determined 'class position' that is derived from the relative control of consumer goods, means of production, assets, resources and skills that produce an individual's income within a given economic order, 'status' is designated as an effective claim to social esteem in terms of positive or negative privileges and is rooted in lifestyles, formal education and occupational prestige (Weber, 1978, pp. 305–6). According to Weber, status may relate to, but is not solely determined by, class position because factors such as money and property 'are not in themselves status qualifications, although they may lead to them' (ibid., p. 306). A group of individuals may share the same status according to an upbringing and education that 'create[s] a common style of life' (ibid.), but their class position may vary greatly according to their wealth.

In China, wealthy private business people and public sector employees with stable incomes are the main target groups for housing consumption, and thus the main housing-status-group members. Compared with wealthy business groups, public sector employees have lower incomes. However, the state launched a series of policies to allow public sector employees to realize their fringe benefits through market transactions. As a result there are different degrees of wealth and political power among the housing-status-group members, as well as varying access to different types of valuable resources. In terms of personal wealth, they are not all super rich – many of them have modest but stable incomes. In terms of political power, not all of them occupy powerful positions in the administrative hierarchy. As far as social status is concerned, they enjoy advanced status but engage in different occupations: mid- or high-ranking public servants, professionals and private entrepreneurs. Therefore, despite the fact that as members of the housing-status-group they share the key characteristic of home ownership in high-status gated communities, it is the route through which they acquired the gated community residence that constitutes their 'status honour'. As Weber notes, 'a specific style of life can be expected from all those who wish to belong to the circle' (1978, p. 932).

Thus, the concept of China's housing-status-groups has more social than spatial meanings. It is not limited to a precise occupational group or distinct analytical category, but is a more inclusive category that includes all beneficiaries of economic reform, whose social distinction results from and is accompanied by their privileged access to economic, political and social resources. Moreover, as this chapter will show, instead of a consumption-based middle class lifestyle, the significance of China's housing-status-groups lies in the heterogeneity of its members, which indicates social class segregation resulting not only from market activities but also from institutional factors such as a hybrid reward system, unequal resource allocation and membership of a privileged group under China's socialist market economy.

This chapter will examine the formation of China's urban housing-status-groups, and to what extent the sphere of consumption shapes their class subjectivities. In contrast with housing consumption in Western industrialized societies, where the formation of the so-called 'housing classes' mainly takes place in a housing market (Rex and Moore, 1967; Saunders, 1990; Kurz and Blossfeld, 2004), housing consumption in China is generated not only by an organically developing housing market, but also by strong state intervention. Housing reform was arguably to be limited to those working in the public or non-enterprise sectors and who had access to welfare housing in the state sectors (Wang and Murie, 2000; Gong and Li, 2003). Those who benefited under the previous distribution system also benefited most from privatization because the opportunities to purchase new housing were largely restricted to the housing that people were already living in at the time of reform (Wang and Murie, 2000). Those working in the non-enterprise and state sectors were also among the first to purchase new apartments in gated communities (Rosen and Ross, 2000; Wu, F., 2002, 2004; Lan, 2003; Huang, Y., 2005; Li, Y., 2005; Li and Huang, 2006; Xu, 2008). Many gated community residents have only relatively modest incomes, but because of their privileged access to property, goods and services provided by their work-units they could become a consumer group for the same quality housing as their wealthy private sector counterparts.

As a result, China's gated community residents constitute two privileged housing-status-groups, representing members of different elite groups who have experienced upward mobility and achieved a privileged social status since reform started. Unlike Marx's class framework that is closely related to production, China's housing-status-groups are situated in a social structure framework where inequalities are generated through market activities in both the production and non-production realms. During the transition from a socialist planned economy to a socialist market economy, China's marketization more directly shapes life chances because socialist redistributive power is less directly involved in economic resource allocation. But certain work-units continue to substantially influence their employees' life chances by generating and distributing rewards, and these better off work-units distribute rewards only among their employees as collective benefits. Therefore, employees' relationships with their work-units have remained essential for each individual's life chances in today's urban China, not only because it provides income, but also because it grants group membership with privileged access to resources and reward distribution.

While housing consumption has led homeowners to a common class, great variations exist in their experience of becoming a member of the housing-status-group. These different class experiences, in turn, may result in various class subjectivities. According to the structuralist explanation, the formation of class consciousness is a result of class experiences over time. People's life experiences shape (or reinforce or undermine) their perceptions, theories and preferences congruent with their class location and class interests. 'Perceptions, theories and preferences are the result of learning from experiences, and to the extent that one's class experiences all push in the same direction, class consciousness will tend to develop a coherent class content' (Wright, 1997, p. 394). In contrast, individualists (Analytical Marxists) see class consciousness as the decision of utility-maximizing individuals who, at a specific place and time, make a choice based on their individual needs or desires.

The rest of this chapter will examine how the life experiences of different social groups contribute to the heterogeneous lifestyles and identities of China's housing-status-group members. The focus here is on the emergence of the new social groups and their influence on the social structure. The main data source of this research is from ethnography and interview data gathered in the north-eastern city of Shenyang between 2006 and 2007. Based on analysis of their path to homeownership, I will specifically explore interviewees' patterns of consumption and leisure activities, their attitudes towards social change, their self-evaluation of middle class identity, and the creation of a quality (*suzhi*) hierarchy among gated community residents. Without denying the significant role of housing consumption, this chapter argues that for China's housing-status-groups, their class experiences and the interests generated within their employment relations more strongly shape their class identity than their experiences and interests as consumers of housing.

THE MAKING OF CHINA'S PRIVATE HOMEOWNERS

In the socialist era, housing allocation was considered a public welfare for urban employees, but not all employees had equal opportunities to be allocated the same size and quality of housing. Access to work-unit housing was limited to employees in the state sector (Logan and Bian, 1993; Logan et al., 1999; Zhou, 2004). The work-unit's size, its bureaucratic rank and the industrial sector it belonged to were positively related to better-quality housing. As the interviewees recalled, the allocation criteria varied slightly among different work-units but, in general, gender (only male employees were considered), work seniority and political and work performance were important in gaining credit for housing allocation. A good reputation among employees also increased the chance of obtaining work-unit housing. By getting married and having a child at a later age, for example, Mrs 19 gained a good reputation in her work-unit for abiding by the government policy of 'late marriage, late birth', thus the work-unit's authority considered her housing application favourably. As a result, she was allocated with housing – which was very rare among female employees in her work-unit. Needless to say, a good relationship with the leading cadres in the work-unit also helped.

Although the housing was allocated to urban employees as a public good, conditions and facilities were generally poor. The house size was quite small, usually no larger than 40 to 50 m^2 for a household with three to five family members. It was very common for residents to share facilities such as a kitchen, toilet, running water, fuel and shower with other households. Because the work-units were the sole housing providers and managers, residents had no option but to endure the poor condition of old buildings and bad locations. One of those interviewed commented, 'Conditions were just enough to live but not enough to enjoy'.

The establishment of a commercial housing market and the availability of higher-quality housing provided a decisive advantage to the urban better off who had the ability to adjust to their changing housing needs. In the cities of China and among high-income groups, 'owning your own home' has become the most important material prerequisite for a good life or a successful lifestyle and one of the observable changes in cityscapes has been the growing number of apartment blocks and villa estates. As found elsewhere, residential satisfaction is one of the most significant predicators for moving home (Rossi, 1980; Hu and Kaplan, 2001; Clark and Huang, 2003; Fang, 2006). Almost all of the gated community residents interviewed expressed dissatisfaction with their old apartment and satisfaction with their new apartment and the environment of their gated communities. Compared to their old housing, their new commercial housing is of larger size and better design – the size of their apartments varies between 90 and 260 m^2, normally with two or three bedrooms, and with better facilities in terms of bathrooms, heating systems, parking and so on.

As the income gap widened after the economic reforms of the 1990s, security in residential areas became a concern for the new wealthy. A gated community with walls and fences, CCTV and 24-hour security guards not only enhanced their sense of safety but also provided a sense of comfort (Webster, 2001; Atkinson and Blandy, 2006). One wealthy businesswoman expressed her concerns:

> We wanted to live in a high-class community because there is not much income difference in this kind of place. If we lived in an ordinary community where both the rich and the poor live together, the poor would envy our money. In this community, we have security because it is gated, and the outsiders can't come in.

The gated community also represents a higher socioeconomic status, a distinct lifestyle and cultural milieu. Many real estate developers put much effort into the sale of a prestigious lifestyle as part of their brand rather than merely promoting their apartments. For private entrepreneurs particularly, the pursuit of status is not limited to wealth accumulation. More importantly, how their wealth is presented contributes to the pursuit of their status. When talking about his housing choice, a successful private entrepreneur said:

> It has to be a gated community, because first, it is safe; second, that is the only way to make sure the status of your neighbours is pretty much the same. Housing in China today is the most important thing. Once you have your housing, you have your life, because that is the only guaranteed part of your social status.

The major consumers for this kind of community are wealthy business-people (mainly private entrepreneurs), high-ranking government officials, managers from big state-owned enterprises and professionals, particularly from finance, law and technologies. For within-the-system employees, their housing consumption today is closely associated with their access to public housing before the housing reform. More than 90 per cent of my interviewees secured public housing from their previous or current work-units between the 1980s and early 1990s. During housing privat-ization in the 1990s, they remained in their apartments and usually spent 10 000 to 30 000 RMB to buy full ownership of their work-unit housing. Many of them subsequently re-sold their apartments at prices four or five times higher. The price at which they sold it normally contributed 50 per cent of the cost of their current gated community housing. Alternatively, some rented out their old apartment when they upgraded to a brand-new, better-quality apartment in a gated community. Those who took on a mortgage debt sometimes used rental income from their old apartment to pay back their loan every month.

In this process, two main factors were influential: the type and quality of the housing people were living in, and access to stable income and subsidies after the housing reform. Among those interviewed many started their career as ordinary workers in state-owned enterprises before the 1980s, because state-owned enterprises were the most resource-rich work-units at the time they entered the workforce, especially in an industrial zone like Shenyang. But most of them switched to other jobs, voluntarily or involuntarily, when state-owned enterprises lost their dominant position in the social economy. Accordingly, some of them had access to public housing provided by their resource-rich work-units when housing privatization was implemented. Therefore, among the public sector employees who experienced housing privatization, the biggest beneficiaries were those who were living in housing provided by a well-resourced work-unit when housing privatization was carried out, because they were the only group who could later cash in their desirable housing at a much higher price in the market. Some of those interviewed had experienced several rounds of housing allocation with a gradual improvement of housing quality, and these people benefited most at the time of privatization. Mr 48 recalled his access to housing resources at different times:

> I was transferred from Beijing to Shenyang in 1985 as an engineer. Engineers were rare at that time. So I was allocated a 49 m² apartment in line with my professional title. It was really considered an excellent apartment at that time. Six years later, I was offered a job in the provincial government office. So I got another 83 m² apartment from the government office. At the beginning I didn't have full ownership, and then in 1996 when the housing reform started, I spent 16 000 RMB buying that apartment in accordance with a series of favourable policies. In 1999, I became a department-level cadre. According to the policies, I was eligible for a 105 m² apartment. So my work-unit sold me my current 123 m² apartment at a high discount.

With the termination of public housing distribution in 1998, some government offices and large enterprises nonetheless developed their own housing estates. In this type of gated community, the apartments are sold to employees at a discount. Although the residents living in these communities may be employed in various work-units, these work-units generally belong to the same supervisory department or to the same government administrative system. In most cases, these kinds of workplace-sponsored housing communities are off-limits to 'outsiders' who are not employees of the administrative system or of a specific work-unit. In addition to cheap housing, residents in these workplace-sponsored communities also enjoy other benefits, such as cheaper management fees or free heating.

Management companies in workplace-sponsored housing communities are normally hired and paid for by the work-unit or the supervisory department and provide better-quality services at lower fees. One retired cadre described conditions:

> We have 210 households here. All the residents here are cadres from XYZ bureau. It was almost like a work-unit housing distribution. If you were a department-level cadre without an apartment, you could get one. Or if your apartment was too small or too old, you could exchange it for a new one here. We got it after housing privatization. So we all had full ownership.

A stable income and access to housing subsidies after housing privatization are also important in acquiring gated community residency. Except for those from private business groups, all of the other interviewees received housing subsidies according to their positions at their work-units and the sectors and ranks of their work-units. Moreover, they all have a pension and medical care, which gives them the security to invest more in housing. In the younger generation, those who are outside the system and who are successfully engaged in market-orientated jobs (such as in private business, high-level management in private or foreign companies, and high technical positions, and so on) are more likely to be able to afford high-prestige commercial housing. Nevertheless, generous housing subsidies and mortgage plans are provided by resource-rich government offices and profitable state-owned enterprises and private and foreign companies, and in particular to young public servants and professionals. To offset the huge increase in housing expenditure arising from the abolishment of the public housing allocation, some work-units, especially government departments and public institutions, offered cash subsidies to their workers. Profitable market-oriented workplaces also use a generous salary package and housing subsidies to attract highly skilled employees (Tomba, 2004). According to those interviewed and working in profitable or resource-rich enterprises, their work-units can provide 30 per cent or more of the monthly cost of a mortgage or car loan to their employees, as well as monthly subsidies. For example, Mr 27 and his wife, who were senior technicians in the telecommunications industry, used up all their savings as the down payment for their new apartment in the early 2000s. For this couple, being able to pay back the mortgage was a far away dream at that time. But in the following years, the telecommunication company offered very generous salary packages for them, and they managed to pay back all their debt, including the 15-year mortgage, in three years. Mr 27 is highly impressed by the economic rewards for their expertise: 'I am blessed that I can use my technical skills and knowledge to make money today'.

   The significant relationship between housing consumption and the formation of China's urban housing-status-groups is that housing consumption has not only created a hierarchy of home ownership, but it has also revealed the privileged access of certain social groups to resources through their relationships with redistributive powers, the market, or both. Those who have been working 'within the system' (such as public servants and professionals) and those who have market-orientated occupations (such as private entrepreneurs) have been advantaged in their access to housing resources, which in turn has led them to their class position. The material well-being or class interests of China's urban housing-status-groups merge as both an outcome of consumption and as a result of group privileges obtained from the hybrid economy. Better off work-units were able to distribute better housing in the socialist period, and policies during the reform period of the 1990s further favoured employees who wished to buy the houses that they were occupying, while a number of subsidy schemes were provided by either the government or employers to urban residents. Those outside the system secured their privileged access to housing resources mainly through their success in the competitive labour market. The complexity of the formation of China's urban housing-status-groups, in turn, leads to a diversified set of class markers, including members' lifestyles and subjectivities.

CONSUMPTION AND LIFESTYLE

For Weber (1978), lifestyle is the most typical way through which members of different status groups seek to define their boundaries – that is, through which they establish cues or markers of inclusion and exclusion. Cultural taste and consumption are considered aspects of lifestyle that symbolically communicate 'distinction' and thus produce a form of hierarchy that is set apart from that of mere economic advantage (for example, see Bourdieu and Passeron, 1977; Bourdieu, 1984; DiMaggio, 1994). Consumption of material and cultural goods serves as a primary way in which individuals become connected with, and thus integrated into, the social structure. Despite their different access to housing resources, a majority of China's housing-status-group members living in gated communities eventually acquired the type of home ownership that contributes to their privileged class position, which differentiates them from other social groups by the walls of their residential compounds and the social boundaries of housing consumption.

Housing consumption is intertwined with the high expense of education, which is another big expenditure for the urban wealthy (Lin, 1999; Rosen, 2004a, b). As found in most developed societies, school is a central tenet of class formation and maintenance. In post-reform China, the expansion of educational opportunities led to a more competitive job market with a pool of candidates with higher qualifications (Bai, 2006). This kind of pressure made parents invest more in their children's education. This investment is focused on achieving both a higher level and quality of education. After-school classes include subjects tested in the university entrance examinations, such as mathematics and English, as well as non-tested lessons that are nonetheless believed to be 'good' to improve a child's quality, such as piano, painting, dancing and even taekwondo. Most of those interviewed sent their children to between two and five different after-school classes every week in order to guarantee that their children 'won't lose out at the starting point', and children's education was considered the biggest household expenditure. Meanwhile, university fees have risen incrementally since the end of 1990s. University tuition and other fees can amount to hundreds of thousands of RMB per year depending on the course undertaken, rank and location of the university. With the belief that better education leads to higher-paid jobs, parents are keen to send their children to the high-ranking universities, and to study more expensive majors such as law, engineering and computer science. The expense is even higher for postgraduate education. Almost all interviewees had already sent or planned to send their children to high-ranking universities in China or overseas. After calculating all kinds of educational expenses for her school-aged son, Ms 70 came to a conclusion: 'Based on today's situation, kids from poor families have a hard time getting a good education'.

In addition to direct investment in education, many parents consider buying an apartment in a neighbourhood close to a good school. Shenyang has officially abandoned the system of exam competition during the years of compulsory schooling, which means students now enrol in local schools based on their residency registration. When asked why they moved into their current residences, more than half of the interviewees mentioned a good school in the neighbourhood as the crucial criterion. Some interviewees proudly stated that the real-estate price in their neighbourhood was almost 30 per cent higher because there was a good school in the neighbourhood. The search for high-quality education starts as early as primary school. Although primary school enrolments are only available to children living in the neighbourhood, in some situations when there is a school with a good reputation in a nearby neighbourhood, parents will use personal contacts to help their children to get into that school and by quietly paying higher fees.

Despite common consumption patterns such as housing and education, stratified consumption is found in expenditure on daily necessities and leisure activities. The existence of this heterogenic consumption pattern is largely determined by the fact that within-the-system residents rely more on the material benefits provided by their work-units, while those outside the system are more connected to the market through their consumption. For example, some public sector employees have privileged access to goods provided as work-unit welfare, so they do not necessarily need to purchase the goods or services they desire. Car ownership is a clear example. All the private entrepreneurs interviewed possessed at least one car, and the majority owned two cars. Very few public servant interviewees owned private cars, but their work-units usually provided cars and drivers for their transportation to and from work, and this was a common entitlement among the 'departmental and higher'-level cadres.

Leisure is, historically, an important form of conspicuous consumption (Veblen, 1939). A central feature of contemporary consumerism is the expansion of leisure activities, because leisure activities are also considered important for the formation of class culture and identity because of the interpersonal relations created through participation in them (Hsiao, 1993; Chua, 2000). Leisure has become not only a serious business, but also a preoccupation, especially among the younger members of the middle class (Robison and Goodman, 1996; Pinches, 1999; Wang, Y., 2003). Studies of urban middle class taste in liberal democracies have assumed that wealth would lead to a middle class leisure and taste, and to community-centred networks (Havighurst and Feigenbaum, 1959). The findings of this research suggest instead that the leisure activities of China's urban housing-status-groups are occupation-based rather than community-centred. For instance, tourism is another important indicator of consumption and leisure. Private entrepreneurs and professionals outside the system tend to travel on their own or with their families, while within-the-system employees are more likely to go on trips organized by their work-units. Usually, the travel costs of the work-unit-organized trips are very low or even nil as they are provided as a work-unit benefit. A majority of within-the-system interviewees travelled with their work-units at least twice a year. This benefit is also available to retirees, but is restricted to the ex-employees of the work-units. On the other hand, short trips organized by gated communities are usually poorly attended.

The result of these heterogeneous lifestyles and consumption patterns is that China's housing-status-groups have less in common than the more consumption-based middle classes in Western societies. Gated community residents have relatively little interaction with each other because of both the physical structure of the apartment buildings and the accelerated pace of everyday life in a competitive market economy. Many residents, especially younger ones, rarely spend much time at home. The heterogeneity of residents also creates boundaries between them; those who work in the same sector get to know each other more easily, those who work in different sectors less so. But in general, communication among residents is low. For example, Ms 33 used to live in a factory residential compound. She misses the pleasant times when she shared dumplings with her 'working class neighbours' on summer evenings. In considerable contrast, she rarely has a chat with other residents in the high-end gated community she is living in now, especially with her wealthy neighbours:

> In this community, all kinds of people, those from other cities, those from the countryside, those from different work-units, all live here. People's personalities, thoughts and mentality are all different. Some people don't like socializing. Some think they are wealthier, so they don't want to socialize with you. Some prefer to keep their background a mystery, so they don't want to socialize either. We public servants do not look down on private businessmen. But there is always some distance. We don't have anything in common to discuss, and some of them are hard to get along with, not like the work-unit workers.

Despite some shared consumption patterns, such as housing and education expenses, the stratified consumption of leisure activities, which is considered a marker for structural class formation, has a divisive effect. In fact, there exists a bifurcation of consumption patterns largely determined by the fact that the 'within-the-system' groups rely more on the material benefits provided by their work-units, while those outside the system rely more on the open market for their consumption. Despite the common image of the 'good life' often associated with gated communities, China's urban housing-status-groups have not yet become members of one undifferentiated 'status community' where the lifestyle of one's neighbours becomes the social context for one's own lifestyle. In this sense, consumption and leisure activities among China's urban housing-status-groups illustrate more the effect of (employment) group membership influences and are not a marker for class formation.

ATTITUDES AND IDENTITY

Economic growth and the evolution of a consumer society in China has generated widespread assumptions that these developments have led to a new middle class with spending habits to match their expanding aspirations. Various studies have considered the new rich consumers in China as the foundation of China's (new) middle class (Goodman, 1996, 1999; Davis, 2000; Zhou, 2005). They provide information not only on how these consumer groups dress, spend and live, and on what they buy, drive and eat, but also on their anxieties about maintaining their lifestyles. The exceptional interest in China for finding and explaining the middle class also reflects the attitude of the Chinese government, which sees the middle class as a force for economic growth and social stability (Li, Q., 1999, 2001; Zhu, 2005; Li, H., 2006; Liu, 2006).

Impressed by the dramatic changes in their everyday lives, the housing-status-groups are grateful to economic reform. The most frequent summary of change in their everyday life was: 'I never dreamed of the apartment and community like this before'. The higher return to education, in terms of both economic rewards and in-kind rewards, brought satisfaction and gratitude among public servants and professionals. Looking at his life today, Mr 49 is very satisfied:

> I am from the countryside. Only a few people from countryside could end up like this. I benefited from the reform. Looking at society as a whole, those who have knowledge benefitted most. Because the space has opened up, you can fly to wherever you want. And there is more respect for knowledge now.

While they are satisfied with their current situation, the urban housing-status-groups recognize the unequal distribution between them and other social groups, in particular, the workers in non-profitable state-owned enterprises (SOEs) and the retrenched. A retired cadre was angry about the widening gap between workers and cadres: 'Under Chairman Mao, workers' pensions and medical care were the same as cadres. Everything was guaranteed. But today, you see, cadres have got everything, cars, a house, and money. What do the laid-offs have today? No wonder they feel left out'.

As they have benefitted from economic growth and the development of the market economy, members of housing-status-groups are more likely to attribute their satisfaction to the state's policy changes that made market development possible. The rapid social change and dramatic improvement of some social groups' lifestyles, together with the widened inequality gap between different social groups, has caused some insecurity about their current situation. Thus, the stability of this beneficial situation over a certain period of time is also a major concern in the urban housing-status-groups. Although the various privileged status groups might attribute their upward mobility to different paths, they share the dominant state discourses of the importance of retaining economic, political and social stability. Therefore, they believe problems like widening income inequality and the miserable situation of laid-off workers should and will be solved gradually and, more importantly, they want this problem to be resolved without damage to their privileged status.

According to Weber (1978), privileged status groups always use their monopoly power to ensure the security of their economic position by exercising influence on the economic policies of political bodies. The urban housing-status-groups have accepted and become supporters of the state's call for 'constructing a harmonious society', in that they use the same rhetoric and discourses of 'harmonious society' that focuses mainly on social stability. Earlier studies on the 'harmonious society' discourse mainly focused on the state's strategies to create political and social stability for economic development (Li, S.M., 2005). The 'harmonious society' discourse is the privileged social groups' strategy for maintaining their privileges based on their exclusive access to resources that are unequally distributed to other social groups. The policy deliberately sought to assure those who benefited from reforms that their situation was secure, and thus eliminated this constituency as a potential challenge to the state's authority.

Given that their consumer power is rooted in the redistributive rewarding system, housing-status-groups within the system will always act to secure their privileges and stabilize the status quo. A public servant is optimistic about the future of the working class: 'Workers in SOEs are a bit worse off, but it is hard to avoid that. That is the short-term pain during the reform. It won't last long. It is hard to predict what will happen, we should improve social harmony'. Private entrepreneurs might have been comparatively more impressed with increasing economic freedom, as restrictions on private businesses have been reduced significantly over the past quarter-century (Dickson, 2003a; Krug, 2004). The consistency of state policies over a relatively long period has diminished private entrepreneurs' earlier concerns that a policy shift could destroy many years of hard work overnight. Private businesses today receive more support than restriction from state policies (Tsai, 2002, 2005) and more bureaucrats are also actively engaged in market activities (Duckett, 1998). Thus, like their within-the-system counterparts, the desire of private entrepreneurs to maintain the current environment for business operation is also strong: 'Once our generation has benefited from this, we won't give up so easily. You can't use those who didn't get the benefits to smash those who got the benefits. That's why we need harmonious development'.

Compared with their clearly shared attitudes towards social change, the class identity of the housing-status-groups remains ambiguous despite being labelled as middle class by other social groups and media. When asked whether they think of themselves as middle class, less than half of the interviewees considered themselves middle class and nearly half of them were uncertain about what the definition of middle class should be. Most of them tended to minimize the comparison between themselves and one particular other social group, while being uncertain about what the social structure as a whole looked like. Ms 27, a successful lawyer, evaluated her current situation as follows: 'Maybe we are better off than salaried people in other occupations. Compared to those rich business-men in our community, we are so far behind. That is where our position is. Middle class? Not sure'. One observation here is that their understand-ing of 'middle class' is that it is some kind of a privileged minority and also an indicator of 'doing better than ordinary people', whereas in the West, middle class is generally considered the majority class, rather than a privileged minority. Nonetheless, when asked to evaluate their socio-economic status within their community of residence, a majority of the interviewees saw themselves as middle level or lower-middle level within the community.

Economic factors seem to offer an easier way to identify middle class status. Members of the within-the-system housing-status-groups tend to be more conservative about their status in the social hierarchy, mainly because of their relatively modest income, while private entrepreneurs and younger professionals are more likely to identify themselves as middle class: 'Sure, I am middle class. I have a house and cars and my own store. Income is important. If you have your own house and car, you are middle class in China'. When it comes to occupations, urban housing-status-groups feel that 'other people are the middle class'. There are divergent attitudes between occupations within and outside the system. Both the within-the-system group and outside-the-system group see their counterparts as enjoying more of the advantages that define the middle class. The public servants consider private entrepreneurs to be middle class mainly because of their wealth; while private entrepreneurs consider the power and privileged access to resources offered to public servants by the work-units as determinant factors for achieving middle class status.

There is also a diversified attitude among different occupations within the system. Salaries of employees from non-enterprise work-units such as schools, hospitals and research institutes usually follow the public servants' wage scale, but their work-units do not distribute the same fringe benefits that the government offices do. In recent years, state policies were designed to raise the salaries of public servants, which also benefited some of those non-enterprise work-unit employees. Although a majority of them are satisfied with a wage scale that is often identical to that of the public servants, they are dissatisfied with the wide range of fringe benefits distributed by the government offices to the public servants. This usually leads to them ranking public servants – a group with the same salary – as having higher status.

A comfortable lifestyle without pressure is also considered part of the definition of 'middle class'. The insecurity caused by the dramatic social changes has made the long-term stability of a better-off situation more desirable than the current material benefits. That explains why the public servants are most often considered the 'real middle class' in China. Some professionals do not consider themselves as middle class because of the high expenditure on their children's overseas education and their feelings of insecurity with regard to their jobs. Private entrepreneurs, although they are more likely to identify themselves as middle class, are the most insecure about their future in the social structure. For them, stability has become a determinant for being middle class in China: 'The concept of middle class, I think should mean a stable and comfortable life. No debt. It is just a life without anything to be worried about'. This kind of stability is expected to lead to a satisfaction with life. One middle-aged businessman did not consider his job as stable: 'A middle class person should have a stable job. My job is not. I think if a couple are public servants, or they both have a stable business, they should be middle class. Middle class should be considered as long term, not short term'. For many of them:

> the real Chinese middle class are those who work at the government offices. After five or ten years when they achieve a certain administrative level, they become middle class. Some professionals, like doctors, are also middle class because they can live in a stable situation for years. They have higher economic reward, and they also have better social resources, and more importantly, they are very stable.

QUALITY (*SUZHI*) HIERARCHY

In addition to divided middle class identities another form of social hierarchy has developed among urban housing-status-groups based on what in China is known as *suzhi* (quality), a Chinese variant of 'cultural capital'. In today's China, the notion of 'individual quality' is perceived as a critical element of classification among different social groups (Anagnost, 2004; Kipnis, 2007). Generally speaking, 'high quality' is associated with a university education, good manners, a white-collar job and an urban residence. Recent studies have pointed out that the *suzhi* rhetoric draws a sharp distinction between the educated middle class on the one hand and the unemployed or the rural migrants on the other (Hsu, 2007; Anagnost, 2008). Hsu (2007) notes a transformation of hierarchy 'from one based on the logic of state socialism to one based on the logic of *suzhi*' (p. 22). Tomba (2008) points out that the state has propagated stereotyped models of 'quality' behaviour, which takes middle class modernity as exemplary. The *suzhi* hierarchy also exists among China's urban housing-status-groups, commonly recognized as better off or privileged social groups.

When asked to evaluate other residents in their community, most interviewees started with evaluations such as this: 'Generally speaking, the residents' *suzhi* in this community is high. But not everybody who lives here has a high *suzhi*'. A *suzhi* distinction was drawn mainly between two occupational groups: residents who were employed in the public or foreign investment sectors and residents who were self-employed – that is, public servants and professionals on the one side, and private entrepreneurs on the other. The public servants and professionals saw themselves as 'high-quality' people (better educated and better behaved), and labelled the wealthy businesspeople, and in particular non-high-tech private business owners, as 'low quality', mainly because of their lower education and what the well-educated salaried residents considered to be poor manners: the use of coarse language and selfish behaviour. Many interviewees complained that their private business owner neighbours only cared about their own interests and ignored other residents' benefits and feelings. Mr 35 explained:

> Both the human and natural environment are good in this community. The human environment is people's *suzhi*, by which I mean, people's education, mentality and morality. For example, urban people have a higher *suzhi* than rural people, because they are better educated and they see more things and communicate with more people in the cities. The residents here are teachers, public servants and businessmen. The teachers and public servants have a higher *suzhi* than the businessmen who are selfish and isolate themselves.

The educational background of residents marked the most significant differences in the *suzhi* hierarchy. 'Higher-quality' professionals were generally deemed to be the people who had been the beneficiaries of housing reform and subsidy policies and who, as a consequence, lived in residential areas they could otherwise not afford (Tomba, 2009a). This *suzhi* hierarchy became a barrier for socialization among residents. People tended to communicate with residents who were considered of similar or higher *suzhi*, rather than of a similar socioeconomic status. In particular, those who live in mixed communities, which accommodate both workplace-sponsored residents and commercial housing residents, feel the segregation more obviously. The well-educated private entrepreneurs obtained greater respect and they did not consider themselves in the same group as the more poorly educated private entrepreneurs who had started their businesses at the early stage of reform as a marginalized group. As a resident in a workplace-sponsored community, Ms 47 is satisfied with the *suzhi* of the other residents:

> The residents' *suzhi* is high here because all of residents here are public servants. Now as long as you have money, you can move into those other fancy gated communities. But having money doesn't necessarily mean having a high *suzhi*. Those postgraduates, they have high *suzhi*, and they will make good money later. Their wealth would validate their high *suzhi*. But those who are doing illegal business, they could be very rich but their *suzhi* would be very poor.

Suzhi has gradually become a marker of class position in China. Public servants, professionals and entrepreneurs all think education and *suzhi* are important. The label of 'low *suzhi*', does not prevent private entrepreneurs from stressing the importance of education. Some private entrepreneurs consider themselves middle class not only because of their wealth, but also because they sent their children to university and in some cases postgraduate schools. The ideal type would be those whose *suzhi* grew together with their wealth accumulation. Ms 29, a young businesswoman, is proud of being successful in her private business, but she is reluctant to consider herself as 'high *suzhi*' or middle class, because she barely finished high school:

> No, I am not middle class. Middle class is a concept of spiritual civilization and high *suzhi*. It is accompanied by a good education. There are some university professors living in our community, they are middle class. They have a high salary, spend more, and they have good manners and *suzhi*. The growth of your wealth should be accompanied by improved *suzhi*. There are also people with fast money living here. They are all poorly educated. There is no way to communicate with them and have a nice conversation, never.

Private entrepreneurs are considered the wealthiest group, but lower in *suzhi*. Yet, the private entrepreneurs do not agree that public servants have a higher *suzhi*, because of the widespread perception of government officials' corruption problems. In one mixed community, the residents in the work-unit buildings turned down a request to establish a joint homeowner committee with the commercial building residents, mainly because the work-unit residents considered the wealthy residents in the commercial buildings as 'fast money with low *suzhi*'. As a result, the two groups of residents went ahead separately to form their own homeowner committees. Thus, in this mixed community, subsidized and commercial housing identical in quality are built next to one another, producing a mix of different types of owners who pay different prices for the same apartment and different management fees for the same services, and who also are engaged in different homeowners' committees that deal with the same issues such as organizing resident activities and helping to solve problems in the residential areas.

Suzhi is gradually becoming the most important criterion for the evaluation of other social groups within the community, and it also influences people's housing consumption choices. When asked whether, when looking to purchase a home, they considered what their potential neighbours would be like, most people responded that they expected their neighbours to be 'higher quality', or 'just like us' in their *suzhi*. The high price of gated community apartments excludes people with insufficient financial resources, and the *suzhi* hierarchy often separates the private business owners from the professionals and public servants. People prefer to have professionals and public servants as neighbours; they are considered trustworthy because of their transparent occupational background and their willingness to share information with other residents. Thus, higher *suzhi* has become a commercial brand for workplace-sponsored communities to attract outside buyers for apartments that have been placed on the market. Many outside buyers chose workplace-sponsored communities such as 'public servant communities' mainly because of the homogenized resident composition and their 'high quality' despite having to pay nearly 30 to 50 per cent more to get in. One young couple reported:

> One main reason we moved here is because two-thirds of the residents here are public servants. I bought commercial housing in this community, so I paid the market price that is 30 per cent higher. They all are public servants, thus we assume they are people of much higher *suzhi*. We love to live with this kind of people.

Given that most homeowners are new to the experience of property ownership and have bought apartments in new, large developments rather than in their previous neighbourhoods, locality-based interests are expected to determine patterns of interaction between neighbours, in particular, collective actions carried out by homeowners over disputes related to property rights (Read, 2003; Tomba, 2005; Rocca, Chapter 6 this volume). During this process, *suzhi* has become a rhetorical weapon when disagreements or conflicts emerge among the two sets of residents. Those who support collective action are criticized as low-quality residents by those who are against collective action. As long as disagreements exist, people talk about their opponents as low-quality people. The bifurcation of the urban housing-status-groups and the constant use of *suzhi* terminology in conversations erodes trust among residents, which in turn exerts a negative influence on their collective actions.

Public servants and professionals seem to rely more on the official authorities (e.g., their work-units or higher-level government) to help in solving problems. They feel angry when their rights are violated, but the anger is often overshadowed by the sense of responsibility implied by 'we government people'. Also, they are not willing to cooperate with their 'lower-quality' neighbours because it is always 'hard to communicate with them'. Their dependency on the redistribution mechanisms for their current socioeconomic status has also led to a preference for top-down processes of conflict resolution. Such attitudes affect their willingness to engage in collective action. Their responses are often based on careful calculation of the social costs of such activities, because they are worried that participating in collective action might be considered as 'low-quality' behaviour by their work-unit authorities and damage their career opportunities.

CONCLUSION

This chapter has examined the new social groups that have emerged in post-reform urban China through housing consumption. Without denying the commonly acknowledged important role of consumption in creating China's urban housing-status-groups, it argues that it is not housing consumption per se that contributes to the making of the urban housing-status-groups, but the complex interplay of market and state in the distribution of resources to create advantages for certain social groups to get ahead and which, in turn, locates their group members in the privileged positions of the social structure.

Despite the fact that home ownership in high-status gated communities is one essential characteristic the housing-status-group members share, they have different lived experiences and they have various strategic alternatives for pursuing their material interests. They lack a shared basis for similar lifestyles and class subjectivities to create coherent class markers. They perceive and defend their material interests in different ways because of widely varying social and political identities defined by their different group memberships within the market and socialist institutions. Therefore, consciousness and practice and the connections between them are important when discussing the formation of class consciousness in today's Chinese society. We should not expect class consciousness and class struggle in post-reform China to emerge in the terms that the Analytical Marxists describe as 'arising from the given, fixed preferences and goals of utility-maximizing individuals, at a particular time and concerning particular issues' (McCall, 2008, p. 152). Housing consumption is an important, but not the only, factor shaping class structure in post-reform China. Housing consumption itself is closely related to the nature of the hybrid economy, that is, inequality generated in the housing market is largely influenced by inequalities caused by the hybrid economy. Path-dependent class experiences have led to heterogeneity among China's housing-status-groups, which includes inconsistent lifestyles and consumption patterns as well as diversified social attitudes and group interests. China's housing-status-groups and their class subjectivities are shaped on one hand by their experiences from their employment relations and on the other by the consumption choices they make. To what extent their lived experiences or consumptions weigh more in shaping their class consciousness depends on the level at which '"a result of common experiences" (are) inherited or shared' (Thompson, 1968, p. 9).

4. White-collar workers: gender and class politics in an urban organization

Jieyu Liu

Feminist discussion on the relationship between gender and class origin-ates in the early debate of the relationship between patriarchy and capitalism. Dual systems theory, one of the prominent frameworks of feminist discourse on this subject, argues that patriarchy and capitalism are related structures of domination that lead to the dual inequalities of gender and class for women (Hartmann, 1979; Walby, 1986, 1990; Delphy and Leonard, 1992). It has been crucial in emphasizing a structural, economic and historical context for the analysis of gender inequalities. However, the theory is criticized for its assumption that patriarchy and capitalism are independent structures. Instead, it has been argued that class and gender relations should be analysed and considered as mutually constitutive concepts (Pollert, 1996; Acker, 2000, 2006).

At the specific organizational level, one of the methods used to achieve the analysis of mutually constitutive class and gender relations is grounded in a processual approach. This approach is closely associated with the way in which concepts of gender and class are defined. Gender is defined 'as a complex and contradictory system of social relations and culture that includes expectations, ideology, social and economic, polit-ical structures, and micro-level statuses, identities and practices' (Martin, 2001, p. 590). The processual approach is crucial to exploring the production and reproduction of gender relations within specific work organizations (Munro, 2001).

While class is widely regarded as a difficult concept to define (see Crompton, 2010), in the organizational setting it may be viewed as the 'enduring and systematic differences in access to and control over resources' (Acker, 2006, p. 444). As Acker notes, class is analysed as a process of social relations within work organizations. Viewed through this prism, research can show the ways in which inequalities are formed and how class relations are interwoven with other relations such as gender (Acker, 2000).

Informed by the existing feminist literature on gender, class and organizations, this chapter aims to examine the intersecting processes of gender and class within a work organization in China. While existing work has demonstrated the structural inequalities, the impact of such 'simultaneity of oppression' (Hull et al., 1982) upon the process of identification and differentiation in the organization has been given less attention. It is argued that it is exactly the mutually constitutive nature of gender and class domination that preconditions the context, and shapes the ways, in which individuals see themselves and interact with each other. In particular, the processes of identification and differentiation create tensions, anxieties and sometimes opportunities for individuals who are at the crossroads between gender and class positions.

SOCIOCULTURAL CONTEXT

In an attempt to introduce a new ideology of equality, when the Communist Party came to power in China in 1949 it legitimized its approach towards women's liberation with legislation on issues such as marriage, labour and land. The Party firmly believed that women's emancipation would be realized through their full-time participation in paid work outside the home and their actions are widely credited with improving women's status. During the Mao years (1949–76) paid employment became a normative feature of urban women's lives; however, research focusing on women's labour at that time has shown that women were mobilized into less-skilled, lower-paid jobs (Wolf, 1985; Jacka, 1997). Moreover, the momentum behind the early reforms did not last and following the commencement of the post-1980 economic reforms, gender discrimination against women proliferated (see Wang, 2000). It has been found that young rural women workers, who made up the major force of labour in foreign-owned factories, were subject to unpleasant working conditions and harassment (Gaetano and Jacka, 2004; Pun, 2005), whilst older urban women workers were more vulnerable to redundancy during the economic restructuring of state enterprises (Liu, 2007).

Class inequalities were naturally key targets under Mao's political campaigns, however, with the exception of the turbulent years of class struggle during the Cultural Revolution, there were still considerable differences in the access to power and economic resources between peasants, workers and cadres during Mao's leadership. Following the post-1980 economic reforms, class inequalities intensified as the gap between rich and poor was legitimized in the modernization discourse and increasingly widened in society. Against a backdrop of considerable social change in China, it seems important to understand how the gender and class influences played out in the micro-processes of modern organizational life. While existing studies on micro-level employment conditions in China have focused upon the experiences of migrant workers in factory labour regimes (Lee, 1998; Pun, 2005), this chapter considers an office setting, because the burgeoning white-collar industry is an aspiration for many (both male and female) Chinese graduates.

A COMPANY IN EAST CHINA

This chapter is based upon data collected through an ethnographic study of a company situated in the Yangtze River Delta of East China.[1] The Delta, which includes Shanghai, is one of the economic development zones designated by the state and has enjoyed rapid economic growth during the post-1980 economic reform period. The company is one of the major state-owned foreign-trade companies in the region. It specializes in exporting machinery products and has an annual export volume that is among the highest in the country. Because of its size, stature and profitability, the company is a very desirable employer locally for university graduates. During the economic restructuring of the late 1990s many older staff took early retirement from the company, and as a result the age structure of the company is relatively young, ranging from 22 to 45 with the majority in their late 20s and early 30s. In 2008, when the fieldwork was undertaken, the company occupied two floors of a skyscraper and employed approximately 75 staff split into four departments: sales (48), finance (6), central administration (6) and technical support (15). The data was derived mostly from in-depth interviews and observational notes taken when I was working as an intern in the sales department for six months. The company staffs were aware of my identity as a researcher and thus I was given considerable freedom to walk around, attend meetings and talk to staff.

ORGANIZING WORK

Roles and Responsibilities

The sales department, which in itself was subdivided into various sectors depending on export region, was generally viewed as the core of the company. In the sales department there were two types of position: sales manager and sales assistant. The role of sales manager involved meeting clients, negotiating sales deals and other auxiliary market expansion activities. As the company's sales were export-orientated, the opportunity to bring in new deals mostly arose when sales managers attended biannual Chinese trade fairs and overseas trade product exhibitions. For the rest of the year, a sales manager's duties mainly involved the day-to-day management of existing clients and deals. It was commonly understood that a sales manager who excelled would be promoted to sector sales manager and therefore be responsible for all staff (including managers) in an individual regional sector. The role of a sales assistant involved looking after all aspects of an order such as negotiating with suppliers, organizing transportation and payments and managing client queries. At the company there were 13 male sales managers and one female sales manager; 24 female sales assistants and ten newly recruited sales assistants (four men, six women).

The official company justification for the gendered division of labour in the sales department (between predominantly male managers and predominantly female assistants) was an historic difference in qualifications and a twofold gender discourse relating to technical ability and spatial arrangement. Before the millennium the division between male sales managers and female sales assistants was marked and accounted for by the difference in qualifications (the former with university degrees and the latter with vocational school degrees). However, over the five years to 2008, the educational background of women sales assistants changed considerably, with the majority holding a university degree. In the most recent recruitment round, all six women had graduated from famous Chinese universities with two having Masters degrees in science. Nevertheless, the female graduate recruits were still channelled into specializing in foreign trade procedure operations, which could realistically only lead to an experienced sales assistant role. This was in contrast with their male counterparts who started as assistants but were given more varied opportunities and were expected to develop into future sales managers.

To account for the discrepancy between women's educational qualifications and their vocational destiny, management invoked a particular twofold gender discourse. The first part of the discourse was built upon a gendered assumption in respect of machines and technology. Management claimed that since the company exported machine parts, men were naturally better at technical know-how than women. However, given that many women sales assistants held a good engineering degree and the export machinery was not unfamiliar to them in the way that men had expected, this explanation seemed to have only limited value.[2]

The second part of the discourse represented the defining reason for such a gendered division of labour. I was told by the management that it was not safe for women to go on business trips and, as noted above, these business trips were a key managerial task and the way in which new sales were generated. To consolidate the gender discourse, management gave the example of the chaotic state of some African countries, and cited internet and newspaper horror stories of robbery, violence and rape incurred during business trips that were circulating in the office. This was despite the fact that many trips were also made to American and European countries.

It is worth noting that this spatial arrangement between men and women has some striking similarities with the experiences of women workers in pre-communist China. Traditionally, the proper place of women was closely linked with the inner domain of the family while the proper place of men was associated with the outer public world. As a result, in the earlier twentieth century, women who worked in paid labour outside their family's (inner) space were seen to do so at the risk of violence and disgrace (Rofel, 1999). The views of contemporary urban white-collar Chinese management suggest that the boundary between the workplace and household has been redefined, but that the gendered association of 'inner' and 'outer' remains strong. Underlying the modern gendered spatial arrangement is the belief that women are physically weaker and less capable than men and require protection in the public world. It is the naturalization of gender that validates this spatial discourse.

In the sales department, it seemed that a male clique played a hunter role, with associated glory and prestige, while presiding over an almost exclusively female subsidiary support network. This gendered organizational logic requires a re-questioning of the association between women and work in the Chinese context. Although urban women had been established as full-time lifelong paid employees from the late 1950s and the contemporary generation of young women has a recognized working identity, from interviews with male managers it was found that the concept of 'work' needed to be further differentiated into the sub-terms 'career' and 'job' to understand the varying gendered expectations.

One male sales manager explained to me what he considered to be the motivating force behind women's desire to be sales managers:

> Some women in the company want to become sales managers, in fact, they don't know how hard-working a sales manager is, what they see is the income difference between two positions. It is exactly the income gap that motivates

the women to desire to be a sales manager. It is not because she wants to achieve any sense of success by being a sales manager.

Another male sales manager held similar views on the relationship between women and work: 'work is important to women but it doesn't need to be challenging, it just needs to be easy and stable work so that women have something to do with their time'. The male interviewees considered women's work in the sense of a job, that is, a simple matter of work equalling income, or even just a hobby to kill time. In contrast, for men, the male interviewees implicitly considered work in the sense of a career, that is, a means to take on challenges and to gain success and one of progression and continuous work. This subtle division was also aggravated by the fact that women were still considered mainly responsible for the domestic domain despite their mobilization into work since the late 1950s. According to Acker's theory of gendered organizations there is a gendered nature to common concepts such as 'job' and 'worker' in organizational logic. These concepts assume a particular organization based upon the image of a white man who is dedicated to 'his full-time life-long job, while his wife and other women take care of his personal needs and his children' (Acker, 1990, p. 149). In the Chinese white-collar context, the concept of career is closely linked with a masculine image, fighting for success at work, with family responsibilities taken care of by his wife.

Related to the gendered associations of job and career is the greater importance that marriage is considered to hold for a woman. As the male deputy manager put it, using a Chinese idiom: 'the biggest fear for a man is to enter the wrong occupation while the biggest fear for a woman is to marry the wrong man'. As a result of the culturally embedded difference between the gendered weight attached to work and family, the company turned a blind eye to female staff who used their family responsibilities to defer demands at work. Although the embedded managerial attitude allowed women to juggle the demands between work and family, it reinforced the gendered expectation at work and the gendered organization between domestic life and social production.

Remuneration

The organizing principles and practices of work have resulted in a vertical segregation by gender and have significant class consequences for women's access to the company's profits. As Acker (2006, p. 450) puts it 'wage setting and supervision are class practices'. The wage structure of the company consisted of a basic wage, welfare allowances and a bonus. The first two components were calculated based on a number of factors such as educational level, years of service and positional pay grade. The lowest level pay grade of a sales manager equalled the highest level pay grade of a sales assistant. The major differential in take-home pay between grades was due to differing bonus entitlements.

The bonus of a sales manager was equal to 15 per cent of the profit contribution of all deals completed, and in a good month this could be more than a sales assistant earned in a year. Sales assistants, who may have made a significant contribution to the successful completion of a deal, did not receive a bonus based on profits. The bonus of a sales assistant was set within a fixed range with the exact figure determined by their line manager's assessment of their work performance. While a sales manager's income was subject to market conditions, the income of a sales assistant was subject to labour control.[3] In order to downplay the injustice felt by the assistants, management frequently tried to highlight the volatile nature of the markets in company-wide meetings to reinforce a notion that the sales managers' bonuses were unstable.

In addition to the officially documented wage structure, there was an unspoken, opaque practice that was crucial to the economic polarization in the company: the annual distribution of dividends from company shares. Although the company was officially classified as state-owned, up to 30 per cent of its registered share capital was held by management staff and, unbeknown to sales assistants, sales managers were invited to buy company shares at a discounted price.[4] Since the company was both highly profitable and had grown considerably in a relatively short period of time through dividends, several managers had become millionaires. As one male sales manager (aged 30) said 'I have enough money even to provide for my grandchildren'.

When I asked if management was planning to allow assistants to buy company shares, the general manager said 'all sales managers are included; however, it won't become a rule to include sales assistants. Whether to give or not is arbitrary. If the management felt a certain assistant had behaved well, we would give some to her'. In 2010, during a follow-up visit to the company, one woman (sales assistant) interviewee had recently been invited to buy some shares in the company (albeit a tiny fraction of those held by sales managers). While the interviewee could not afford to buy the shares on her existing wage she was able to borrow the capital from her parents. She was warned solemnly by management not to reveal details of the purchase to others in the company.

The analysis of the organizational principles and practices of work and the distribution of remuneration in the sales department shows that the organization hierarchy between sales managers and sales assistants constitutes and replicates dominance and subordination relations that are characteristic of class. The income gap between sales managers and sales assistants is polarizing, with a class hierarchy built upon a vertical segregation by gender. The legitimization of gender segregation has been established through gendered associations of career and job, and naturalized gender stereotypes. Finally, the secretive practice of share and dividend distribution obscures the polarized positions between all managers and (most) assistants and, in doing so, jeopardizes solidarity among assistants.

CONSENT AND RESISTANCE

In the gendered and classed hierarchy of this Chinese white-collar company, how do female sales assistants respond? This question is addressed below by applying a feminist appropriation of Gramsci's theory of hegemonic ideas focused upon class relations (Gramsci, 1975). Pollert (1981) used Gramsci's theory through a lens of gender to explore the collision between ideas as both 'received' from dominant class and gender stereotypes, and those created through lived experiences during her study of female factory workers in England. She demonstrated that the contradiction between hegemonic ideas and common sense that comes from an active 'making sense of the world of lived experiences' (Gramsci, 1975, p. 89) were central to the continual interplay between women's consent and resistance to their experience as wage workers and as women. In the modern Chinese company used in this study, the concept of contradiction is embedded in women's attitudes towards the management's ideological hegemony on the gendered division of labour in the company.

When asked if being a woman shaped her life choices, a 24-year-old sales assistant with a university degree in engineering replied with frustration: 'not until now in the company. I was always expected to excel academically. But now the company thinks of us so differently. My heart sank when my line manager said to me in the annual review meeting, "don't work so hard; you also need to have time to find a good husband"'. Many women sales assistants rejected the gendered expectations at work. One said 'the company has very different expectations based upon sex, but I feel men and women are of equal importance at work'. Another complained: 'the sex stereotype is so strong. It appears that we women are naturally less capable than men. As a matter of fact, women are actually more capable than men'.

On one level, many women rejected the assumption of men's mental superiority over women at work. This questioning of male and female abilities arose from the women's own experiences of growing up as an only child in their family (as in Gramsci's notion of actively 'making sense of the world of lived experiences'). Studies have found that an unintended consequence of the one child policy is that there are no gender differences in educational development between single-girl and single-boy families in urban China (Tsui and Rich, 2002, p. 74). On another level, women sales assistants seemed to accept the justification that women are not suitable for business trips. One important reason is that they had hardly any experience of going abroad so they took for granted that what was described to them was factual. Furthermore, the assumption of a weaker female body has wider resonance in gender discourse in China. For example, Croll (1985) pointed to the fundamental contradiction between Maoist gender rhetoric, that woman can do whatever men can do, and the widely accepted belief that women are physically suited to lighter jobs. As a result men's physical superiority over women was hardly ever questioned in the company, producing a biologically determinist understanding of gender-naturalized segregation of work and also limited space for women's resistance.

The naturalization of gender creates obstacles for women in the fight against the gendered division of labour. As a result women sales assistants resorted to a resistance strategy to deal with their unequal treatment. In company meetings management attempted to promote an initiative ideology among employees that emphasized individual responsibility for various aspects of trade procedure and, in doing so, reduced costs and maximized profits. The benefits of promoting such an ideology were obvious to the management since the dividend was a key source of income. However, women sales assistants were not keen to take the initiative. As one put it, 'since they (management) didn't treat us well, why should we help them to save money? We should treat ourselves well'.

Since their career plans were disturbed, many young, single, women sales assistants prioritized their own pursuit of self-development; for example, they learned piano, studied a new foreign language and some even secretly started online enterprises. These women valued the challenges and experienced satisfaction and success from these activities, which they felt went some way to counterbalancing their unjust treatment at work. Other, married, women sales assistants with childcare responsibilities placed priority on the family. As one woman put it, 'the company hoped for our loyalty, but instead we put our loyalty at home'. These married women are fundamentally different from the family-oriented women type classified by Hakim (1998).[5] While these women strategi-cally established a family orientation as an act of resistance, through a vicious circle, this reproduced the gender expectations of management (i.e., the association of women and family) and reaffirmed their subordi-nate position at work. This resistance strategy was built upon a gender construction that simultaneously created opposition to management exploitation and trapped the women.

CLASS CONCIOUSNESS

Women sales assistants were aware of their disadvantaged economic position and frequently joked bitterly during the interviews about their status in the company: 'although the company is so glorious from the outside, there is a huge difference inside. We are not white-collar workers; actually we are just blue-collar workers that happen to work in the offices'. I was also told about their story of fighting for welfare provision back in 2002. According to Chinese labour regulations, the employer should have contributed to a pension, medical and unemploy-ment fund for all staff. However, all sales assistants were deprived of this welfare entitlement at that time. The sales assistants therefore initiated a united campaign for the welfare contribution and, after half a year of persistent requests to the head of the Central Administration Office, sales managers and other senior staff, the company acquiesced. From this incident, it is evident that the subordinates had the group solidarity to fight for their interests. However, there was no appetite to fight against the hierarchical division of labour based upon gender. Instead, the class consciousness of sales assistants seemed to fluctuate in different contexts, contingent upon the presence of a gender order. This is examined through consideration of two pairs of manager–assistant relationships.

The first pair consists of a 30-year-old male sales manager, Yang, and a 25-year-old female sales assistant, Qing. Yang was married with no children. Qing was single. The micro-level interactions between them were embedded in symbolic family relations. For example, when Yang was about to go on business trips, he would often say to Qing, 'look after the things within the family well'. Yang also acted as an 'older brother', often enquiring into Qing's private life, such as where she lived, where to go on dates and so on.

Qing could not do the same to Yang. Although Qing could assert some autonomy and power in managing the tasks done in the 'family', their

relationship was heavily reliant upon the roles and expectations associated with their gender identities. The expected gender order between the
pair made this arrangement so natural that a power relation was barely
perceived to exist. In this pair overt conflict was minimized and the
unequal position between them was obscured by the 'natural' gender
order.

In contrast, the only vertical relationship that consisted of a *woman*
sales manager and a *woman* sales assistant was less harmonious. The
sales manager (albeit low level among managers), Wang, was 29 years
old and married with no children. The sales assistant, Li, was 27 years
old and married, also with no children. In this pair, there was not a
convenient symbolic family relation to draw upon. While Wang spoke
well of her assistant and put her forward for a special reward in the
company, Li and other assistants referred to Wang as the 'exploiter',
criticizing her for making Li work harder than other managers. (Although
from observational research it seemed that Wang allocated similar tasks,
and a similar volume of tasks, as other male sales managers.)

Since involvement in homo-social activities among women was a way
to demonstrate one's popularity, one tactic that the sales assistants used to
fight the 'exploiter' was to exclude Wang from informal encounters both
at work and outside work. In the dining hall at lunchtime, most female
sales assistants sat in groups or pairs, but more often than not Wang sat
alone or with male managers. During interviews Wang confided that she
felt lonely and isolated at work. The difficulty in the Wang/Li relationship lay in the fact that Wang could not extract any power from her
gender, and instead she had to assert only the authority that came with
her position. In effect women sales assistants saw Wang's authority as
'unnatural' while male managers' authority was taken for granted. In this
pair, class politics were pushed to the fore.

On class consciousness, the Marxist framework identified a necessary
move for the proletariat in the class struggle, from being a 'class in
itself', that is, a structurally created entity, to a 'class for itself', a class
conscious of its position and mission (Lukacs [1922] 1968). Comparing
the two pairs of relationships just discussed, it seems that when faced by
male managers, women sales assistants would act as 'a class in itself',
while in front of a female manager they became 'a class for itself'. Such
transformation is closely dependent upon the presence of a gender order,
showing the dynamic and complex relation of class with gender.

AT THE CROSSROADS

The way gender and class are infused in the company means that being a woman would entail a subordinated class membership while being a man entails a dominant class membership. Such a pattern made the lives of men and women who did not comply with such normalization in the company problematic. Zhao (30 years old and married) the head of central office administration (i.e., not part of the lucrative sales function) was the only woman at senior management level in the company. Through an analysis of her feelings towards male managers, female sales assistants and her male clerical assistant, there appears to be a fluidity in and between identity categories. Zhao's position at the crossroads of identity categories created particular frustrations, as well as spaces for coping strategies.

Zhao's department supervised trade transactions, managed personnel and undertook general administration, such as the organization of meetings. Other senior managers viewed these as 'housekeeping' activities and so considered the department ideal for a female manager to run. This clearly irked Zhao; however, despite her annoyance she invoked her gender identity to strategize in the all-male management environment. She explained, 'I think as a woman I have some advantage. If I make mistakes, the other managers will say, "she is just a woman, the weaker sex, let her go". If I try to put forward my plans, they will tolerate and accept them, "no need to be difficult with her"'. Indeed, she succeeded by invoking her gender vulnerability to protect herself and to make her voice heard in the paternalistic environment. However, this strategy paradoxically reinforced and reproduced the gender order endorsed by the male management circle.

Since one of Zhao's tasks was to promote morale in the company, helping to build good relationships in the work force and in particular among female sales assistants was constantly on her mind. Unfortunately, as Wang found, being a woman made it difficult for her to command respect: 'Look at Chen [another male senior manager], as a man, he can easily establish his authority. But for women, whether it is due to jealousy or lack of respect, I always feel the opposition from them. I need to readjust myself when I interact with them'. She gave a detailed example:

> They (women sales assistants) often gathered in the toilet[6] discussing the food, the make-up and pets etc. I feel these topics are so low brow. But in order to get close to them, I tried to appeal to their interest by talking to them about what they were interested in.

In effect Zhao tried hard to downplay her class identity and attempted to bond with the assistants on the basis of being a woman. Although she could maintain a brief informal dialogue with the assistants, the distance between them was carefully guarded by the latter. One of the male senior managers mocked this attempt to integrate, referring to her as the 'mole'.

Zhao's position at the crossroads between gender and class created a further particular challenge when she interacted with the male clerical assistant in her department:

> Feng [29 years old and married] is almost the same age as me. But when I am in front of him, I don't know how to express it, I feel he is the older brother, I am just a young girl. I said to myself, how come I become so unconfident. I find it hard to assert authority in front of him. I need to show extra confidence but no matter what I try, I still appear as a woman.

Gender dictates the kind of power that a female boss is able to exercise in the Chinese context. As a relatively young female senior manager, Zhao's 'weaker' gender status dilutes any power she can draw upon from the class position. Such modification of power is closely embedded in the process through which class hierarchy is formed according to gender segregation within the company.

Feng serves as an example of men who were at the crossroads of gender and class in the company. Although young men started out as sales assistants in the sales department, they were channelled into sales management positions over time. Male staff in the finance and technical support teams were viewed as being equipped with a specialism and treated with respect. However, there was limited potential for promotion and development for men (or women) in the Central Administration Office, and as such Feng was effectively in a similar position to that of a female sales assistant in the sales department.

During interactions with his boss Zhao, Feng was able to take the subject position and assert power in their relationship on the basis of his gender. This was done implicitly; for example, he always addressed Zhao by name only, unlike the other sales assistants who added their manager's title when addressing them. It was also done explicitly; for example, he openly joked about Zhao's dress and accessories while women sales assistants only did this behind the backs of their male managers. However, his success of drawing upon his gender power was contingent upon the fragile status Zhao held as a result of her crossroads position. Within the same class membership, however, his gender identity did him no favours.

Due to the association of gender and class, a man was expected to be on the right career track, with a successful future to fight for. Non-conformity with the hegemonic masculine norm made Feng's life difficult among women clerical staff. As one sales assistant confided with contempt for Feng's role: 'a man was doing this kind of work!'. At one informal gathering after lunch, in his presence, one female sales assistant said: 'Feng is so frugal, he couldn't afford to buy us ice creams'. She played upon his failure to conform to the hegemonic masculine image (successful and wealthy) to exert power over him in public. Feng initially tried to answer back but ultimately just smiled awkwardly. Paradoxically, in the end, the crossroads between his gender and class membership opened an opportunity for Feng. When a vacancy came up for a position as administrative director at a newly opened company factory, Feng was selected to take on the post. Although not advertised, it was implicitly understood that it was the incompatibility of his situation with the gendered class arrangement in the company that helped Feng attain the promotion, rather than his performance and ability.

The infusing of gender and class not only created the 'simultaneity of oppression' (Hull et al., 1982) in the company, it also preconditioned the ways in which individuals saw themselves and interacted with each other. For example, the gender identity of male managers helped to consolidate their dominant class position while the inferiority of the female manager's gender status made her dominant class position fragile. Furthermore, tensions, anxieties and sometimes opportunities arose for individuals (both men and women) who were at the crossroads between gender and class membership.

CONCLUSION

This chapter has outlined the ways in which gender and class interact in shaping people's experiences through an ethnographic study of a white-collar office setting in China. By focusing on micro-level processes and interactions, the underlying research found that increasing polarization is taking place in white-collar work. In the company studied, the organization hierarchy between sales managers and sales assistants constituted and replicated dominance and subordination relationships that were characteristic of class. This class hierarchy was built upon a vertical segregation by gender.

The legitimization of gender segregation was established through gendered connotations of 'career' and 'job' and naturalized gender stereotypes. By making sense of their own experiences in upbringing and education, women sales assistants began to question gendered expectations at work. However, a biological determinist understanding of gender naturalized men's physical superiority over women, which, in turn, limited women's potential for resistance. As a result, women workers increasingly became white-collar proletariats.

This empirical study of a modern Chinese work organization provides an opportunity to demonstrate the ways that the local, social and cultural context is crucial to understanding micro-level organizational experiences. On the one hand, the wider sociocultural understanding of gender and work closely influences the organizational logic among management. On the other hand, the micro-processes by which gender and class are infused in this specific organization shed light upon the wider economic transitions during the reform period. While gender has become a marker in the new labour regimes in the economic reforms (Lee, 2005), gender is also increasingly playing an important role in class formation in China.

NOTES

1. This work was supported by the British Academy (Grant Number: SG48096).
2. Western feminist studies have shown that male technical superiority was socially constructed: it was not gained by men innately but was appropriated by them in their lifetime through social practices such as the definition of tasks and the selective design of tools (Wajcman, 1991).
3. Sales managers had much more flexibility over time and space for work in comparison to sales assistants who were closely monitored by line managers and personnel officers. For example, all interviews with sales managers took place in their work time (sometimes in a café or in a private office) while all interviews with sales assistants happened in their personal time.
4. During the economic reforms, state-owned enterprises were encouraged to be registered as limited companies with shares and became listed on the market; this company went through the same process but was not listed on the market.
5. Hakim (1998) stated that women were naturally divided into family-oriented type and career-oriented type.
6. As sales assistants work in an open plan office, toilets have become a place for socializing with each other without male/senior interference. Sales assistants generally use online messenging services to arrange toilet breaks in their work time.

5. The socioeconomic status, co-optation and political conservatism of the educated middle class: a case study of university teachers

Beibei Tang and Jonathan Unger

In the literature on democratization, the rise of a large middle class is often seen as a prerequisite for the development of civil society and a well-functioning democracy (for example, Moore, 1966; Lipset, 1981). In East Asia, the cases of Taiwan and South Korea have often been cited as examples (Chou and Nathan, 1987; Cheng, 1989; Huntington, 1991; Koo, 1991; Shin, 1994). But China is a counter-example. China is ruled by an authoritarian regime that maintains its rule not so much through blatant force but rather through the legitimacy it enjoys. In particular, the influential urban educated middle class in China has little liking for democracy, as will be seen in these pages. It has been co-opted, and serves as a base of support for the current leadership of China. Contrary to the political science hypothesis that the growth of an educated middle class leads to democratization, China's middle class backs the status quo.

A couple of decades ago, it was argued that one of the salient factors undermining the prospects for Chinese democratization was that its educated middle class was relatively small. But it has grown very rapidly since then, spurred by a very rapid expansion of university and post-graduate education and by the priority placed on expertise by the government and by business. In the major cities of China today, the social influence of the educated middle class is pervasive. Their numbers are large enough that they set the tone and tastes of respectable urban society.

A small minority of the well educated, such as independent attorneys and high-tech entrepreneurs, are self-employed. A larger number work for private businesses, be it as lawyers, accountants or IT specialists. But the great majority of the educated middle class are salaried employees of one or another type of government-funded institution. They are high-school teachers and academics, doctors, engineers and the skilled white-collar staff of state-owned industries, as well as government administrators and specialists of all kinds. A national survey of urban households in 2002 revealed that 91 per cent of university-educated professionals held state-sector jobs, as did 81 per cent of university-educated managers (Wang and Davis, 2010, p. 161). Many of them do not earn salaries comparable to those earned by highly valued experts and executives in the private sector. But much of the public-sector-educated middle class has good incomes. And as public employees, they are what the Chinese refer to as 'within the system', and accordingly they often have access to valuable non-monetary benefits and perquisites that are exclusively distributed to 'within-the-system' employees.

The educated middle class was not previously so materially fortunate. At the time of the Tiananmen protests in 1989, large throngs of middle class protestors joined angry university students at a time when practic-ally all of the middle class was publicly employed. China's educated middle class had good reason to be angry. Salaries were low, and sour jokes circulated about private barbers earning more with their razors than public hospital surgeons. They were bitter that the sons and daughters of senior Party officials were doing well in private business, which they thought smacked of corruption, and rumours circulated about how these 'princelings' were grabbing hold of public property. Members of the educated middle class were furious that when it came to determining living standards, 'political connections' took precedence over their own expertise and loyal service.

But in the decades since, as China's economy has expanded at a breakneck pace, there has been a deliberate government policy to favour members of the educated middle class through their pay slips and fringe benefits. Year after year, those on government payrolls have been offered higher salaries. They no longer have reasons to hold grievances on this score. The educated middle class has enough cash at its disposal to buy cars and, starting in the early 2000s, the sale of cars began to jump at a rate of close to 40 per cent a year. State employees who in the 1980s could not afford a refrigerator or colour TV or even leather shoes (many could only afford cloth shoes) and who lived in dreary tiny flats up six storeys of stairs have now gained a material life that they had never imagined possible. They do not want to upset the political apple cart.[1] If the government's plan was to co-opt the educated middle class, the policy has worked.

This chapter examines one particular occupational group within China's educated middle class – the academics at universities and research institutes. Through in-depth interviews conducted between 2007 and 2009 with current and retired university academics in the cities of Shenyang and Guangzhou, it examines the changes in the circumstances of these intellectual professionals: their current socioeconomic status, their sources of income and material dependence on both 'post-socialist distributions' and market activities, and their perceptions and attitudes towards the status quo and current regime. The interviewees represent, roughly, three generations of intellectual professionals: a senior generation who worked for their university during the socialist planned economy of the Mao era, a middle-aged generation who experienced major changes in their work-units under China's post-Mao economic reforms, and a younger generation who joined the university in more recent years. The interviews focused on each generation's access to resources through the market economy and through the post-socialist 'within-the-system' distribution of benefits, and on how their identities and perceptions of their socioeconomic status have changed through their experiences over time.

THE GOVERNMENT'S POLICY CHANGES TOWARDS INTELLECTUALS

Under Mao, the Chinese Communist Party provided leadership positions to persons identified as 'reds' (based on their loyalty to Party goals and a good family class label) (Unger, 1982; Walder, 1986; Andreas, 2009), and needed educated professionals to fill crucial non-leadership positions in industry, public administration and education. Because of their expertise, these educated professionals of the 1950s were entitled to benefits provided by their workplaces, such as larger and higher-quality housing. However, the professionals' political loyalty to the regime and their class status were suspect (Kraus, 1981). They were targeted for 're-education' under Mao, and with the swing toward more radical policies starting in the latter half of the 1960s in the Cultural Revolution, up to Mao's death in 1976, the privileges of the professionals, including academics, were greatly reduced or eliminated. In particular, the wages and non-monetary benefits of the younger generation of professionals became similar to those of ordinary workers. Nor did the professionals wish to differentiate themselves by dressing differently or leading a privileged lifestyle. To do so would have opened them to charges of possessing 'bourgeois' inclinations. It was a period of deliberate social and economic levelling.

Practically all urban residents belonged to a work-unit (*danwei*), and for most people, including the educated professionals, a job in a *danwei* was all-encompassing (Lü and Perry, 1997; Bray, 2005). Jobs were almost always held in the same *danwei* for life; there was effectively no labour market. The *danwei* not only provided the sole locus of a person's career, it also provided employees with accommodation (ergo, they and their families lived and socialized with their workmates), as well as healthcare, access to strictly rationed consumer goods, and entertainment (even movie tickets were distributed through the *danwei*).

In this system, what counted in terms of access to material goods or to better-than-average housing depended principally upon whether or not you belonged to an elite work-unit. Influential work-units had the connections and funding to construct more and better housing for their members and to secure privileged access to rationed goods. Since little was accessible through the open market, what counted for 'within-the-system' employees (and almost every urban resident fitted somewhere in this 'within-the-system' hierarchy of work-units) was this structure of 'socialist distribution'. In a period when people played down their educational credentials and professional status, they often drew their status within society from the particular status of the work-unit to which they belonged. A guard, driver or clerk in a prestigious work-unit had a more enviable status than did a university-educated employee in a work-unit that was poorly situated in this hierarchy. Even today, when most resources are accessible through the open market, the legacy of this 'socialist distribution' remains, and a prestigious work-unit still has an impact on its employees' social status.

Since Mao's death and the rise of Deng, the priorities of the Party-state's agenda have shifted from those of revolutionary transformation and a socialist planned economy to modernization. Expertise began to be praised as the most important force for the country's modernization. The new national Party leadership reintroduced strict examinations for admission to elite secondary schools and for all universities (Unger, 1982; Zang, 2001), and educational credentials gradually became prerequisites for a wide range of managerial and administrative posts. The same emphasis appeared in Communist Party recruitment after 1980, when the Party began to make special efforts to admit well-educated people into its ranks. Initially, to justify this policy change, the Party leadership declared intellectuals to be members of the working class as 'mental labourers'.

As has been noted, however, their continued low living standard in the 1980s resulted in frustration and anger, especially when poorly educated private businesspeople and children of cadres became considerably better off than doctors, highly skilled administrators and university professors.

Accordingly, to redress the disparity in incomes, a few years after the suppression of the social and political unrest at Tiananmen in 1989, the government took a series of important steps to elevate the status as well as the living standards of the highly educated. The great expansion in the ranks of educated government officials further blurred the distinction between 'reds' and 'experts' (that is, between political loyalty and expertise), and intellectuals have come to be regarded as peers of the political elites rather than a threat. The intellectuals' contributions to the policy-making process gradually became more welcome, and many have been given opportunities to work for policy-making institutes and think-tanks, to publish in official newspapers and journals, and to provide consultations for policy-makers (Zheng, 2006, p. 250). As a consequence, the upward social mobility of the well educated has been accompanied by their attainment of political credentials. Nationwide, by the end of 2010, about 37 per cent of Party members had university degrees, far more than in previous decades (Wang, 2011).

MATERIAL DEPENDENCE

At government offices and public institutions such as universities, schools and hospitals, the basic salary scale is set by the government, and salaries depend mainly on position and seniority. In the 1980s, a low salary was the main and normally the only source of income for academics. But starting in the 1990s, universities were allowed to adopt a bonus system to assuage the material grievances of academics and to end decades of a relatively egalitarian but low system of salaries for university employees. As found elsewhere in China, while base salaries remained largely regulated by the government, the distribution of bonuses led to significant differentials in wages between employees engaged in the same jobs and also generated income inequality among employees of different work-units (Wu, X., 2002; Xie and Wu, 2008).

In 2007–09, at the time of our interviews with academics, their basic monthly salary stood at only around 2000–4000 RMB depending on their position, and retirees normally received 90 per cent of their basic salary as a pension. But none of the interviewees could calculate their basic salary when asked. Their fixed basic salary contributed only a portion of their actual salary. What made a significant difference was the bonus salary. The universities have absolute autonomy in designing the bonus scheme, including various activities to generate bonuses as well as the amount and methods of income distribution. With the additional bonus salary, the interviewees' monthly salary at the Shenyang universities amounted to about 4000 RMB on average and 5000 RMB in Guangzhou.

In addition, in recent years a meritocratic trend has appeared in the public sector as a result of a rising demand for skilled professionals. Today, outstanding young employees of universities, such as award-winners, project leaders and those with overseas degrees and research experience, are allocated resources that were once only available to senior faculty members. For example, University H awards from its own budget 10 000 RMB for each publication in a top-ranked journal. Also, individual academics who manage to organize a competitive research team and obtain outside funding for it receive 36 000 RMB a year as a reward from the university. Academics recognized as Distinguished Professors also receive annual rewards ranging between 30 000 and 80 000 RMB.

Academics' Income from Market Activities

Since the 1990s, China's turn toward the open market has led to a 'commercialization of education'. In addition to funding allocated by the government, most universities have boosted their finances by expanding enrolments and by charging relatively high tuition fees. In addition to their formal tertiary education programmes, many universities have also adopted a strategy of setting up profit-making educational subsidiaries. Universities today allow their colleges and departments to operate non-degree professional training programmes and classes, tapping into a growing market demand. The income from these programmes and classes is partly paid to the university and partly kept within the college, while the rest is distributed as bonuses among college staff. As a result, colleges offering courses in high demand, such as business management and professional skills training, are much better off than those that do not have such classes to offer. Interviewees suggested that bonuses offered by the better-off colleges can be 20 times higher than those of 'poor' colleges at the same university. In this scenario, university employees' salaries no longer depend on a fixed salary scale and a bonus system per se, but also on the profitability of the market activities of their section of the university.

Another source of income derives from the individuals' personal engagement in market activities. Apart from their work inside the university, many academics moonlight as consultants and participate in well-paid research projects for government offices or enterprises. This extra income is associated with the value that the market attaches to the individual academics and their particular discipline. However, the status of the university as a leader in the academic field also gives individuals an edge in the consultancy and research market. Government offices as well as enterprises normally prefer to pay more to hire researchers from highly ranked universities to carry out research projects. Thus, the status of academics' 'within-the-system' work-unit facilitates their competitiveness and success in the 'outside-the-system' labour market. The extra income from 'outside the system' can constitute 50 to 70 per cent of their annual income. For those whose college fails to distribute decent incomes, this extra income becomes crucial to their economic well-being.

Compared with intellectual professionals in the 1980s, who were angry with income inequality generated by market activities, the younger generation today appreciates the market opportunities. Mr F, a young university lecturer, owns two flats in newly developed, high-end gated communities in Guangzhou. Mr F's 3000 RMB monthly basic salary was of little help in buying the expensive apartments, but since 2003, when he joined the university, Mr F also has been working as a part-time real-estate planner and consultant in a well-paid moonlight job. Mr F summarized the relationship between his two jobs:

> A work-unit cannot give you everything you want any more, and so you need to rely on the market. A work-unit offers me a platform from which I can board the market. With my salary, I can't make ends meet, so I have to do other things to support my family.

Mr F in fact does more than make ends meet; by combining two sources of income and benefits, he does very well.

The aspiration to attain a high living standard is not confined to salaried academics like Mr F, but also applies to today's university students. They are, after all, the incoming generation of the educated middle class, and most of them look forward to their own material futures. In one survey of university students, about half said that making money is as important as, or more important than, having ideals or friends. In another survey, 83 per cent of the students at a teacher training university chose 'A modern person must be able to make money' as the most commonly selected value statement (Rosen, 2004b).

Resources from 'Post-socialist Distribution'

Despite the enormous changes that have occurred in post-Mao China, for a publicly employed educated middle class person, privileged access to 'within-the-system' resources often remains as important or more important to their living standard as their monetary income. Housing remains a prime example, despite the termination in the early 2000s of public housing distribution. As Beibei Tang discusses in Chapter 3 of this volume, favoured public-sector employees continue to enjoy privileged access to housing resources. In the period of Mao's rule, under a system of 'socialist distribution', accommodation and other desired resources were distributed by work-units based on criteria such as length of service that gave relatively equal access to both white-collar and blue-collar *danwei* members. By contrast, in the system of 'post-socialist distribution', access today is weighted heavily in favour of the more valued members of the work-unit – high-ranking administrators and favoured professionals.

Access to superior housing is by far the most important of the distributable resources and, compared to other public-sector employers, universities hold a unique advantage – exclusive use and management rights over the land they occupy. Under the socialist planned economy, universities obtained land-use rights through administrative channels according to central capital investment plans. Since the 1980s, many universities have converted this into de facto ownership rights in the new land leasehold market, becoming powerful 'socialist land masters' (Hsing, 2009, p. 34). During the housing reform of the late 1990s and early 2000s, universities often developed their own high-standard residential compounds on campus. They then sold the apartments to employees at discounted prices, and continue today to provide highly subsidized management services.

For employees of resource-rich universities, the ostensible termination of public housing distribution in the early 2000s did not lead to the loss of privileged access to housing resources. Ways are quietly found to maintain the practice, and these rely on close relations with the local government. In 2011, China's two most elite universities – Peking University and Tsinghua University, which are located close to each other – announced that each university will provide about 5000 'self-built' apartments to their employees at discounted prices. These 'self-built' apartments will be constructed on land allocated by the local government to the two universities for their 'employee housing' projects. The apartments will be sold to their employees at one-third or one-half of the market price – which is expected to save the employees of each university about 6 billion RMB in total (Lan, 2011; Yang, 2011). As part of the agreement with the university, the employees who purchase these flats are not allowed to sell the apartments in the market, but only to other employees at the university. Thanks to the hefty subsidies to enable them to purchase the apartments, fortunate members of the salaried public-sector middle class such as these university academics can afford to live in accommodation of a similar quality and style to that of businesspeople who earn several times more. As in other prestigious gated communities found in Chinese cities today (Low, 2001, 2003; Li and Niu, 2003; Tomba, 2004; Wu, 2005), the university residential communities enjoy a protected environment away from chaotic city living and enjoy high-quality services that contribute to a 'high-status' lifestyle.

Like housing, health care in urban China for private-sector workers has often been transformed from a public good into a user-pays system. But universities, like other elite public-sector employers, still provide generous health schemes – together with the services of an on-campus clinic. If members of the university staff visit the clinic, they pay only 10 per cent of the medical bill. If they go to a hospital, the university will cover 80 per cent of the medical cost. In contrast to other occupational groups (especially private business owners and workers), who worry about the prospect of expensive medical bills, interviewees at the two universities expressed satisfaction with the social security benefits provided to them as 'within-the-system' employees. In this privileged 'post-socialist distribution' scheme, retired professors and high-ranking university officials enjoy even better public health care that requires them to pay only 5 per cent of clinic fees and 10 per cent of in-hospital treatment costs.

While they recognize the advantages of public-sector employment, younger employees who have recently joined the non-prestige universities in Shenyang and Guangzhou do not enjoy access to heavily subsidized flat purchases and therefore face a much more challenging housing situation than the older generations. Most universities now only provide rented apartments to new staff members (within-the-system employees only) for the first two to three years after they join the university. The rent is highly subsidized by the universities, and the tenants pay only a symbolic fee. The dwellings are normally one-bedroom apartments (usually $30\,\text{m}^2$) for singles and two-bedroom apartments (usually $50\,\text{m}^2$) for families. Sometimes single employees have to share an apartment if the university faces a housing shortage that year. The lease is usually not renewable, and the tenants will need to move out to make room for newly recruited employees. In some cases, if the tenants want to stay, they are required to pay rent at the market price, which is now very high in China.

After the termination of subsidized sales of public housing in the early 2000s, the universities in our Guangzhou and Shenyang case studies, like other public-sector work-units, started to contribute to a Housing Provident Fund (HPF)[2] for their employees. The university contribution normally amounts to about 500 RMB per person per month based on the employee's salary scale. Given that the amount of this HPF contribution is fairly small in relation to the current market price for a flat, the better-off universities in Guangzhou also offer up to 3000 RMB in rental subsidies per year to those who have joined the work-unit since the early 2000s, and thus do not own a flat through the previous highly subsidized purchase scheme.

CENTRALIZATION OF ADMINISTRATIVE POWER AT UNIVERSITIES

With increasing financial resources available, the government education offices have augmented their power to intervene in the operations of universities. In recent years, the appointments of university presidents have been decided by the educational supervisory government departments, and there are frequent exchanges between the positions of university presidents and officials of education departments (Xinhua, 2010). In addition to providing the leadership personnel, the Central Government offices also control the distributions of resources to universities. In some cases, the positive outcome of a research funding application largely depends on close relations between the academics and the officials in charge (Wang, 2010).

University presidents and the other administrative leaders who have been appointed to run universities control access to the scarce, rationed rewards such as housing, non-wage benefits and even promotions. They also increasingly control functions that university academic departments used to manage, including academic programme design, enrolment plans, research funding, teaching plans, and so on. A recent academic survey showed that nearly 63 per cent of respondents believed the academic committees in Chinese universities have no say in the decision-making about academic resource distributions (Xinhua, 2010). Facilitated by the marketization of education and by what is known in Chinese as the universities' increasing 'administrativization', a new powerful interest group of education managers has emerged.

The shift of power toward higher-level administrators inside universities has resulted in increasing competition for administrative positions. Because of administrative control over the access to research funding, administrative leadership often leads to a more successful academic career. A middle-aged professor recently promoted to a senior administrative position at his university expressed surprise at the large number of invitations and nominations he quickly received from highly ranked academic journals and prestigious academic committees inviting him to become a member of editorial and advisory boards, based on his administrative title rather than his academic achievements. The importance of administrative power has attracted more members of the younger generation to endeavour to gain administrative credentials, and in doing so they curry favour with the university administrations and embrace the political status quo.

THE SECURITY AND PRESTIGE OF PUBLIC-SECTOR POSTS

As a direct result of the emerging market economy in the latter half of the 1980s and the early 1990s, a considerable number of skilled employees at state-owned enterprises and institutions moved into private-sector employment, attracted by higher economic rewards in the open market (Davis, 1992, 2000; Zhou et al., 1997; Lu, 2004). However, private businesses have faced a more challenging competitive situation at the later stages of the reform period. With the rise in wages in the public sector, the gap in economic rewards between the private and public sectors started to close. Moreover, regardless of the housing difficulties faced by some of the younger generation, as public-sector employees they enjoy welfare benefits not accessible to private-sector employees, while the self-employed have to arrange for their own welfare. As a result, the greater job stability, welfare benefits and rising salaries make public-sector jobs more appealing than in the early stages of the reform period.

Although most public-sector employers, including the universities, have jettisoned the system of life tenure and have obliged employees to enter into non-tenured contract employment, public-sector work-units are still considered more reliable providers of job security. Some of the younger interviewees started their careers in a private enterprise, but then switched to a university because of uncertainty about their future at the private enterprise. Mr M, a young university lecturer, shared his rationale for leaving a well-paid job in a big private enterprise for the lecturer position:

> Although a private enterprise can offer a higher salary and bonuses, it's the kind of place where you trade away your youth. The work there is too demanding for someone to remain too long. Once you reach a certain age and your contribution diminishes, they'll kick you out. I would have made more money if I had stayed in the firm. But when I turn 40 or 50, what can I do then? There's no security there. Or a firm can go bankrupt so easily, and you can lose your job any day. Do you know how hard it is to find a job these days? Stability is the top priority, followed by a good salary.

A 2011 poll of university graduates shows that most of their votes go to publicly owned enterprises for the top 50 'best employers' (Jiang, 2011).

Job stability has also resulted in a higher level of credit and a higher status for public-sector professionals. For instance, when urban residents apply for a mortgage through a bank, they are normally required to provide evidence of employment by way of a letter from their employer. Due to the lack of a reliable income tax reporting system and efficient credit assessment tools, the banks lay more trust in the employer than in an individual's actual or declared income. Stable, profitable and well-resourced work-units, such as universities and government offices, provide their employees with credentials as trustworthy borrowers. Some banks even approve mortgages to public servants and university staff with nil down payment because they trust their work-units will guarantee them a stable and decent income over the long term. One university staff member emphasized how his identity as a '*danwei* person' even helped him in social relationships:

> No matter what we do today, we need a letter stamped by the *danwei*, otherwise things won't go very smoothly. So for example, when I introduce myself to other people, people trust me more when I say: 'I work at University X' than if I say: 'I am a researcher'. They trust us because they trust our *danwei*.

The privileges offered by membership in resource-rich work-units such as high-ranking universities tend to increase the individual members' sense of being a '*danwei person*'. This *danwei* identity is strongly associated with the *danwei* moral economy and the idea of 'taking care of one's employees' (Chan and Unger, 2009). Through their role in the distribution of rewards, university employers help academics to maximize their 'within-the-system' privileges and provide institutional back up for their market activities. For Ms X, a middle-aged university lecturer, the *danwei* culture is a very important and treasured part of public employment:

> If one day, our university becomes private, our *danwei* culture will be gone. The state wants elite professionals, so the state allocates a large budget to our university. So our university doesn't need to be too careful about profits, like private enterprises do. It doesn't mind giving us some welfare. The culture of the *danwei* will only last as long as public ownership lasts. In China's state-sector economy, at least two types of *danwei* will survive: government agencies and big monopolistic state-owned enterprises. In China, we are still *danwei*-owned individuals. If my *danwei* is good, my life is good.

In short, the growing importance for professionals of being with a 'good' employer is that the status of their work-unit, rather than just their professional occupations per se, leads to a better material life. This in turn forms a material base for this group's acceptance, and even support, of the status quo and the current regime.

Overall, the academics we interviewed considered monopolistic state-owned enterprises and government offices to be even better off work-units than their own. These state-owned enterprises were seen as more desirable because they offered both high salaries and generous welfare to their employees through substantial state investments and state-assisted monopolization of their market. One interviewee emphasized the importance of these enterprises' monopolistic nature:

> They don't seem to have any pressure from market competition, because even if they don't perform well, the state will help them. A friend of mine works there. He even gets a shopping voucher worth a few thousand RMB from his *danwei* every month. But other enterprises are quite different. They have to fight to survive in the market.

Not surprisingly, monopolistic state owned enterprises have gained in popularity among university students. For example, by 2011, China Mobile had been voted at the very top of the list of 'best employers' by final year university students for three consecutive years (Jiang, 2011).

Most public service work-units such as universities offer three- to five-year contracts to their employees, though in the majority of cases the contracts are automatically renewed. But government offices offer life-time employment, which makes them envied for providing the most stable employment. Although the government's policy is that teachers' welfare should be in line with that of public servants, the reality reveals significant differences in salary and other benefits. When comparing his financial situation with that of his public servant friend, one lecturer observed:

> Last year, both government offices and universities raised salaries. My monthly salary was raised by 500 RMB. But my public servant friend got a raise of 3000 RMB. And they also get a contribution of 2000 or 3000 RMB to their personal Housing Provident Fund, while we only get 400 RMB. That's why everyone today wants to become a public servant. Their *danwei* offers both more stability and better material benefits.

Thus, high prestige, rising salaries, stability and all sorts of material benefits have given government office jobs the reputation of a 'golden rice bowl', and have attracted more and more well-educated young people. This has raised the bar, in terms of higher education qualifications, for recruitment to such jobs 'within the system'. A postgraduate degree is now required for an increasing variety of positions, along with political credentials (Party membership), relevant working experience and high performance in specially designed exams. In 2009, despite the requirements being set increasingly higher and an upper age limit of 35 for applications, 1.46 million applicants registered for the exam for national public service positions, with an acceptance rate of 1:93 (Yang, 2009).

While well-educated younger professionals aspire to public-sector posts, do they also look up to private businesspeople? Some Chinese-language publications lump professionals and private entrepreneurs together as China's admired 'new social strata' (for example, Chen, G.J., 2004, pp. 96–7; Lu et al., 2009, p. 201). However, well-educated professionals do not deem themselves to be of a social status similar to the bulk of private businesspeople. Apart from the wealth gap, a discourse of 'quality' (*suzhi*) differentiates the two groups. The salaried professionals tend to feel superior to many of the businesspeople who crowd the same shops and restaurants that they do. They view the latter, if they are not well educated, as *parvenus*, and hold in disdain their supposed lack of taste. The educated middle class perceives itself as being of a superior status.

The urban populace of China agrees. Even though China's bookstores are filled with books on how to do well in business, surveys show that the most highly admired occupations are those of the salaried educated middle class. In 2000, the anthropologist William Jankowiak (2004) asked hundreds of young adults in one large city to lay out dozens of cards, each bearing the title of an occupation, in descending order from most to least admired. The four most admired occupations turned out to be those of professor, lawyer, doctor and secondary-school teacher, which were listed above the province's Party Secretary, the mayor, an international businessperson or the director of a joint-venture company and far, far higher than a low-level official (who ranks below a barber).[3] A 2005 survey showed that professionals and high officials were considered as the two most 'desirable occupation' categories, especially among the well-educated groups (Tang, 2009). If the middle class professionals feel they deserve a high status, they are not alone in believing this. The rest of the population admires them and aspires to be like them. The views of the educated middle class influence the views of Chinese society as a whole and, in line with this, their political attitudes carry weight society-wide.

THE POLITICAL DISPOSITION OF CHINA'S INTELLECTUALS

The evidence from this examination of university staff indicates the dependence of China's intellectual professionals on the current regime, the formation of their identity as being 'within the system', the rise in their social status and the gains they have made in their material living standards. As has also been observed, well-educated government administrators have done even better. Together, these findings help explain why the educated middle class largely supports, rather than challenges, the current regime. In contrast to the late 1980s, when the older generation of intellectual professionals, including academic staff, joined in protests calling for liberalizing reforms, the educated elites in China today have reweighed the costs and benefits to themselves. Their material dependence on the post-socialist distribution system through their membership of public institutions has increased the personal cost of challenging the current regime. Their dependency relations in their public-sector employment and their identification with highly educated public servants as a whole have decreased their incentives to dispute the current system, and their greatly enhanced living standards give them a stake in the status quo. As a result, the educated middle class today aligns itself with and reinforces the Party-state.

Throughout the twentieth century, Chinese governments have generally been wary about the potential for political discord posed by intellectuals and university students, who in the past have been at the forefront of organized unrest. This political opposition by intellectuals and students reaches back to the liberal May Fourth Movement protests of 1919 and the 1920s, to the communist-aligned student agitations of the 1930s and 1940s, to the Hundred Flowers Movement outcries of 1957 against the Party's deadening style of rule and, more recently, the Tiananmen protests of 1989. In view of this past, China's rulers have learned to worry about the potential of the educated as catalysts and organizers. The feeling within China today, valid or not, is that any surge of major social unrest would be incapable of toppling a government – that it would be leaderless, disorganized and local – without their participation. But today there is very little chance of mass participation by the urban educated in social unrest. They have been co-opted by the system. In fact, now that their material livelihoods and status are secure, if there is another outbreak like the Tiananmen protests of 1989 many of them would prefer to be on the other side of the barricades – on the government's side. This is the distinct impression that the authors of this chapter have gained from conversations and interviews during the past decade with members of the educated middle class, including but not confined to academics.[4]

Our discussions over the past decade with Chinese academics and with other members of the educated middle class have led us to believe that many of them literally do not want democracy – that is, multi-party elections for the nation's top leaders. This impression is confirmed by a survey of three major cities that showed that a mere 25 per cent of middle class respondents disagreed with the statement, 'Competition among several parties in the election of government leaders should not be allowed' (Chen, 2010, p. 345). This is not a newly formed opinion. Two decades ago, many of the students and older members of the educated middle class who participated in the Tiananmen protests held this view. They did not and do not want China's rural majority to play a decisive hand in deciding who rules. Many of them hold the rural population in disdain, believe farmers would be swayed by demagogues and vote-buying, and feel they are not yet ready to participate in elections. This is ironic, since villagers have been the only people in China who have been allowed to cast secret ballots to elect their local leader.

Many members of the educated middle class are now, and were at the time of the 1989 Tiananmen protests, vaguely pro-democratic just so long as democracy can be put off to a future time. In the late 1980s the then Communist Party Secretary Zhao Ziyang favoured a policy called 'neo-authoritarianism', under which the Party would act as a benevolent autocracy until such time as the middle class had developed sufficiently to predominate in a democratized polity (Sautman, 1992). Until then, China would remain in a state of tutelage, much as Sun Yatsen proposed in the 1920s. This was the programme of the Party elite's reform camp, and it drew support from among the urban educated.

During the Tiananmen protests of 1989, what the university students and their middle class supporters such as academics wanted, instead of multi-party democratic elections, was political relaxation in ways that concerned themselves. They wanted to be able to play a role in organizing their own clubs and associations. They wanted 'personal space' – that is, to have the government not interfere in their personal lives. They wanted access to more interesting magazines and films, and the freedom to have public intellectual discussions (just as today they want their own websites and access to web chat rooms). As patriotic citizens, academics and other intellectual professionals wanted their expertise to be listened to in the making of government policy. They also wanted what they considered a more just distribution of incomes, in which they would be beneficiaries. In all these respects, they are largely getting today what they wanted then.

If anything, at the time of the 1989 Tiananmen protests many of them were more in favour of political liberalization than they are now. At that time, they admired Gorbachev and the political reforms he was carrying out. But the collapse and dismemberment of the Soviet Union in the early 1990s and the corruption and plunging living standards that soon followed under Yeltsin's rule soured China's educated on the idea of Party-led political liberalization along Gorbachev's lines. By the mid-1990s, young Russian women were flowing into China in large numbers to work as prostitutes, in what many Chinese considered shocking evidence of Russia's penury and humiliation. Many of the urban educated who had demonstrated against the government in 1989 began to feel relieved in the 1990s that China had followed Deng Xiaoping's policy of economic rather than political reform.

Their writings today in academic journals and high-brow magazines are often imbued with a sense of satisfaction. There are, of course, exceptions, but many of the educated middle class seem to consider the low living standards and lack of security of China's farmers and workers as the necessary price to be paid for China's globalization and modernization. They perceive the current distribution of salaries and living standards as rational and justifiable and consider that they themselves deserve their current status.

At the time of the 1989 Tiananmen protests, much of the educated middle class was, of course, in favour of the right to protest. But now that they have obtained what they want, their mindset has also changed in this respect. In a survey of three major Chinese cities, only 23 per cent of the middle class respondents disagreed with the statement, 'In general, demonstrations should not be allowed because they frequently become disorderly and disruptive' (Chen, 2010, p. 342).

Nevertheless, many among the educated middle class still think of themselves as progressive and pro-reform, albeit in modest ways. They are apt to shake their heads in dismay at China's environmental problems and express hopes that the government will give greater priority to the issue. Many of them were shocked in 2011 when railway officials sought to cover up the cause of a fatal collision between high-speed trains (such train tickets are expensive, and so passengers are all middle class and above) and many tens of thousands expressed themselves on the web in support of greater government transparency and accountability. Those with specialized expertise are often eager to offer suggestions on how to enact this or that incremental reform. What pass in China for academic papers are often really policy prescriptions on how to improve one or another aspect of China's physical or administrative infrastructure, or to relieve traffic congestion, or to provide for a more effective education curriculum.

A small number of writers go further. They worry in print about corruption, about the awful working conditions faced by many millions of migrant workers, and about the plight of farmers. Gutsy journalists, bona fide members of the educated middle class, have written exposés about the seamier side of the Chinese economic miracle, and television programmes exposing corruption and cheating are popular. But these are loyal expressions of concern; the authors sincerely worried that exploitation, corruption and grinding poverty might lead to instability. China's top leaders have publicly expressed similar concerns about corruption and the difficult situation of struggling farmers. Barely any of this investigative journalism hints at displeasure with the national leadership, and this does not just seem to be a question of censorship. Even most of the relatively small group of investigative journalists and critical academics appear to live comfortably within the boundaries of China's status quo.

There is one issue over which a part of the middle class, including some academics, at times feels at odds with government policy, and that is when national pride is at stake. They harbour concerns even though the government itself has consistently pushed patriotism as a means to prop up the populace's overall political support. Chinese leaders tend to play this card less fervently or blatantly than American presidents often have, but at times when Chinese pride is injured the government has reacted angrily for domestic audiences. It did so in 1999 when the Chinese embassy in Belgrade was bombed by American planes (Gries, 2001; Hillman, 2004); it did so twice when Japan rewrote textbooks to picture Japan's military behaviour in China during World War II in a softer light; and it did so in 2008 when the Olympic torch (which in Chinese was called the 'sacred flame', its sacredness identified with China and Chinese national pride) was attacked on its travels round the world by pro-Tibetan demonstrators (Nyiri et al., 2010). By encouraging nationalism at home at such moments, though, Beijing has run the risk of seeming too mild in its diplomatic reactions in the international arena, and a portion of the middle class feels uncomfortable whenever this occurs.

But the grumbling at such moments has been fleeting. Few among the educated middle class actually seem to put great importance in nationalism as a personal ongoing political concern. China's educated middle class is open-minded regarding foreign influences, both in their professional work and more generally. They look approvingly on most things foreign and modern and are eager to sample foreign foods, fashions and fads. The best of the university students (a disproportionate number of whom come from educated middle class families) eagerly prepare for the TOEFL (Test of English as a Foreign Language) and IELTS (International English Language Testing System) exams so that they can study abroad at a postgraduate level, and many are quite happy ultimately to settle abroad, with their parents' encouragement.

Whatever their qualms over this or that government statement or policy, most members of the educated middle class find little to be irritated about on a daily or ongoing basis in regard to the Central Government. This is quite unlike earlier times. Under Mao in the 1970s, when the government had direct control over almost all economic activity and was responsible for all services, it naturally took the blame whenever there were shortages or inadequate services. This was a problem all communist political systems have faced. But as the Central Government in China has pulled back from dominating everything directly and has devolved responsibilities to lower levels or to the private sector, it can no longer be blamed by the populace for the various frustrations of daily life. Instead, it is now the private employer, or the school head, or a *local* official who is perceived as blameworthy, and the Central Government is no longer so much the lightning rod for people's frustrations and anger.[5] This is especially true among the educated urban middle class, which has little to feel resentful about in any case.

Instead, when members of the educated middle class see the national leaders on the evening television news, they generally perceive the leaders in a favourable light. The current leaders fit the image of the type of people the middle class want to see in charge. As of 2011, the President and Party Secretary, Hu Jintao, the Prime Minister Wen Jiabao and their designated successors were all university-educated technocrats who rose to the very top through what has increasingly become a Party meritocracy. They look like members of the educated middle class, and share many of its values. When people from the urban educated middle class bother to think fleetingly about politics they do not, by and large, favour some imagined alternative political system. This is, to a large extent, *their* leadership.

Their favourable view of the status quo and the Chinese leadership is not new-found. It was also evident a decade ago in the early part of the 2000s. For instance, summarizing a large survey of political attitudes in Beijing, a 2004 book by the political scientist Jie Chen concluded that, among all urban groups, 'those who perceive themselves to belong to the middle class and who are government bureaucrats are more likely to support the incumbent authorities' (Chen, J., 2004, p. 152).

The Chinese educated middle class has, as a whole, become a bulwark of the current regime. As a consequence, regime change or democratization should not be expected any time soon. The rise of China's educated middle class blocks the way.

NOTES

1. On the attitudes of China's urban population towards their government see Chen, J. (2004) and Whyte (2010).
2. The Housing Provident Fund (HPF) is an employment-based, nationwide, compulsory savings plan for the purchase of private housing. Under this system every worker in state work-units is required to set up an account in the local HPF management centre. Employers and employees are required to contribute the same amount to the employees' HPF account. Almost all universities in China, as public-sector work-units, are required to contribute to the HPF. On top of the HPF contribution, individual universities can offer other subsidies from their own funding sources. The subsidies can be used for either savings or rental payments, according to employees' own preferences. Details of HPF are discussed in Wang and Murie (1996, p. 985) and Zhang (2000, p. 343).
3. A similar more recent survey showed the mayor at the top of the prestige ladder, but he was followed closely by the engineer, scientist and university teacher.
4. One of the co-authors has engaged in such discussions with Chinese intellectual professionals going back into the 1980s.
5. This shift of attitudes among China's farmers is discussed in Unger (2002, pp. 214–15).

6. Homeowners' movements: narratives on the political behaviours of the middle class[1]

Jean-Louis Rocca

The 'middle classes' have become a hot topic in Chinese society. Researchers, officials and journalists have largely adopted the idea that China needs a strong middle class to pursue modernization. Admittedly, points of view are diverse concerning the definition of this group of people – in terms of level of income and education, type of job, lifestyle and relationship with the state, but everybody agrees on the tasks it has to assume: to stimulate domestic consumer demand, to raise the quality of the population, to introduce modern lifestyles and to contribute to political change (Li, 2006; Goodman, 2008a; Rocca, 2008, 2009). The middle class is supposed to be the only force that can contribute efficiently to democratization. It is an idealistic class, conscious of its rights and ready to defend them but, at the same time, clearly opposed to any political clash. As it relies exclusively upon rational solutions to solve social and political conflicts, the middle class could play a vanguard role without jeopardizing social stability (Tsinghua daxue ..., 2010).

This understanding is supported explicitly and implicitly by modernization theory (Lipset, 1959, 1960; Rostow, 1960; Moore, 1966; Inkeles and Smith, 1975; Inglehart, 1997; Huntington, 2006), which considers that industrialization improves the likelihood of democratic transition by increasing the levels of education, by stimulating urbanization and occupational specialization. These phenomena contribute to the emergence of relevant political actors and create social pressure for democratization. Roughly speaking, during the stage leading up to modernity, economic growth is supposed to give birth to a new social class – one that most scholars confusingly call both a bourgeoisie or middle class, though strictly speaking these are not the same – which compels the state to introduce a democratic system with regular, free and fair elections.

This has apparently been documented by many case studies in Western and East Asian countries (Goodman, 2008a). Under this theoretical framework, the question at stake is whether all middle classes have the capacity to assume the same historical role their counterparts did in the development of other countries: that of changing or strongly contributing to a change of polity.

The objective of this chapter is not to enter into that controversy. It is mainly to contribute to the assessment of its heuristic value by asking two questions. First, is the role of the middle classes and particularly that of the new middle classes (white-collar, managerial and professional workers) in the democratization process so clearly established? Second, is the political behaviour of the Chinese middle classes comparable to that of its counterparts in Western and East Asian countries, or does it confound its expected role?

In such a short chapter, it is unthinkable to deal with the Chinese middle classes as a whole. Not only because we would need to take into account the behaviour of very different groups of people, but also because we could not avoid the huge and controversial question of the definition of the Chinese middle class. Moreover, following Boltanski in his seminal book, *The Making of a Class*, I consider that the 'middle class' has no existence in itself: it is the result of a social construction in which individuals, groups and institutions play a prominent role, and in which social imaginary and material constraints are of equal importance (Boltanski, 1987).

In recent years, many foreign and Chinese researchers have emphasized 'homeowners' as representing the politically conscious vanguard of the Chinese middle classes. One of the reasons for this focus lies in the growing number of social conflicts that have mobilized people to defend their property rights. According to a survey of 100 estates, conflicts over property rights occurred in 80 per cent of them (Chuan, 2009, p. 3). Another reason to deal with this specific group is linked to the idea, largely widespread in intellectual and political fields, that the struggle for 'property rights' could lead to the struggle for 'citizens' rights' (Chen, 2009). Not only has the level of income and professional status of this group given them the capacity to enter into the ranks of property owners, but their level of education has enabled them to become aware of social evils. Occupying a prominent social status, homeowners are considered to be in possession of the resources to organize themselves and to enact protesting strategies (Tomba, 2005, 2009b).

Finally, homeowners' movements are particularly well documented. In recent years, numerous journalists and scholars have written articles on the subject, and research groups have been specifically set up to study this field. Internet forums are full of references to different aspects of conflicts occurring in *xiaoqu* (housing estates). For the purposes of this chapter, I have also paid particular attention to 'grey literature', in particular, theses written by students from Tsinghua University as well as different non-published studies by Chinese scholars. In particular, I will use results of research conducted by a group of students led by Professor Shen Yuan of Tsinghua University. I also had the opportunity to conduct 11 in-depth interviews with people who have participated in home-owners' movements, and more than 100 shorter interviews with members of the Beijing middle class about conflicts in *xiaoqu*.[2]

SOCIAL MOVEMENTS AND THE MIDDLE CLASS: SOME HISTORICAL ELEMENTS

Did the new middle class contribute to democratization in developed countries? I will successively deal with the situation of the middle classes in Western countries and in East Asian countries.

Middle Classes and Democratization in Western Countries

From an historical point of view it is completely wrong to say that, in Western Europe and in the United States, the new middle class is the father of democracy. The new middle class grew quickly in the beginning of the twentieth century (in the US) and in the 1950s and 60s (in Western Europe), periods when democracy was well established.[3] On the contrary, before World War II, the embryonic new middle class was not particularly struggling for democratic rights in any Western democracy.[4]

This mistake, which is very widespread among scholars, is probably due to confusion between the 'bourgeoisie' and the 'middle class'. Be that as it may, if the relationship between the bourgeoisie and democracy is still a matter for debate, there is no doubt that there is no correlation between democratization and the growth of the middle class, at least in Europe and in the United States.

Concerning the role of the middle class in the process of political change, the conclusions are more balanced but very confusing. C. Wright Mills is probably the most quoted author with regard to the middle class. Most scholars use his book as the main piece in arguments that emphasize the role played by the middle classes in political change. Yet, if we read Mills carefully, we discover the opposite point of view: that the new middle class has no political role to play. He writes 'Whatever history they [the new middle class members] have had is a history without events; whatever common interests they have do not lead to unity; whatever future they have will not be of their own making' (Mills [1951] 2002, p. ix). Further, he argues (p. xviii) that:

> The political problem posed by these people is not so much what the [political] direction may be as whether they will take any political direction ... Estranged from community and society in a context of distrust and manipulation; alienated from work and, on the personality market, from self; expropriated of individual rationality, and politically apathetic – these are the new little people, the unwilling vanguard of modern society.

Mills argues that the middle class has blurred boundaries and is highly fragmented. 'White-collar groups are differentiated socially, perhaps more decisively than wage-workers and entrepreneurs' (p. 73). 'For these classes are diversified in social form, contradictory in material interest, dissimilar in ideological illusions; there is no homogeneity of base among them for common political movement' (p. 351). In brief, Mills suggests, 'the new middle classes will continue to grow in numbers and power, and although they will not become a force that will rise to independent power, they will be a major force for stability in the general balance of the different classes', and 'they are natural allies and shock troops of the larger capitalist drive' (pp. 290–91).

Likewise, for Bourdieu the main character of the middle class is its dependence on work as well as on the other aspects of social life (Bourdieu, 1984). The members of the new middle class are confronted with an unstable world, and they are never sure where they are situated on the social ladder. They imitate the bourgeoisie and strive to avoid falling in the category of 'workers'. What they want is to obtain the symbolic and material rewards attached to the bourgeois condition. They reproach the dominant class for using 'tricks' (such as social capital, money, cultural capital) instead of using 'normal ways' (such as education, personal efforts and talents) to maintain their position in society. In this struggle, laws and regulations are supposed to be efficient means for guaranteeing 'fair competition'. This is all they can do as far as politics is concerned:

> Their desire for social recognition and their proleptic identification with the dominant class are revealed in the nature of their demands, which give priority to the symbolic aspects of existence, not only because affronts to the dignity of the 'person' are felt more acutely by those who are freed from the most brutal forms of oppression and exploitation, but also because their very concern for dignity inclines them to demands which testify to the dignity of the demander. Thus the fear of losing all they have won, by trying to get all they have been promised (particularly through education and qualifications),

does not fully explain the form taken by petit-bourgeois bargaining strategies. The ordinary means of the workers' struggle, strikes or demonstrations, are for them a last resort, which they will consider only when driven to extremities by excessive injustice ('If need be, we'll take to the streets'). They prefer symbolic weapons, starting with campaigns for 'education', which sets up a relation of domination, or 'information', in which they have inordinate faith, and that particular form of collective action which is achieved through the 'association', a strictly serial grouping of individuals assembled solely by the same 'cause', the same desire to deliver a sort of ethical summons. (Bourdieu 1984, pp. 456–7)

The Ambiguities of New Social Movements

In the 1970s and 1980s, the emergence of new forms of social movements attracted the interest of many European researchers. For them, these movements were contemporaneous with the emergence of a new society (post-industrial, post-materialist, post-modern, complex, etc.), in which 'traditional' demands for material benefits were replaced by demands for more participation, more autonomy, more control over labour organization, a better quality of life and the ability to express identities (for example, sexual, ethnic, linguistic, cultural, in consumption and gender relations) (Bell, 1973; Inglehart, 1977). The general increase in education and income levels among the European population after World War II gave rise to a large group of middle-range wage earners that launched very specific social movements. This rapidly increasing group of people struggled against new forms of domination that not only defined behaviours at work but also moulded every aspect of social life and even created 'programmed' identities (Melucci, 1978; Touraine, 1978). As a result, if certain aspects of the new social movements can be considered simply as reactions against the marginalization of particular groups or attempts to access the political field, the main objective of most of them is quite different: it is to strive for the modernization of archaic institutions (culture, neighbourhood, family, prison, psychiatry, consumption, sexuality, environment) that repress free expression of identities and especially of symbolic identities. The fundamental motive of protesters is to recognize themselves, to be recognized as subjects of their own life and to satisfy individual needs in their specificities (Kriesi, 1995).

However, some scholars have contested whether these movements reflect the opinions and interests of a specific category called the 'middle class'. Middle class politics is characterized by variability, inconsistency and fluidity and the mere existence of 'middle class politics' is highly questionable (Abercrombie and Urry, 1983; Oppenheimer, 1985). The emergence of 'new social movements' is not connected to the development of a 'service class', a group that would be the core of the middle class (Bagguley, 1992). The 'new social movements' are led by intellectual radicals and advanced detachments rather than by a class (Duyvendak, 1995; Cleveland, 2003). In the 1970s and 1980s, most left-wing intellectuals had lost confidence in the capacity of the working class to destroy capitalism and sought a new revolutionary force. From this perspective, the middle classes represented a serious option. But, contrary to the hopes of left-wing intellectuals, middle class protest movements did not aim to overthrow the capitalist system but to reform the system to protect the interests of certain social categories to the detriment of others.

Why is the middle class not a revolutionary class? First, the new social movements paid little attention to the demands of the lower classes. On the contrary they developed a specific protest culture that is at odds with that of the working class. No matter what lifestyles, behaviours, social expectations, political ideas or cultural tastes are concerned, the middle classes aim to distinguish themselves from the lower classes.

The second problem concerns the structural tension that exists between individuals and collective action. A movement is collective but the logic of action is determined at the individual level (Melucci, 1982, pp. 91–2). As a consequence, both the involvement of individuals and the endurance of a movement are very fragile. A new movement is easily subject to manipulation, treason and break-up, which can nourish criticisms against the behaviours and the trajectories of the leaders. Moreover, as long as the system gives people the opportunity to satisfy their individual needs, they will be ready to accept it and to give up more radical demands.

Third, in post-industrial societies, it is very difficult to oppose 'state' and 'society' and many new social movements have been subjected to a process of institutionalization. For instance, in Western Europe, governments have created ministries for the environment, for women's rights, and so on. Some activists have become politicians and some associations have become partners of the state (and of the European Commission), receiving funds and obtaining influence on public policies (Tarrow, 1989; Spanou, 1991; Dalton and Kuechler, 1990).

Finally, demands for the recognition of identities have been naturally and gradually 'hijacked' by business interests. The success stories of green and fair trade products, of 'authentic' and local goods, the emergence of ethnic or gay businesses, the development of a 'well-being' industry (for example, new age activities, personal development, psychic therapies) prove that identities can be transformed by capitalism into new means of wealth accumulation.

Economic Miracles and Middle Classes: East Asian Countries

Many researchers have popularized the idea that the middle classes have played a determinant role in the third wave of democratization (Hunting-ton, 1991; Glassman, 1997) and particularly in the democratization of Asian countries (Hsiao, 1993). In South Korea, the middle classes have allegedly played a determinant role in the collapse of the authoritarian rule (Han, 1989; Kim, 2008). In Taiwan, they are said to have been the main force in the struggle for the creation of the first Chinese democracy (Tien, 1996; Diamond et al., 1997, Chapters 5 and 9; Chao and Myers, 1998). However, the supporters of this argument do not take into account an impressive quantity of research and materials that challenge, or at least weaken, the 'middle classes' thesis (Jones, 1995, 1998). It is not meaningless to remark that Koo (1991, p. 491) whose works are usually used in support of this thesis, has, actually, a more subtle stance on this matter. For him:

> the role of the middle classes in democratization is fluid and variable, not necessarily because of their inherently inconsistent class interest but because the democratization process is a complex and protracted process and because different segments of the middle class respond to this political change differently. The transition from authoritarian rule is composed of a series of different 'moments' or conjunctures, each of which raises different issues, a different form of conflicts, and a shifting balance of power among classes. Responses to these changing political contexts varied not only between the working class and the middle class, but also among different segments of the middle class.

Roughly speaking, if many segments of the Korean middle classes were in favour of democratization before 1987, after that date they supported more authoritarian forms of governing by fear of instability (see also Dong, 1993).

For Englehart, the middle classes did not play a specific role in the democratization of Thailand compared to other classes. A part of the elite, that is to say, a coalition of military and bureaucratic interests, decided that an electoral system would preserve stability more efficiently than a dictatorship. Englehart (2003, p. 254) writes:

> Economic growth in Thailand was based on foreign capital, and created a globalised economy sensitive to the confidence of international markets. A perception that these capital markets favoured democratic regimes and polit-ical stability changed the political calculus in Thailand, shifting it firmly toward liberal democracy in the wake of the 1997 currency crisis.

As for the middle classes, they supported protests against corruption and for more democracy but adopted more cautious attitudes as soon as stability was disturbed (Englehart, 2003; see also Ockey, 1999).

In Taiwan, the triggering factor was the success of the reform policy on the mainland. The Nationalist Party and the elite were forced to abandon the fiction of reconquest and to focus on the 'national question' (Mengin, 2000). As such, the democratization process has been largely controlled from the top (Nathan and Ho, 1997). In the 1990s, the middle classes were not particularly in favour of democracy as they were strongly associated with the Nationalist Party and industrial bureaucracy (Metraux, 1991). This does not mean that the middle classes opposed the process of democratization or did not support the social movements that flourished in the 1990s, but simply that they were not the driving force in the process of political change.

HOMEOWNERS' MOVEMENTS IN URBAN CHINA: SOME FINDINGS

As it did elsewhere in China, the 'Notice Concerning the Deepening of the Reform of Housing System in Cities and Towns and the Speeding of House Building', dispatched in 1998 by the State Council, paved the way for the spread of housing system reform in Beijing. Under this notice, the welfare system was abolished, and housing was commodified and governed by market forces. The main building pattern has taken the form of housing estates made up of big towers and shaped as gated communities. In 2007, Beijing had 5000 housing estates ('Wuquanfa shishi … ', 2007), 4000 of which housed more than 10 million people inside the fourth ring road (Chuan, 2009, p. 4). In these gated communities, all flats are privately owned. Some are rented out by their owners.

This reform has given birth to a new stratum of homeowners and to a new source of conflict. Property rights are clearly guaranteed by law but, until 2003, no regulations were in place that could tackle the issue of estate management and, in particular, the management of common areas (such as warehouses, parking lots, shops and lifts). However, even after the promulgation of the 'Regulations on Estate Management' in March 2007, most aspects of collective life in housing estates have been left vague. Three interest groups are in charge of *xiaoqu* management and are regularly in conflict. The first interest group is the homeowners themselves, who are both individuals and members of a community of homeowners – a double identity, both components of which have only very recently emerged. The second interest group is made up of real estate companies and management companies, which are generally connected and sometimes belong to the same 'business group'. The third interest group is made up of the residents' committees, the street bureaux and the local Beijing Construction Commission, which are responsible for the control and the supervision of all aspects of the estate's social life.

These three groups do not have the same strength. Not only do the 'market' forces and administrative institutions – the second two groups – enjoy massive resources but they have close ties. Consequently, local administration is rarely supportive of the point of view of homeowners even if, in certain cases, it sincerely tries to arbitrate the dispute. Moreover, the regulations that control the way estates have to be managed are clearly partial to real estate and management companies. The homeowners are supposed to be the rulers and to have the ability to change management companies quite easily but in reality any decision requires the approval of a large majority of homeowners, which can rarely be achieved. Because of the difficulties of mobilizing numerous people, it is quite easy for the interest group to divide and rule.

Strangely enough, while the adoption of regulations, circulars and rules in the beginning of the twenty-first century is a response to the increasing number of protests, it has led to an explosion of legal and administrative cases. Figures from six district courts from 2003 to 2007 reveal a sharp increase in the number of cases concerning the management of estates. At a grassroots level, complainants have immediately understood the importance and usefulness of legal tools for action against malpractices. But the promulgation of new regulations in 2007 has had the opposite effect: a decline in the number of cases (Chuan, 2009, p. 13). As for the number of complaints concerning disputes in estates received by district construction commissions, these rose sharply during the period 2002–04, remained steady during 2004–06 and dropped afterwards (ibid., p. 14). In this case, it seems that the progressive legalization of the management of *xiaoqu* has constrained local administration and companies to negotiation in order to prevent legal action and protest.

The typology of conflicts has to be divided into conflicts with the real estate companies and with the management companies (Chuan, 2009; see also Huang, Y., 2005; Tan, 2008; Liu, Z., 2010). In the first case, the main reason for conflict lies in the clauses of real estate contracts, which often do not specify who owns what, the floor size of the flats or the ways in which real estate companies can operate in the sector. In the second case, three types of conflict can be distinguished. The first concerns the quality of services provided by the management company. The management company considers itself the master of the *xiaoqu*, the only body that can manage it efficiently. It is a profit-making enterprise and as such its spontaneous attitude is to provide less to gain more. Under such circumstances, the problem of power imbalance between homeowners and management companies gives rise to numerous conflicts. Many homeowners complain about the manners (or behaviour) of management company staff. Homeowners interviewed for this study complained: 'They are impolite and sometimes brutal' (interview with homeowner, December 2009). 'That is very strange, as a homeowner I am one of the managers of the estate and they infringe my rights in relying on regulations I am supposed to have passed' (interview with homeowner, January 2009).

The second type of problem relates to the level of management fees. Many management companies charge too much money when they carry out maintenance work. It is difficult for homeowners to know how the company uses the money they pay. Conversely, many homeowners refuse to pay fees, which creates many difficulties for the company and leads to the disconnection of utilities such as electricity, water and heating. The question of ownership rights on the common parts or facilities is the third source of conflict and probably the one that leads to the fiercest protests. The renting of these spaces can bring in a lot of money and 'who is entitled to receive this money' has become a very 'hot' question. According to a survey, the management companies use common facilities for making money in 90 per cent of estates ('Zhongguo shehui ...', 2006).

To a certain extent, this divide between real estate and management companies is artificial, not only because they usually have close ties but also because, according to the Beijing Construction Commission, 80 per cent of conflicts in estates have been generated directly or indirectly by developers from the beginning of the operation (Huang, Z., 2005, p. 9) and 70 per cent of the cases tried by the court of Xuanwu originate from problems inherited from real estate companies (Gao, 2007; see also Read, 2008).

Protesters' Motives

The reasons for participating in a protest movement lie usually in a feeling of having been a victim of injustice. Confronted with a 'problem', protesters consider that they have been treated incorrectly. Sometimes, they get the feeling that they have lost their dignity. We can give many examples from actual cases: a developer wants to build on a piece of land that was originally supposed to be a garden; an argument with a young security guard about a parking space degenerates into a fight and finally a group of guards give the homeowner a beating; a management company increases the management fees and refuses to start up heating until homeowners pay their bills. Suddenly, some people have the feeling of looking down into the abyss opening under their feet:

> Life is no longer secure and everything can happen if we cannot enjoy some sort of protection. We have money, we have a family, a good job, everything seems to be OK and suddenly everything collapses. We discover we are nothing, a small thing, and some people can do all they want to do and we cannot stop them. (Interview with a homeowner, December 2009)

The discourse can be further elaborated, especially when activists or movements' leaders are concerned. These activists refer to more general principles they would like to defend, such as the respect for laws and regulations, the rights of citizenship and property and the dignity of the person. They oppose everything that prevents people and situations from being appraised on the 'quality of person' or on 'talents'. 'Laws and regulations have to protect the good people. We have fought for getting some properties. We are educated people, working people, contributing to the wealth of the society. We are respectful of laws and regulations and then we deserve to be protected by them' (interview with homeowner, February 2010). 'I do not put up with these people [developers, management companies, small cadres] who know each other very well and use networks to protect their business. They have no knowledge, no qualities, they just give bribes and make money' (interview with homeowner, December 2009).

For a small number of leaders – for example, those who are devoted nearly full-time to homeowners' organizations, giving advice, organizing meetings, discussing with officials – the homeowners are the vanguard of a 'broader' middle class movement. But even these people do not go beyond their own interests. When they are asked if they are ready to fight for the rights of migrants or poor people, they are not very enthusiastic. 'The situation of migrant workers is not very good and very fair, but the situation is complex in China. Property is the most important thing to protect. If you protect property you protect everything. In Western countries, everything is based on property, including human rights' (interview with homeowner, February 2010). Moreover, some conflicts are linked to the presence of migrants in the neighbourhood. They are seen as being responsible for the sharp increase in criminal cases in recent years. Most owners feel that despite an impressive number of guards, security systems, and so on, they do not feel safe. 'The guards let rag-and-bone people wander in the compound because they receive some money' (interview with homeowner, January 2009). 'The management company has opened shops in the compound and now everybody from outside can come' (interview with homeowner December 2009). Sometimes, the basements are rented to migrants for sleeping or to companies for stocking goods, which gives 'outsiders' access to the premises. In addition, homeowners have reacted very promptly to the renting of 'deprived houses' (*pingfang* 平方) to migrants in the neighbourhood outside the compound, and put pressure on the residents' committee and the street bureau. To the real estate companies' great delight, the deprived houses have eventually been destroyed, giving developers a new opportunity for business. Security can become a source of conflict among homeowners themselves. Some of them are in favour of using collective properties to make money as long as the money goes in homeowners' pockets. Other people put security above all.

Chinese researchers consider that the significance of homeowners' movements goes beyond the simple defence of a particular group's interest. In fighting for their own rights, they would also fight for citizens' rights (Rocca, 2008). Yet homeowners, be they leaders, activists or participants, do not have a 'universal' approach to various rights and laws, except on rare occasions when the discourse shifts to 'lofty ideas' during meetings.[5] As far as I know, there are no attempts in Beijing to link homeowners' movements with movements against 'pull down and move out' measures, or movements launched by migrant workers. What interests most homeowners is the value of their property. The destruction of a garden, the lack of security, the increase of management fees, the construction of a new building, the inefficiency of the management company and so on, all contribute to the depreciation of their properties. The point is not that they insist on the pragmatic aspect of their demands but that they emphasize the fact that global considerations for the protection of rights and dignity can not be isolated from materialistic interests. Considering that property is a central element of a citizen's identity, homeowners cannot but be particularly sensitive to the value of their properties. They are obsessed with laws protecting properties and by their ability to defend these rights, but only as members of the class of proprietors, that is to say, the people who should constitute the core of Chinese society. To a certain extent, the attitudes of homeowners' associations can be characterized as *juridisme*, that is to say, that they have a will to solve everything through laws and regulations. 'In Western countries, laws and regulations solve all the problems citizens can meet. Strong people cannot do what they want to do. There are clear limits. In China, we have to struggle hard to protect our rights' (interview with homeowner, November 2008). During meetings, much time is spent in

analysing every problem that homeowners can address in their compounds. Everything has to be ruled by laws, nothing must remain in
darkness. Transparency must be the rule.

The opinion homeowners have on the situation in China is generally
negative. 'In China there is no freedom of speech, newspapers are
controlled by a one-party system, we cannot set up associations. Vulnerable groups cannot organize themselves'. And, 'In China, powerful
people control everything whereas the people are weak' (interview with
homeowner, January 2009). 'If you have money, you are powerful, you
can make money, if you have money you are powerful. It is as simple as
that. The people cannot change that. We need more democracy, the
ability to express our discontent with authorities, the right to reveal
malpractices' (interview with activist, February 2010). However, as we
will see, there is no demand for the setting up of a large-scale election
system.

Scope of Movements

Another striking characteristic is the limited scope of the homeowners'
movements. The focus of action is centred on the *xiaoqu*, and to belong
to the *xiaoqu* is perceived as an identity. The residence is a living place in
which everybody has to be involved, contributing to a harmonious life in
common. By definition, the reference to a specific identity leads to a
strict differentiation between 'us' and 'them', 'them' being the 'enemy' as
well the people living outside the compound. The notion of *xiaoqu*
identity is connected to 'self-government', which is claimed by the
leaders of homeowners' movements, as well as by the official discourse
(Zou, 2009):

> We should be the masters of the residence. As proprietors of the premises, we
> should be granted the rights to control everything within the residence. The
> management companies should obey our decisions. Residents' committees
> and street bureaux should respect our decisions as long as they are in
> accordance with laws and regulations. (Interview with homeowner, January
> 2009)

The '*xiaoqu* homeowners' committee' is not the exclusive organizational
form of a homeowners' movement, but usually the emergence of a protest
movement leads to the setting up of such a committee (they also use the
term 'association'). However, it is not a spontaneous organization but an
official one and, to a certain extent, a compulsory form of representation
for homeowners. As such, it is supposed to follow a process of formation:

the constitution of a homeowners' assembly, the election of the committee and approval of the committee by the local administration. That is why, under certain circumstances, a homeowners' movement is led by a 'committee' that has no legal existence, or by a group of people which is a de facto informal association. Whatever the situation, the participants feel that they are members of an association of people defending only their own rights and, to a certain extent, defending their 'territory' and then aiming at dealing with problems geographically defined by the *xiaoqu* and the limited time-frame required to resolve the issue at hand. That is, they are not interested in protesting issues that lie beyond the boundaries of their *xiaoqu* or beyond the time-frame required to solve local problems.

In 2007, only 10 per cent of Beijing housing estates had set up a homeowners' committee (Tan, 2008, p. 1). The proportion had climbed to 20 per cent in 2010 but remains modest ('Beijing xinjian ...', 2010). One of the biggest problems that homeowners' movements face is to develop at all. In an attempt to 'institutionalize' the discontent of homeowners, the regulations adopted in 2010 (see below) are aimed precisely at allowing more *xiaoqu* to organize themselves. The objective is 'to improve homeowners' self-governing mechanisms' and more precisely to ease the five difficulties they are facing: that it is difficult to initiate committees, to prepare meetings, to put decisions on record, to make policy decisions and to change management companies ('Beijing xingui ...', 2010).

Indeed, the fact that homeowners' organizations are embryonic is a double-edged sword. On the one hand, it limits the scope of action but on the other hand it can lead to uncontrollable actions. In Beijing there have been some attempts to coordinate the initiatives of homeowners' committees at city level. But the organization (see below) clearly aims to provide technical support to new committees, or to help *xiaoqu* to organize themselves, to do research and survey the situation of homeowners and to negotiate more efficiently with the authorities in order to improve laws and regulations. The homeowners' protests are considered by the activists as a collection of *xiaoqu* movements expressing a locally rooted identity. 'Our objective is to help each proprietor to use his rights against every infringement. Every *xiaoqu* must become a self-governed place' (interview with activist, May 2009).

This situation creates a tension between the overall objectives of the activists – to force local power, to implement laws and policies – and the basic day-to-day concerns of homeowners: problems with bins, lifts, parking places, fees, and so on. Most leaders of committees and/or movements complain that homeowners are only interested in petty things and are not willing to discuss or support principled demands. 'They behave like clients expecting services. When their interests are not at stake, they do not move' (interview with leader of a committee, February 2010). Some participants, including some who have had prominent roles in homeowners' movements, have left the field of protest because they are sickened by the egotistic behaviour of their neighbours.

Forms of Protest and Mobilization of Resources

In the light of most theories on social movements, homeowners' movements are very modern, meaning that even though there is no doubt that spontaneity plays a certain role in the triggering of movements, participants and leaders are mobilizing resources with efficiency and celerity. They have very quickly understood how to strengthen their position.

The repertoire of actions used by homeowners is largely devoted to small-scale, moderate forms of protest. They are obviously wary of being involved in 'mass' demonstrations. Of course, one of the main tasks of movement leaders is to mobilize a significant proportion of homeowners. But the task is usually difficult because most people work long hours and have no time or energy for extra activities. Usually, only 10 to 20 per cent of residents participate in their homeowners' movement, sometimes less than that. The degree of participation is not homogeneous. The number of participants and the degree of participation decline as the movement goes along. The launch of actions is generally preceded by time-consuming homeowners' meetings.

Most actions are carried out 'within the system'. Activists negotiate with the developers and the management companies, inform and put pressure on local institutions, circulate and present petitions, write documents and collect laws and regulations. In order to reinforce their position, they contact newspapers and important people. The objective is not to extend the movement in terms of number of participants or to get the support of public opinion, but to try to increase the pressure on the developers and the management company. The main resources they try to mobilize are linked to government and market. The tactic is then to show that the struggle takes place within the context of the government's policies and the principles of the regime. 'We are respectful of the social stability, we are supporting the government's policies. We do not want to make trouble, we want to live in peace and security' (interview with homeowner, April 2008). Other, more aggressive means can be mobilized in case of failure. A complaint can be lodged against a company with the local court, a small-scale demonstration can be organized in the neighbourhood or in front of the local administration's buildings, some people may even go on a hunger strike. But these actions are rare and limited in scope. Even the demonstrations gather only dozens of participants. Sometimes, participants shout slogans but usually they prefer to write slogans on banners. The objective is to be 'viewed' in public space, to warn local authorities that more radical means of protest could be used.[6] Violence is used only as a last resort, and usually as a reaction to violence used against them.

Whatever the means and the modes of action chosen by a movement, such as documents, slogans, articles or petitions, all use the words of official discourse. Once again, it is important to prove that the demands go hand in hand with the regime's objectives and that everybody speaks the same language: rule of law, social harmony, defence of property, small prosperity, social mobility, social justice, social stability, civilized society, raising of population quality, and so on.

The creation in 2006 of the *Beijingshi yezhu weiyuanhui xiehui shenban weiyuanhui* (Bidding Committee for the Association of Beijing Homeowners' Committees) illustrates the complex relationship between the state and the homeowners' movement. In August 2006, an Association of four committees representing 32 committees submitted to the Beijing Construction Bureau that a Beijing Association of Committees should be set up. After some days, the Bureau answered that the case was being 'handled for consideration' by the administration, but after that the Association never received any official notification. After a while, it decided to call itself 'Bidding Committee for the Association of Beijing Homeowners' Committees'. The Association does not depend upon any governmental department. Its members grew to 76 committees in 2007 and 142 in 2010. In addition, some activists who have not succeeded in setting up a proper committee participate in the activities of the Association. The member committees receive information, are invited to attend meetings and lectures and they can enjoy advice and support in case of conflicts or legal problems. The Association strives for more cooperation between committees, and the sharing and spreading of experiences, notably through internet forums. According to the leaders' statements, the Association has become a 'social network' by struggling for the creation of a 'homeowners' identity' and to a certain extent by taking the official discourse at its word on the 'building up of community'.

However, the picture of an association firmly opposed to 'power' in order to give birth to an autonomous 'civil society' and to change 'politics' does not fit very well with the complexity of the relationships with the state. Actually, the Association has become a recognized representative by the local and central administrations. Yet, nearly from the beginning, disagreements have appeared among the four initiators and later on between the 12 people – the four initiators and eight new representatives who joined the leading group after one year – who manage the Association. These disagreements can be considered as the consequence of a 'power struggle' between individuals but, as such, the phenomenon is symptomatic of the importance of the structure in the political arena. Moreover, the disagreements mainly concern the nature of the relationship that the Association should establish with the authorities. 'Should we collaborate with the government?', 'Can we get better rights protection without establishing long-term cooperation with the authorities?' became the main questions at stake. One of the conveners has developed close relationships with the Chinese Association of Social Work and, at the beginning of 2010, organized a Forum on 'management service and homeowners' that aimed at allowing 'harmonious victory for everybody'. Homeowners' representatives, the Chinese Association of Social Work, the Ministry of Civil Affairs, the Association of Management Companies, consumers' associations and the Beijing Construction Commission attended the event. The initiative was sternly criticized by two other Bidding Association leaders who delivered an open letter stating that the Association had no direct link with the Forum. Whatever the answer to the above questions, there is no doubt that the Association and its different committees have become government 'partners' and that in spite of the intensity of conflicts occurring (or because the intensity of some of them) it has become difficult for the local government as well as the Central Government in Beijing not to involve them in the reshaping of communities (Liu, 2010). It is also quite clear that the Central Government puts pressure on local governments (and in Beijing, the two are quite close) to give more influence to the Association. The fact that the Forum took place in the Great Hall of the People is not without symbolic significance.

Another danger to the independence of homeowners' movements lies in the support that the committees receive from private enterprises. Admittedly it is not 'regular' sponsorship, but as some leaders are private entrepreneurs, it is easy for them to collect funds to finance activities. In one case, we have found participants working in the staff of a real estate company. Certain leaders and participants find it difficult to accept that they are dependent on 'state' and 'market', the two 'targets' of the homeowners. Real estate and management companies are part of the 'market', and municipal construction commissions, street bureaux and courts are state organs. In other words, activists gradually discover that their 'enemies' are not so easy to define and that independence is difficult to achieve (Shi, 2008).

Enemies and Friends

Some Chinese researchers insist that homeowners' movements should extend their scope and not limit themselves to the use of laws and regulations. Under a context in which the rule of law has not yet been firmly established, citizens face serious difficulties when they lodge a complaint with a court or when they appeal to the Letters and Visits Administration for help.[7] Actually, the success rate of such action is very low. Homeowners have to create a real space for social movements to be able to build up social and political legitimacies by using media and by getting more influence in the political apparatus.

However, this does not mean that better protection of homeowners' rights does not remain the main objective of the movement. More precisely, to force local authorities – residents' committees, street bureaux, letters and visits administrations and local courts – to apply existing laws and regulations and to strive for their improvement seem to constitute the core of the movement. The idea is that homeowners need legal protection in order to avoid infringement. Every aspect of these movements is designed as an overall attempt to put the higher authorities in an uncomfortable situation. Homeowners reproduce and distribute laws and regulations protecting their rights, publicize articles published in the media that support the movements or criticize developers and management companies. They get in contact with local people's assembly representatives and sometimes National People's Congress members, and reveal misconduct and malpractice by local authorities. The problems they face seem to originate from political archaism at local level. 'Chinese society has deeply changed. Property has become a very important element of the economic and social development. Before, nobody was homeowner, now most of people own a flat and sometimes several flats. But in certain parts of the society, nothing has changed. Local authorities can behave exactly the way they did before' (interview with homeowner, July 2008). 'China is now one of the biggest economies in the world, but a citizen can be hit by anybody who has power, his rights can be infringed without any chance to be protected by the law' (interview with homeowner, September 2009).

Consequently, enemies and friends are clearly defined. Friends are people 'within the system' who can help homeowners to make more efficient legal protection and who contribute to the defence of property rights. They are in contact with lawyers to take advantage of the resources that laws and regulations can provide them.

From the homeowners' point of view, the Central Government is on the right side of the picture. 'Our leaders are good, no problem, the direction given is right' sums up the general attitude of the people I interviewed. 'The problem is that they are unable to implement good principles at grassroots level because of corruption' (interview with leader of a committee, February 2010). The enemies are therefore the 'local cliques' constituted of what one Chinese researcher calls a 'real estate interest group' including two main characters (developers and management companies) but also street bureaux, department of housing management and local courts (Zhang, 2005). 'All these people have common interests, they help each other. They give money to important people, they make a lot of money from our property. In China, power belongs to a very small proportion of people' (interview with homeowner, January 2009). Yet, it is important to differentiate this type of behaviour from those of the national leaders. 'How is it possible that a good government like that tolerate this situation? Why in Beijing, central leaders are so efficient and local officials so dishonest? I do not understand' (interview with participant of a movement, June 2009).

The line between participation in movements and political protests is never crossed. Of course, it is possible that this is for tactical reasons: political demands could lead to a breakdown in the negotiations with the authorities. However, it is also clearly linked to the fact that homeowners usually consider entering the political field to be dangerous – dangerous for them, but also for Chinese society. 'China does not need a change in political regime. It needs stability'. 'The quality of the population is too low to have elections in China. Peasants, migrants cannot understand what being a citizen means in terms of political rights. They would vote for silly people or dangerous people. We cannot rely upon them'. 'Elections for what: look at the mess in Taiwan or in Africa, look at what is happening in Russia? No, we are not ready to vote, we need to keep going with economic development and to improve' (interview with homeowner and university professor, November 2009). Some people consider that homeowners' movements could be a step on the long road to democracy but they consider that the number of people who have the ability to attend such movements is too small for the moment.[8]

Leaders and Participants

The most active participants in homeowners' movements are generally few, a maximum of a few dozen. Sometimes, the movement is limited to several people supported by different people at different times. Most leaders complain about this situation. They have the feeling of wasting time, energy and money and of taking personal risks for people who try to escape responsibilities at the first occasion. 'Finally I spoiled my time,

I got problems with the police, I have neglected my family for nothing. My neighbours were very happy to see me solve their problems with the management company, but they let me down when personal involvement was needed' (interview with activist, April 2009). However, if some people have given up out of disappointment, many other leaders have continued to invest time and energy in the field of 'movement' and sometimes become 'experts' in social movements. This is the case for retired officials but also for businesspeople or intellectuals and technicians who help *xiaoqu* homeowners to set up associations. At the same time, some of them give advice to local governments to help solve or to ease conflicts.

These 'deeply involved' movement leaders have a lot in common. They have a good family background, whatever the nature of the background: a rich family before 1949 that encountered major difficulties during the Cultural Revolution and finally regained prominent status afterwards; a poor working class family that became powerful after 1949; a family of intellectuals, and so on. They have all received a good education and, whatever their sector, they have been very successful. A third characteristic is their high degree of 'politicization'. Depending on their generation, the circumstances of politicization can be different: socialist experience in the 1950s, the Cultural Revolution and 'Up to the Mountains, Down to the Villages' movement, the June 1989 movement, and so on. But all of them consider their involvement in homeowners' movements as a continuation, through different means (avoiding political clashes), of their political activism. At last, they have very good connections in the political apparatus as well as in the business field. Even if they can involve themselves in actions that apparently contest social order, they do not want to challenge the political regime. 'R', who has participated in a hunger strike, is in reality a very moderate activist (Chuan, 2009). And 'X', who seems to be an extremist, refusing to negotiate and criticizing the system violently in private, also gives conferences to officials (interview with homeowner, May 2010). I present below the pictures of five leaders that strikingly highlight these common characteristics.

Chen Bing is one of the conveners of the 'Bidding Committee' set up in 2006. The son of university teachers, he was a student in Beida's (Peking University) International Relations Department at the end of the 1980s. He travelled in the United States after the May 1989 movement. After his return to China he started business in the advertising industry. In 2002, he tried to set up a committee in his own *xiaoqu* and after countless difficulties and obstacles succeeded in 2004. After that experience, he has become a well-known columnist in newspapers, magazines, radio and television, delivering analyses and advice concerning estate management. Some of his demands have been introduced into the Property Law promulgated in 2007. For him, the issue of homeowners' committees is a cause that cannot be circumscribed to a simple question of 'protection' of 'rights'. He devotes himself to 'social progress', he promotes 'the development of socialist democracy and the legal system', 'the construction of a harmonious society and of a civil society'. He advocates the respect of rights granted to citizens by the constitution. Considering that aim, he sees homeowners' committees and assemblies as a very good starting point.

'Z' was born in 1954 into a landlord family and he had a harsh time during the Cultural Revolution. However, he graduated as a film director and made a lot of money in the cultural industry and then in the car rental industry. He set up a committee and is also one of the creators of the 'Bidding Committee'. He is a member of the Beijing Assembly of the Chinese People's Political Consultative Conference (CPPCC) and is perceived as an extremely moderate activist. He refuses to oppose the government and considers that, given the force of the state apparatus, the best solution is to negotiate. He has developed huge networks with business companies and management companies. He sees himself as a mediator and apparently plays this role very well (Liu, 2010, pp. 33–5).

'Q' was born in 1958. He obtained a degree in economics in 1982 and worked as a secretary of the Youth League in an administrative organ. He shifted to business after that. Through his network, he made a lot of money. In 2010, he became a member of the Democratic Party. He comes from a working class family but quite an exceptional one: his family enjoyed the privilege of receiving a mango from Mao Zedong during the Cultural Revolution. With this kind of background, he was easily admitted to university. He later became the manager of several companies. He considers that the committees have to be managed as companies even if they are non-profitable organizations. They need money. They should develop networks with 'market forces' and have a perfect organization with an efficient labour division. In 2008, he has set up his own management company with some activists of the 'Bidding Committee', which has led to lots of criticism from the other members (ibid., pp. 35–6).

I would also like to give two other examples concerning two home-owners' movement activists who are only involved in *xiaoqu*-based conflicts. The first one is a retired official, himself the son of an official, who was shocked at the bad quality of the services provided by the management company of his *xiaoqu*. He has been physically (though slightly) assaulted by security guards. But he succeeded in changing the management company after numerous actions (petitions, a sit-in), partly because he had good connections with colleagues still working in administrative organs. According to him, his status prevented him from being mistreated inside his compound by what he calls 'hooligans' and, as soon as the movement developed and forced local administration to intervene, he became the right person to negotiate with. As a retired official, he considers that his duty is to contribute to the implementation of a legal system in China and to give people some means by which they can protect their rights and reinforce social justice. The second example is a successful designer who was in his last year of secondary school in 1989. He was detained for several months after the 1989 movement and was refused entry to university. Finally, he opened his own business. His father and mother were teachers. He considers his involvement as a continuation of his political involvement in students' protest movements of the 1980s:

> I do not want to deal with politics any more; it is too dangerous and useless. The system is too strong, the Party is too powerful, what we can do is change small things that can influence people's everyday life. Now, nearly everybody is a homeowner. Then, if we succeed in providing legal protection to property, we can contribute to the protection of citizens. That is very important. (Interview with homeowner, June and July 2007)

Leaders or activists put themselves in what we could call a 'mediating' position: they are simultaneously situated within the political apparatus, within 'the market forces' and in the field of social movements; they strive for social justice and defend the public interest, but they are also seeking personal interests, in terms of material as well as power-related interests. For that reason many participants or ordinary homeowners complain about the motives of some leaders or leading participants. Some of them use their positions as 'homeowners' representatives' to obtain benefits for themselves. They take advantage of residents' resentment, and organize a movement to fire the management company and hire another one with whom they are acquainted (Huang, Z., 2005). In one case, the representatives of a homeowners' committee embezzled the money collected for organizing collective activities (interview with activist, May 2009). Sometimes, leading participants obtain a discount on management fees for themselves in exchange for which they calm down homeowners (interview with activist, October 2010; see also Huang, Z., 2005, p. 27). In another set of cases, some people who have experienced disappointment, deprivation or frustration at work, in family or in society find in a homeowners' protest movement an opportunity to give vent to their spite.[9] They usually give up as soon as they see their influence declining. Finally, people complain that some representatives have adopted arrogant manners and look down on them since they have become public figures. 'They are dealing with important people now, they are not really interested in our petty problems anymore'.[10]

CONCLUSION

In Western countries as well as in Asian societies, the role of the new middle classes (white-collar, managerial and professional workers) in the democratization process is not well established. In East Asian countries, certain parts of this social category have supported democratization at certain historical moments – like other social categories – and have opposed it at other moments. In these countries, democratization appears mainly as a top-down process in which the elite have played the determinant role. The middle classes seem not to have a 'politics'. They are in favour of political change as long as it serves their interests but shift easily to more conservative attitudes as soon as stability is threatened.

The politics of the Chinese middle classes are quite similar. As 'new social movements', homeowners' movements rely upon a collection of individual interests in order to 'modernize' archaic aspects of the social reality. The leaders of the movements tend to become professional and are gradually integrated into the political system. As for the participants, not only are they very difficult to mobilize but their involvement is limited to the defence of the *xiaoqu* and the construction of a harmonious courtyard. That does not mean that these kinds of actions do not change politics, it means that angry homeowners do not want to overthrow the regime. They struggle for 'liberalization' – the process of making certain rights that protect both individuals and social groups from arbitrary or illegal acts committed by the state or other forces – and not for democratization – the process whereby the rules and procedures of citizenship are applied to political institutions (O'Donnell and Schmitter, 1986). If we use the term 'political change' to mean 'change of political regime', it is clear that homeowners are not willing to assume the role of 'destroyers' of polity. But if we use 'political change' to evoke a reshaping of the relationships between certain social categories and the state, it seems that the middle classes can play a crucial role in that matter. In other words, if we get rid of the myths of democratization and we look at what the very objectives of the new social movements are, homeowners' movements appear quite promising. They have allied with some powerful people and ruling groups, they promote liberalization, which is the objective of the vast majority of the population, they are able to convince the political apparatus to adopt new laws, and they increase their influence on the decision-making process. It is probably less exciting for observers than to wait for 'big change' but it may be more efficient in a long-term perspective.

Why is some 'major change' difficult to imagine as long as the consensus is respected? Because of the way homeowners are thinking about 'politics'. The scope of what is 'politically thinkable' is narrow. People hope change comes but not at the price of instability and it is a fact that elections are perceived as a source of instability, not only because of the intrinsic source of unpredictability they generate, but also because of the high proportion of rural dwellers in the electorate. The class struggle also takes place at that level even if it is fictional for the time being.

China may be in a sort of 'Thermidorian moment' (on this notion see Bayart, 2008) in which the revolutionaries continue to aim at changing the Chinese society, but are no longer against the society. The state has to take the 'social', its inertia and needs into account. Nobody wants to go back to the socialist revolution period but few want to experience a democratic revolution. This is the reason why homeowners advocate more freedom but refuse democratic elections. The 'modernization' of China has become the task of revolutionaries. For that, China has to remain a unified and harmonious nation. The political realm must express this unity and avoid all sources of segmentation. To participate in social movements is a means to continue to deal with politics without challenging the unity of the nation.

NOTES

1. This chapter has a story and a starting point: a discussion I had with a Chinese student. She came to me after a course I was teaching (on theories of social movements) in Tsinghua and expressed her confusion about what appeared to her as insoluble contradictions. Her fieldwork findings were at odds with the theoretical framework she was using ('Western thought' she said, in fact, modernization theory). Members of the middle class are supposed to behave as citizens defending universal principles and general interest but in fact they focus a lot on personal and group interests. 'Society' interests are supposed to be contradictory to 'state' interests but in fact at grassroots level it is usually not so easy to separate the two. Let us try to clear this student's confusion.
2. I have also referred to discussions I had with Judith Audin and Aurore Merle, who are doing extensive research on this issue. However, the analysis developed in this chapter reflects only my personal point of view and has generally nothing to do with the views of the students and scholars mentioned above.
3. Except in Spain and Portugal.

4. Most were involved in 'third way' activism, that is to say, an attempt to find another way between capitalism and communism. Some of them got close to fascist or 'national-socialist' groups.
5. But very quickly discussion goes back to the basics: vernacular problems faced by people in compounds.
6. I have witnessed two cases of 'demonstrations', one at the entry of a *xiaoqu* in Dongcheng, the other one in front of an official building in Chaoyang.
7. The Letters and Visits Administration depends on the State Council and has bureaux in the different levels of government and administration in the whole country. Its main task is to receive complaints from the public concerning malpractices committed by officials.
8. During my eight years of teaching in Beijing, I have had discussions on democracy with nearly 200 people from all walks of life. Of that number only three declared that they considered a representative system of government with competitive elections could be beneficial to present-day China and that the government should establish it immediately. Needless to say the discussions took place in private.
9. One interviewee informed me that in one *xiaoqu* in Chaoyang, a retired teacher was accused of being active in the committee in order to compensate for the situation in his own family where his wife and son look down on him (interview with homeowner, May 2010). See also Huang, Z. (2005, p. 25).
10. This is a recurrent opinion expressed in interviews.

7. Institutional determinants of the political consciousness of private entrepreneurs

Hans Hendrischke

INTRODUCTION

The role of the bourgeoisie and the middle class has been a favourite topic for historians and social scientists alike as the middle class is inextricably linked to such sociopolitical concepts and events as industrialization, nation, state and revolution, and in particular with the French Revolution. Although true class consciousness in the Marxist tradition is only ascribed to the proletariat (Lukacs [1922] 1968), it is the consciousness of the bourgeoisie that matters for the 'birth of modernity', and in particular the birth of the modern nation state (Fehér, 1990).

For an understanding of the political role of China's emerging middle class there are good reasons to revisit the economic and political origins of the European bourgeoisie and class consciousness. The concept of a bourgeoisie raises pertinent political and economic issues when looking for an equivalent of the European bourgeoisie in contemporary China. Is there any likelihood of the emergence of a bourgeoisie in China – a class that controls both the economy and the state and asserts itself against an *ancien régime* that impedes economic development, or is this concept in itself an untenable simplification? Attempts to trace the role of the bourgeoisie in preparing the ground for the French Revolution have led to a more complex understanding of state–society interaction and class formation (Higonnet, 1990). Studies of the French Revolution have shown that the bourgeoisie was closely involved in the formation of the nation state and the transition from indirect rule to direct rule by a modern centralized government (Tilly, 1990).

China's situation is quite different. The 'Golden Age' of China's bourgeoisie (Bergère, 1989) came at a time when the Central Government was greatly weakened after the fall of the Qing dynasty and before the new Nationalist Party (*Guomindang*) asserted its military and bureau-cratic power during the years 1911 to 1927. China's bourgeoisie never assumed political power or played a role in forming a centralized nation state as the civil war and the communist revolution brought an end to the many local traditions of entrepreneurial development. The collapse of the Soviet Union and the subsequent confirmation of China's capitalist development path reignited the debate about the role of the middle class in establishing a market economy and reviving entrepreneurial expertise.

For contemporary China, class is debated in the context of modern-ization and democracy in which the causality that dominated the French Revolution, as well as the collapse of the Soviet Empire, is reversed. Change in China is not coming from a new class overthrowing an *ancien régime*, but through gradual economic and political change that creates popular demand for transparent governance and, in consequence, for democratic reform of the existing political and economic system (Chen and Dickson, 2010, pp. 3–4). In this scenario, the concept of middle class has become depoliticized, as class is predominantly analysed in terms of global income stratification (e.g., Ravaillon, 2009) and culture and behaviour following Bourdieu (1984). The rich and multi-faceted studies on the middle class in China (see, for example, the contributions in Goodman, 2008a; Li, 2010a) are inspired by similar contemporary studies in the US, UK and Australia, which have likewise discarded the political potential that the bourgeois middle class had shown in the European Industrial Revolution (Goodman, 2008b). The question of whether China's middle class will seek a political mandate to secure its economic gains has been narrowed down to a focus on the 'entre-preneurial end' (Dickson, 2010) of the Chinese middle class as the closest equivalent to a bourgeoisie.

The 'entrepreneurial end' refers to private entrepreneurs who are part of the middle class in that they are excluded from the political elite that wields political and economic power through control of the central Party-state and the central state-owned enterprise sector. Private entre-preneurship does therefore not include state entrepreneurs, that is, members of the political elite who hold political appointments as leaders of large state-owned or privatized enterprises originally linked to the central Party-state. Private entrepreneurs as a group comprise a variety of local entrepreneurs, who are embedded in their local communities in multiple ways through their enterprises, which are registered at township and county level and in third and second tier cities, and which numbered 9 million in 2011 (Hu and Ma, 2012). 'Private entrepreneurs' and 'local entrepreneurs' are therefore used interchangeably in this chapter.

Private entrepreneurs have emerged as a new economic elite only since the start of economic reforms, and are concentrated in the economically advanced coastal provinces. The question of how the old, political elite will accommodate the new, economic elite is crucial for the further economic development and the long-term political stability of the People's Republic of China (PRC). The answer is complicated by the dynamic political and economic environment in which these elites interact. Politically, the role of private entrepreneurs is controversial, while the old elite is linked to the Chinese Communist Party (CCP), justified mainly by ideological and historical reasons. Economically, private entrepreneurs compete to varying degrees with state entrepreneurs, whose enterprises are backed by the Central Government and central policies for strategic, social and commercial reasons. Geographically, privatization and the spread of private entrepreneurship is an ongoing process, as enterprise privatization and the required institutional development spread from the coastal provinces to China's hinterland in central, western and north-eastern provinces. Interaction between the political and economic elite is therefore an unfolding and dynamic process that needs to be analysed from different perspectives.

Sociological studies based on empirical data from interviews and surveys have shown that these old and new elites, rather than being opposed to each other because of their different political outlook, have become closely intertwined within the space of one generation (Walder, 2003; Walder and Hu, 2009). Even more surprising, the two elites can be functionally related with one generation using their established political positions to pave the way for their offspring to move into entrepreneurial positions (Goodman, 2000). These survey- and interview-based studies also show that elite mobility predates economic reforms and the communist revolution. These findings are underpinned by detailed local studies (see Li, 2010b). The results of sociological studies do not therefore support assumptions about the potential for political elite conflict and radical regime change, assumptions that are either inspired by modernization theory or hypothetical scenarios, mostly from a political science perspective (see Heilmann and Perry, 2011).

Some recent research in political science has taken a pessimistic turn as researchers who expected private entrepreneurs to demand regime change in favour of electoral representative democracy found little support for political activism. While not excluding political change in the long run, the current consensus is that the Chinese Party-state has co-opted private entrepreneurs by offering privileges and favours in return for political acquiescence. These studies of the political attitudes of private entrepreneurs generally refer to the central Party-state without being specific about a division of roles between state and Party. A recent major study of endogenous institution building from below by local entrepreneurs (Nee and Opper, 2012) has challenged this approach, arguing that it is state-centred because it fails to acknowledge the impact of local market forces on private entrepreneurship.

This chapter will take this critique of the state-centred approach as a starting point to argue that co-optation at the central level only captures a minor part of the institutional environment in which private entrepreneurs operate. In particular, and keeping in mind the local roots of private entrepreneurship, this chapter will explore how the local embeddedness of private entrepreneurs impacts their political outlook and choice of political allies and strategies.

The next section will review the role of private entrepreneurs in institution building from the political science perspective. The section following will examine the local environment of private entrepreneurs from an institutional perspective, in particular the role of the local state and the local Party functionaries in that environment. The discussion will draw these approaches together and assess their implications for the potential political strategies of private entrepreneurs. The conclusion will return to the question of political consciousness by considering how economic and political interaction within highly structured formal and informal institutions informs the political strategies of private entre-preneurs, assuming that their political consciousness will necessarily reflect the complexity of their institutional environment.

THE STATE-CENTRED APPROACH

One of the most prominent research topics in political science, in terms of numbers of studies and influence on public discourse, are studies of the political attitudes of entrepreneurs and their relationship with the political elite and the central Party-state. Several book-length studies have addressed these questions in rich detail (e.g., Pearson, 1997; Dickson, 2003a, 2008; Tsai, 2007; Huang, 2008; Chen and Dickson, 2010), including detailed political surveys on specific questions (e.g., Dickson, 2008, Ch. 8). There is a current consensus that, at least for the time being, China's central political elite has been able to use its political and economic power to co-opt the private entrepreneurial elite (Dickson, 2010) and to keep it from becoming an active political force demanding electoral representation.

At the same time, the informal ad-hoc nature of co-optation is a weakness as co-optation lacks the predictability and stability of a constitutional regime. This leaves the future of private entrepreneurship under perennial doubt with hard to answer questions such as: Is the central political elite likely to represent the economic interests of the emerging private entrepreneurship in the long run? Will the central elite promote a stronger state-owned enterprise (SOE) sector? Will private entrepreneurs under changing conditions demand democratic reforms in order to secure their economic interests?

The sustainability of co-optation between the political elite and private enterprises is therefore crucial. The state-centred approach makes its claims on the basis of political evidence: As private entrepreneurs show no signs of political opposition, the state must be successful in appealing to their self-interest, in particular by providing a stable political environment and intervening on their behalf in economic and legal matters. So-called 'red hat' enterprises run by Communist Party members are often presented as the main beneficiaries as they can tap into the political network of the Party-state for their own benefit. Dickson (2008) develops a hierarchy of co-optation mechanisms, ranging from policy statements, to admission into the Party, to self-organized business associations. This account is based on the assumption that the Party is the central political actor while entrepreneurs only play a passive role.

Political support for private entrepreneurs dominates the domestic media, as this publicly confirms the state's commitment to policies that reversed many previous restrictions on economic activity and private enterprise. At a constitutional and legal level, central political and legislative support has gradually consolidated the legal status of private enterprise. From a starting point in the early 1980s, when there was no legal protection for private enterprises, to the current comprehensive body of legislation (including a company law that was revised to take account of private corporate interests, to constitutional amendments), the central Party-state can point to a steady process of improving property rights and increasing procedural security.

Private entrepreneurs also benefit from political support when they are granted public social status through membership of the Communist Party or of representative bodies such as the National People's Congress or the Chinese People's Political Consultative Conference at various levels. Similarly, public functions in the All-China Federation of Industry and Commerce or the various business associations give symbolic status to the private entrepreneurs who are invited into these roles.

At the individual enterprise level, the Party-state grants privileges or special concessions to private enterprises by supporting business deals with SOEs or facilitating access to bank credit and other resources. Put together, this range of options has enabled the central Party-state to institute what has been labelled 'crony communism' (Dickson, 2010) to describe the collusion between Party-state officials and entrepreneurs.

Co-optation reflects an environment where private entrepreneurship is excluded from formal institution building at central level:

> Whether this is described as the helping hand government, local state corporatism, or the developmental state, there is an underlying notion of the government's decisive role in devising and shaping the emerging institutions enabling and motivating China's economic miracle. It is generally thought that China's development mainly rests on a state-directed process of institutional change, wherein efficiency-enhancing formal rules and policies are instituted by political elites. (Nee and Opper, 2012, pp. 3ff)

From an economic perspective that takes into account the local embeddedness and the informal environment in which the private sector operates, the incentives from co-optation are limited, as they are best suited to an economic environment where markets are weak and the state is strong. They work less well in an environment of strong markets where private entrepreneurs have been engaged in informal institution building. Seen from a local enterprise perspective, the legal and constitutional support only formalized ex post the institutions that private entrepreneurs had already established informally through their own entrepreneurial networks (ibid., p. 6). The usefulness of co-optation and economic patronage of the private sector by the political elite is questionable.

Another explanation for the political acquiescence of private entrepreneurs is proposed by Tsai (2007, 2011) who introduces a local dimension in the discussion of private entrepreneurship. Tsai argues that private entrepreneurs have a voice in local institution building by colluding with local authorities in devising coping strategies to circumvent regulatory restrictions on their operations. These adaptive informal institutions over time find their way into formal institutions and modify those in the interest of private entrepreneurs (Tsai, 2011). While agreeing with Chen and Dickson (2010) that private entrepreneurs are not the harbingers of electoral democratic change for China, Tsai (2005) shows in a large number of examples that private entrepreneurs can take an active role in transforming their institutional environment through intermediation of local government, which links adaptive informal institutions with the formal institutional building process at central level. This gives private entrepreneurs indirect political agency as they cannot control the consequences of their local institution building.

The importance of local institution building is acknowledged in the wider notion of adaptive governance proposed by Heilmann and Perry (2011). Adaptive governance goes beyond Tsai's notion of adaptive informal institutions in that it acknowledges that transformative institutional change can occur within the governance framework controlled by the Communist Party without political disruption, as Chung (2011) demonstrates, for central–local relations. However, the proponents of adaptive governance tie this notion firmly back into the context of government control by interpreting it as a flexible form of formal institution building within the state-centred approach. Evidence of the flexibility of routine procedures for transformative change under government control is provided by Linda Chelan Li (2012) in her study of rural tax reform.

In summary, the state-centred political science approach limits the analytical scope for exploring the political options of private entrepreneurs by both neglecting the political consequences of emerging markets and by assigning exclusive political agency directly or indirectly to the central state. The state-centred approach does not envisage the possibility that either private entrepreneurs or the local Party-state play an active part in autonomous local institution building.

The fact that the state-centred approach 'cannot explain the emergence and self-reinforcing growth of China's robust private enterprise economy' (Nee and Opper, 2012, p. 5) suggests that it is necessary to turn to the more fine-grained analytical approach of institutional analysis.

THE INSTITUTIONAL APPROACH

The institutional approach can shed some light on the questions raised at the outset, and in particular on the role of entrepreneurs in controlling political and economic power. The institutional contribution can elucidate how entrepreneurs are embedded in their local environment and how little formal control they are able to exercise collectively in comparison with the early European bourgeoisie. The lack of political control coincides with weak formal institutions, in particular legal and financial institutions (Yueh, 2011). As a consequence, Chinese institutions seem to be in perennial transition towards a state that is closer to the elaborate Western (mostly Anglo-Saxon) model of formal institutions. This applies not only to economic institutions, but also political institutions, where, for example, the lack of transparency or so called 'ripple effects' such as corruption, are seen as temporary problems awaiting better formal institutions in order to be overcome. The same logic applies to the legal status and self-perception of entrepreneurs, as will be discussed below.

The perceived weakness of institutions can be observed in many different areas. In most cases, official Chinese policies support these perceptions by reference to the necessity of further reforms. Chinese formal government positions perpetuate the view that entrepreneurs are hampered by a lack of formal institutions. The reason why the lack of institutions does not interfere with a seemingly well-functioning private economy is found in coping strategies, such as reliance on political connections, cronyism and other ad-hoc measures.

One indication that this situation is more than a transition towards better institutions comes from historical research. Research on the history of Chinese firms over the last two centuries has addressed similar problems, such as the lack of legal enforcement or specific issues such weak property rights in limited liability companies. Studies in this area (e.g., Zelin, 2009) have produced detailed insights into informal institutions in a pre-legal space that were able to remedy institutional gaps without recourse to ad-hoc solutions such as personal favours. Zelin (ibid., p. 635) concludes:

> While the pre-1904 Chinese legal code provided no guidance in the regulation of shares and shareholding, the legislative gap was filled by a plethora of sample business contracts in encyclopaedias, trade rules, and other social capital that enabled the formation of lasting partnership agreements enforced by the state. Within particular industries we can likewise detect systems of private ordering governed by industry-based codes of conduct and managed through the arbitration bureaus of local Chambers of Commerce.

In a similar vein, contemporary institutional research in the PRC has recently proposed an alternative view on the lack of formal institutions, a view that assumes that there is an underlying permanent structure rather than temporary institutional weakness. Victor Nee and Sonja Opper (2010) propose the term 'endogenous institution building from below' to explain their observations from a recent sample of approximately 700 firms in the Yangtze region. They find an active culture of self-regulation among local private enterprises, particularly in industrial clusters in Zhejiang.

Self-regulation among these firms has overcome the lack of formal institutions while creating superior incentives for innovation and market performance. Nee and Opper (2010, p. 36) argue that:

> The success of China's developmental state was to recognize the importance of bottom-up economic development. Although the state continues to favour state-owned and controlled firms, it has cumulatively accommodated robust bottom-up entrepreneurial action through macroeconomic policies and legal reform to legitimize the private enterprise economy and secure property rights. Revenue maximization motivates the government's accommodation with entrepreneurs and capitalist economic development. The state would not

have been accommodative, however, if the private enterprise economy was not already established as the most rapidly growing source of private wealth creation, employment, tax revenue, technological innovation and sustained economic growth. The rise of private enterprise-led capitalist economic development was not *because* of the state, but *despite* the state's earlier effort to block its development. (original emphasis)

While Nee and Opper have their view on private firms, Hendrischke and Krug propose an integrated view of endogenous institution building that incorporates firms and local governments into an institutional architecture (Krug and Hendrischke, 2010a, b) which is characterized by institutional embeddedness of entrepreneurial activity. This type of embeddedness has three characteristics: local autonomy, networking and organizational choice. 'Local autonomy' means the ability of local governments to create their own institutions that can deviate from central policies, 'networking' means the ability of local governments to coordinate activities of local market players, and 'organizational choice' means the ability to create procedures and organizations in line with local needs.

The institutional economics approach opens new perspectives on the political situation of private entrepreneurs in three respects: their ability to build informal market institutions from below, their symbiotic relationship with the local Party-state, and their mediated relationship with the central Party-state.

The ability to create markets through endogenous institution building from below gives private entrepreneurs a constituent role in the emergence of China's market economy and, consequently, a strong position in their relationship with the Party-state, as the Party-state depends on them for extending and deepening market reforms. Nee and Opper (2012) argue that the formation of entrepreneurial networks in the Yangtze River Delta depended on private entrepreneurs who created their own institutions and organizational structures. These allowed the entrepreneurs to secure know-how and capital that enabled them to conduct business on an expanding geographical scale without the support, and in fact before the setting up, of market-conforming central institutions. These initial steps taken by private entrepreneurs, with the toleration of local government, led to a process of gradual replacement of bureaucratic allocation by market mechanisms, the creation of incentives that stimulated entrepreneurial activity and innovativeness, and the expansion of opportunities for producers to identify new profit opportunities. Past the initial stages in the 1980s, the ability of private entrepreneurs to build markets from below without the need for the Central Government to put formal market institutions into place ex ante remained crucial as markets expanded into new industries and regions.

This ability strengthened their position with regard to the Party-state's role as a guarantor of property rights and procedural security for expanding markets. It also puts the political co-optation of private entrepreneurs into a different light, as co-optation does not enable private entrepreneurship as such, but rather becomes a form of collusion with individual entrepreneurs or certain categories of entrepreneurs, such as 'red hat' entrepreneurs who might otherwise be disadvantaged. 'Red hat' entrepreneurs – those with political connections who rely on repeat inter-action with state-controlled business partners – can be disadvantaged as reduced interaction with the private and more competitive sectors of the economy carries the risk that 'transactions in state-controlled institutional domains often do not constitute the critical component for survival and profits when viewed from the perspective of the overall range of a firm's business operations in competitive markets' (Nee and Opper, 2012, p. 258).

The role of local governments and the local Party-state can be two-faced. Nee and Opper (2012) refer both to the obstruction of market activities by local governments as well as to their toleration and encouragement of new informal market institutions. Kellee Tsai (2005) describes the involvement of local governments in creating adaptive informal institutions as a way to mobilize Central Government support for private enterprises. Local governments in this context act as agents of the central Party-state, but in different contexts they can also act as principals in the interest of the economic development of their own jurisdiction. Their commitment to local economic interests even leads to jurisdictional competition as described in the literature on fiscal federal-ism (Qian, 2000).

Informal institution building by the local Party-state as a principal in its own right (rather than as an agent of the central Party-state) also involves private entrepreneurs and is one of the situations where it is possible to differentiate between the role of local government and the local Communist Party. Local governments acting as agents of the Central Government are responsible for the integration of private entre-preneurs into the formal institutional framework. At the same time, under dual government/Party leadership, they represent local economic inter-ests. Local case studies (Hendrischke, 2007) show that endogenous institution building from below brings together private entrepreneurs and local Communist Party cadres who have authority to make credible commitments towards private entrepreneurs. The local Party, unlike the local government, has the ability to overcome the constraints of formal institutions in areas such as the allocation of land or the granting of specific privileges, such as access to resources. The local Party leadership is therefore in a situation to make binding commitments to private enterprises that are the functional equivalent of property rights (Krug and Hendrischke, 2010a, b).

The local Party-state is additionally linked to private entrepreneurs through its role as intermediary between central and local institutions, through which it helps private enterprises to overcome the problems of weak formal institutions on the one hand or discriminatory central institutions in form of laws and regulations on the other. The lack of implementation of formal, central institutions means that private entrepreneurs are only able to selectively draw on the support offered by the regulatory framework of the central Party-state. Where encroachment of formal institutions on their interests occurs, they generally have no access to a formal appeal process. Local government organizations fill these institutional gaps by mediating between private entrepreneurs and higher levels of the state hierarchy, for example in securing flexibility in implementing central legislation such as labour legislation through the new Labour Contract Law (Hendrischke, 2011).

As a consequence, China's central Party-state does not have a monopoly on institution building nor on the securing of property rights for private enterprises through constitutional and legal means. These are complemented – if not replaced – through informal institutions at local level that create a community of interest between the local Party-state and private entrepreneurship. Devolution of institution building (as described in the fiscal federalism model) to the local level has important consequences for the national unity of economic institutions, in that it rests less on a formal conformity than on an informal political consensus maintained by the Communist Party. The Communist Party thus maintains a political consensus that is able to accommodate local differences in economic policies and institutions. Local differences emerge through the local embedding of institutions with the active involvement of local Party organizations. Local economic institutions in the first instance evolve endogenously and only then take in exogenous influences (including central policies) as a national or global frame of reference. Local institutions evolve through coordination between private entrepreneurs and political agents.

DISCUSSION

The dependence of private entrepreneurs on local institutions and local embeddedness changes their political situation. As long as they depend on formal central institutions their primary political point of reference is the Central Government. However, as local institutions are able to safeguard economic development, the frame of reference shifts to the local Party-state. Only with these tensions between central and local power structures and formal and informal institutions in mind does it make sense to approach questions such as whether private entrepreneurs are likely to vie for political power, and in what form. Whether representative democracy is a suitable strategy for them will depend on how they define their position in the power hierarchy of the Party-state and where they find allies to influence the mix of formal and informal institutions that define their operational environment, specifically the formation of markets.

Dickson (2008) also captures the flexibility that is inherent in allowing private entrepreneurs to respond to the political offers of state association on their own terms and according to their specific local circumstances. However, an inherent weakness in Dickson's argument is the passive role he ascribes to entrepreneurs as institution-takers. If there was ever to be a democratic change in China, which he does not exclude, the required institutional change would be exogenous in his view (ibid., p. 252). While it is possible to argue that an important social group such as entrepreneurs are excluded from formal institution building, it has been shown above that this does not deprive them of functional political representation where private entrepreneurs achieved their economic role in society by participating in informal institution building at local level.

Institutional analysis identifies three layers of institutions and organizations in which private entrepreneurs take part. The first relates to inter-firm networks, the second to the local Party-state and the third to the central Party-state. Each level has different functionalities.

The inter-firm level forms the basis for the other two as, at this level, private entrepreneurial networks build informal market institutions that are at the core of China's market economy. The basic designs of markets at this level operate without government support and formal legal institutions (Krug and Hendrischke, 2010a). At local government level, private entrepreneurs are actively involved in institution building and interaction with the local Party-state, which safeguards their interests through the building of informal institutions and through mediating the impact of formal institutions imposed from above.

The political consequence is that private entrepreneurs do not have a unilateral relationship to the Party-state, but a multi-layered one that fulfils separate functions. For their political affiliation they need to relate to the local Party-state more than to the central Party-state. The central Party-state provides political status and recognition, and provides legal security in routine circumstances. Outside of these, the local Party-state has to mediate between entrepreneurs and the central Party-state. In summary, the entrepreneurs need to work closely with local governments even where central interests are involved as the centre implements its policies through nested local hierarchies. As the economic interests of the local Party-state are closely linked to entrepreneurship, this also means that the local Party-state depends on private entrepreneurs for its own relationship with the centre.

CONCLUSION

The simplest explanation why the political situation of the Chinese private entrepreneurs is so different from that of the nineteenth-century European bourgeoisie is that the European bourgeoisie could avail itself of the institutional and organizational means of the modern nation state. Chinese private entrepreneurs in contrast are primarily embedded in the local Party-state and only secondarily in the Chinese nation state, which, institutionally, is still indebted to its imperial precursors.

As far as their self-interest defines their political consciousness, entrepreneurs are unlikely to promote an abstract ideology that increases their political dependence on the central Party-state. Their interest lies in informal power sharing with governments at local level for whom central regulations are also part of exogenous institution building, which needs to be mediated with their own form of endogenous institution building. This set-up raises concrete doubts about the ability of Chinese entrepreneurs to create a class in any way similar to their European predecessors.

China's private entrepreneurs operate in a locally defined environment. This differs from the situation of the nineteenth-century European bourgeoisie mostly in the absence of a centralized state able to enforce top-down institutional change, down to the corporate level. Three major differences have come to light that are based on the institutional set-up of the Chinese polity and economy.

First, the political orientation of Chinese private entrepreneurs is primarily local and only in the second instance central. Chinese private entrepreneurs are locally embedded in that for their major institutional concerns, such as security of property rights, access to resources and access to markets they depend in the first instance on the local Party-state. Their access to political representation at central level is also mediated through the local Party-state. The local Party-state derives its legitimization from the central Party-state, but in the nested hierarchies of Chinese local governance, local organizations do not have direct access to central legitimization that would allow them to override their local Party-state, that is, that would give them independent status as political actors.

Second, there is no unified model for China that would cover all local variations of relations between the local Party-state and the private enterprise sector, not least because the relationship is dynamically changing. The only way to capture the dynamic relationship between local Party-state and private entrepreneurship is to define the institutional architecture that holds the two together in a diversified and constantly changing environment. This makes it difficult, if not impossible, to define the political position of private entrepreneurs in static terms of class interest and democratic inclinations. There are also institutional differences between economically advanced regions with longer experience in privatization and regions lagging behind with less developed institutions.

Third, for economically developed regions the case can be made that private entrepreneurs have co-opted the local Party-state to protect and safeguard their interests. The relationship between the local Party-state and local entrepreneurs is a patron–client relationship on the one hand; but on the other, the local Party-state is beholden to local enterprises and has to serve them in terms of the flexible implementation of central legislation and regulation. The relationship between private enterprises and the Party-state is one of political subordination, but it is more balanced and interdependent when it comes to economics.

The institutional approach suggests that interaction between Chinese private entrepreneurs and the Chinese Party-state is highly differentiated and occurs in a much more complex and diversified institutional environment than is shown by the state-centred political science approach. With parallel trajectories of cooperation between the Chinese Party-state and private entrepreneurs, entrepreneurs require coordination with the central Party-state in order to secure the informal autonomy of enterprise networks as well as arrangements with the local Party-state that guarantee de facto property rights and access to basic resources. Finally, private entrepreneurs depend on the local Party-state to mediate their relationship with the central Party-state, on which their political legitimacy, access to the formal regulatory framework and national and international markets depends.

The institutional approach suggests that the economic interests of private entrepreneurs would benefit most from a political structure that protects local economic institutions against central interference. Local institutions have emerged endogenously from below in response to the economic requirements of local entrepreneurship and have been tolerated by an accommodating state amenable to local differentiation. This makes national unification of economic and political institutions a long-term project.

8. Understanding entrepreneurs

Yang Jing and Dai Jianzhong

Within three decades of the implementation of post-Mao reform, market-ization in China has developed, and with the massive privatization of state assets that began in the late 1990s, private entrepreneurs have become a major component of the new economic elite in China (Zheng and Li, 2004). At the same time a new class of largely small-scale private entrepreneurs has also emerged who are responsible for individually owned firms with eight or more employees.

Some sociologists have raised questions about the factors that have shaped the emergence and characteristics of this new class of private entrepreneurs (Chen, G.J., 2004, 2005; Dai, 2004; Chen et al., 2006; Yang, 2007). Where did they come from and why did they choose to take the entrepreneurial path when the private sector was so uncertain until the early 1990s? What are the backgrounds and demographic attributes of Chinese private entrepreneurs, and have they changed with time? What are their distinctive features and how do they govern their businesses? Answering these questions is essential for a better understanding of Chinese entrepreneurs and their impacts on the socioeconomic structure of contemporary China.

THE EMERGENCE OF ENTREPRENEURS AS A CLASS

The period since the early 1990s has been one of extraordinary economic growth. This has been particularly apparent in the non-state sector, which has seen a rapid increase in new job openings and market investment opportunities. Consequently, the domestic private sector expanded quickly as seen in Figures 8.1 to 8.3. Within 20 years, from 1990 to late 2009, the number of private enterprises reached 7.2 million, 9 per cent higher than 2008, and constituted 70 per cent of total registered enter-prises. This number increased to 7.6 million in the first quarter of 2010, which translates to 72 per cent of total registered enterprises (Dou, 2010). The total registered capital of private enterprises increased from around

10 billion RMB in the early 1990s to around 1.3 trillion RMB in 2000, achieving a tenfold increase within one decade. In the first quarter of 2010, 15.3 trillion RMB was invested in the private sector, constituting 26 per cent of the total registered capital (ibid.). In terms of employment, about 70 million employees were hired by private enterprises, 8 per cent up from the end of 2008. In terms of contribution to the labour market, the domestic private sector hired 152 million employees, accounting for 90 per cent of all new employees (State Administration for Industry and Commerce of the PRC, 2010).

At the end of August 2010, the All-China Federation of Industry and Commerce (ACFIC) released a list of 'China's Top 500 Private Enterprises in 2009'. The ranking was based on the revenue of approximately 3600 private enterprises that had volunteered to join a research project and to participate in 12 consecutive years of close study on the operation of the private sector. The threshold revenue for the 'Top 500 Chinese Private Enterprises in 2009' was 3.7 billion RMB, an increase of 23 per cent from 2008. Of the 500 listed enterprises, 126 reported revenues higher than 10 billion RMB. The net profit of the 500 combined totalled 218 billion in 2009 RMB, 33 per cent up from 2008.

Although private entrepreneurs have clearly arrived as a socioeconomic force the composition of the private entrepreneur 'class' is still an evolving entity (Tsui et al., 2006, pp. 17–18). The current debates are mainly focused on whether the entrepreneurs originated from a non-elite class or are reproduced from a more privileged, elite class.

In Central Europe, the evolution of market institutions appears to have outstripped the development of private property. For that reason Eyal et al. theorize 'capitalism without capitalists' as a distinct new strategy of transition adopted by technocratic-intellectual elites in societies where no class of private owners existed prior to the introduction of market mechanisms. However, in China, the accumulation of wealth in private hands is ahead of the establishment of market institutions. Instead of 'capitalism without capitalists', which is the current situation in Russia, China might be cited as a case of 'capitalists without capitalism' (Eyal et al., 1998, pp. 184–93). Having witnessed the rapid growth of the private sector, the future of China's prospects for democratic politics and civil society have become new fields of interest among intellectuals. The CCP government's responses to the establishment and growth of the private sector have oscillated throughout the first two decades of economic reform, and are reflected in the debates between conservatives and reformists over the principal spirits of 'red and political solidarity' and 'expert and economic-growth'.

Figure 8.1 Total number of registered private enterprises in China 1998–September 2009 (unit: 10 000 persons)

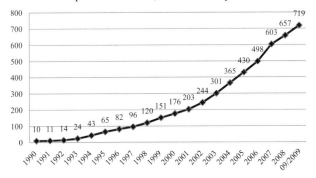

Figure 8.2 Total registered capital of private enterprises 1990–September 2009 (unit: RMB120 billion)

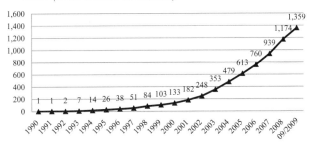

Figure 8.3 Total number of investors and employees in private enterprises 1990–September 2009

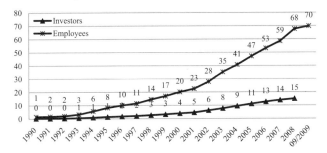

Source: Data presented in Figures 8.1–8.3 are collected from various but reliable resources. From 1990 to 1999 data are from the *Yearbook of Private Economy, 1986–1999*. As the publication of the series was disrupted in 2000, from 2000 onward data are from the reports released by the National Bureau of Statistics of China (NBSC) and the Chinese Academy of Social Sciences (CASS).

Beginning in 1997, the CCP's policy towards private enterprise and private entrepreneurs became more positive. In particular, the recognition of private property in the amendment to the state constitution in 2007 meant that private entrepreneurs were offered another guarantee that they would not be dispossessed. This was something business associations had long lobbied for.

The change in the status of private enterprise has been gradual, though clearly given a boost in May 2000 by Jiang Zemin's lifting of the ban in the CCP constitution that officially prohibited private businesspeople from joining the Party and serving the government. Since 2003, the CCP government has undertaken a determined and extensive effort to recruit entrepreneurs into the Party, a key dimension of the inclusion policy that allows the CCP to adapt, and this is an important factor in promoting organizational change. Some subsets of the cadres in the Party, however, warned that the growing numbers of red capitalists, especially the private entrepreneurs who were co-opted into the Party, were weakening the Party's cohesiveness and betraying its original class nature. The conservatives and observers further asserted that red capitalists are leading agents to promote political change if the interests and policy preferences of the business elites are substantially incompatible with the Party and government officials (Chen, A., 2003, pp. 142–3). Some reformers on the other side claimed that even though there are serious ideological barriers with red capitalists, encouraging Party members to become businesspeople and recruiting entrepreneurs into the Party can also be interpreted as a rational strategy to secure the CCP's leadership. Given that in Western civil society the rise of the bourgeois is regarded as a potential driving force of democratization (Moore, 1966, p. 418), some scholars speculate that continued economic growth and the increasing scale and scope of the privatization of state enterprises might ultimately lead to political change led or motivated by private entrepreneurs (Gilley, 2004; Zheng, 2004). Simultaneously, the other widely held viewpoint is that under the booming private economy and the decentralization of the state's management power, there has been a corresponding transition from 'top-down' state corporatism to a 'bottom-up' societal corporatism within the realm of the local economy (Unger, 1996, pp. 814–19).

Although the current generation of private entrepreneurs may all perform similar economic activities and share common business interests, differences in their social and political backgrounds remain (Chen, G.J., 2004; Tsai, 2005). For example, Chen An has divided Chinese entrepreneurs into two types: parasitic, those whose businesses rely on close attachments with government officials and bureaucratic networks, and self-made, those who survive in the private sector by their own efforts.

Likewise, Dickson (2003a, 2007) also differentiates entrepreneurs into *xiahai* (meaning, 'plunged into the sea of private business', which is a particular term in his studies referring to CCP members who started their own businesses in the private sector), 'co-opted' (which refers to the private entrepreneurs who were recruited by the CCP), and 'non-CCP member entrepreneurs'. He details the different attributes of these three groups in terms of their current status and their political attitudes in comparison with the local cadres. Dickson argues that these different types of entrepreneurs have different patterns of political and economic behaviour and perceptions about achieving their economic goals. (Holbig, 2002, pp. 52–4). Given the relative youth and short life span of the majority of private enterprises, it is not surprising that there is a lack of a common basis for identity and interaction within the entrepreneurs group (Tsai, 2005, pp. 1131–3). Therefore, class formation has not occurred within this group, and it is unlikely that the majority of private entrepreneurs will take up the cause of democracy in China in the near future (Dai, 2004, pp. 335–7; Tsai, 2005, pp. 1152–3).

Some empirical studies (Dickson, 2003a; Ao, 2005) have shown that Chinese entrepreneurs in the last decade or so have established close ties and a series of adaptive strategies for working with local government officials, which essentially prevent them from being a force for change (Wank, 1995a, 1995b, 1996; Unger, 1996; Unger and Chan, 1999; Dickson, 2003a; Chen, GuangJin, 2005; Chen et al., 2006). As long as private entrepreneurs have an interest in economic growth, and their economic success relies on favourable working relationships with local officials, many will 'rely heavily on government patronage for their success in making profits' (Chen, A., 2003, p. 157), and they will remain 'among the Party's most important bases of support' (Dickson, 2007, pp. 827–8). Consequently, most scholars depict a close community of interest and action between government and the business world.

THE DEVELOPMENT OF PRIVATE ENTERPRISE

Different types of marketization took place after the 1989 Revolutions in Central and Eastern Europe (CEE), which not only allowed the growth of a new private sector but also made privatization of public assets state policy (Stark, 1991). In China, market reform had already started in the late 1970s in the form of the Household Responsibility System (HRS). State socialism persisted and the major public sector was well maintained.[1] To control the career tracks of China's leaders, the Party retained the power of its personnel appointment process and the cadre system.

Simultaneously, the Party also encouraged economic decentralization and experimentation, with the aim of encouraging economic growth (McNally, 2008, pp. 116–20). On the one hand, the cadres in the CCP hierarchy system still guide and evaluate the local cadres; on the other hand, the reforms also granted greater autonomy to the cadres in developing local economies (Edin, 2003, p. 38). On the whole, at the macroeconomic level, changes in the strategies and policies of the Chinese government since the early 1980s have created an increasingly entrepreneurship-friendly environment (Li and Rozelle, 2003).

As Walder points out, the key drivers have been marketization and privatization (Walder, 2002, 2003). 'Marketization', refers to the increased competition in labour, commodity and financial markets that has occurred through the destruction of work-units (*danwei*) and their attached privileges and benefits (known as the 'iron rice bowl' in Chinese society), and the guaranteed market for products that maximized employment by ensuring the survival of firms. 'Privatization' refers to the reallocation of property rights from the state to new owners, who range from individuals and households to new corporate firms (Walder, 2003, 2006). Privatization may proceed through the transfer of ownership of existing government-held assets or through investment in new private businesses based on savings or credit.

In the context of China, uncertainties generated from changing institutional structures are both risks and opportunities for the development of private entrepreneurship. China's emergent private entrepreneurs therefore have had to be capable of identifying and creating a promising market, in addition to being talented in making use of institutional rules when starting their business ventures (Yang, 2007, pp. 57–64). Their goal has been to maximize the economic rewards while minimizing the sociopolitical risks by taking advantage of the 'institutional hole' that appears in the interface between state-led development from above and local power from below (McNally, 2008, pp. 120–23). The CCP government's general attitude towards the private economy has developed from encouragement of small-scale self-employed businesses to the approval of the legal protection of private property in 2007 that granted legitimate status to full-scale privatization.

The historical determination of the new private entrepreneurial class suggests several tentative conclusions that can be examined further. During the transition of the political regime private entrepreneurs have come from various backgrounds. However, individual and household business owners, small, private business owners and the bureaucratic elites are the most likely constituents of China's rising affluent class. At the same time political capital is to some extent not as important as human capital upon entry into the private sector. Education becomes a determinant, which indicates the rise of meritocratic values. Overall, personal characteristics, such as cultural capital and former political capital have an important impact on the probability of circulation of the former cadres and administrative managers into the private sector and the generation of new private entrepreneurs.

Education is a key component of the human capital required to facilitate entrepreneurial success. During the 1980s when the development of entrepreneurship had only just been revived, the majority of private entrepreneurs were relatively poorly educated. This group had begun to operate small businesses in the 1970s under the Household Responsibility System, which replaced the Mao-era People's Communes and turned the household into the basic unit of production, distribution and consumption (Oi, 1995). There was a very small proportion of illiterate people, and more than half of these *getihu* (self-employed) were only educated up to junior high school level, a symptom of their relatively humble origins and lower social background. As entrepreneurial developments progressed, increasing numbers of private entrepreneurs were pulled into entrepreneurial activities by factors such as the gradual privatization of state-owned enterprises (SOEs) and township and village enterprises (TVEs), and the merging of state and economy in what has been termed 'local state corporatism' (Oi and Walder, 1999). Furthermore, a larger number of new private entrepreneurs originated from a better social background or a higher social class, and the level of education among entrepreneurs began to improve gradually and consistently. During the late 1990s, the educational level exhibited a sharp improvement.

A number of hypotheses may be tested against the empirical data from the Survey on Private Enterprises and Entrepreneurs in China (SPEEC), which is the main source of information on the new private entrepreneurial class.

Hypothesis 1: People with high education qualifications might be more confident in entering the private sector. Although having a certain educational background is helpful for managing a business, given the large educated population that is gradually getting involved in private business, the positive effect of high education might be less important now than in the 1980s.

Hypothesis 2: Similarly, effects of previous work experience, particularly in positions of management or professional supervision of the industry, have proven to be helpful to people's entry into the private sector.

However, previous experience cannot determine whether or not the business will be successful in the future. In particular, one would expect to see that cadres from the CCP hierarchy are less likely to engage in private business than those who are not. However, administrative personnel from former state and/or collective-owned enterprises (S/COEs) are more likely to engage in private business and some have even been pushed to do so.

Hypothesis 3: Compared to the entrepreneurs' personal attributes, the initial status of their business is a more efficient predictor of business success and the potential for growth.

Hypothesis 4: More investment at the beginning determines the future prospects of the business, especially when most enterprises have been established less than ten years. Thus, a higher value of registered capital would place the business at a better starting point and probably return a higher profit.

Hypothesis 5: If the entrepreneurs' business is based on the established infrastructure of a former S/COE it is more convenient for them to operate a relatively large-scale business.

Hypothesis 6: The industry of the business has various effects on the scale of the business, which is determined by the government's strategic policies and the characteristics of the industry itself. In general, since the competition within any industry has been enhanced, it might be extremely difficult to survive in a sector with relatively loose entry conditions.

ATTRIBUTES OF PRIVATE ENTREPRENEURS

Data for empirical analysis is taken from the Survey on Private Enterprises and Entrepreneurs in China (SPEEC). SPEEC is composed of a series of cross-sectional surveys on private entrepreneurs conducted every two years from 1991 to 1997 and 2000 to 2008.

The sample size ranges from 1946 entrepreneurs in 1997 to 4098 in 2008, with an average response rate of over 80 per cent. The purpose of the SPEEC project is to study the development strategy of private enterprises as the Chinese government has been incrementally relinquishing its control over the private sector. The survey covers the private entrepreneur's family background, work history, political attitudes, income, current family information, housing conditions and the operation of the enterprises. A specific part of the questionnaire refers to political events, with particular reference to policy changes occurring at the time of inquiry. This will be the main focus of the empirical study.

In order to efficiently capture the effect of time, cases with selected variables were merged and further divided into three major groups according to the major shifts in state policy: entrepreneur respondents who registered their businesses before 1992, 1992 to 1997, and from 1998 onward. Since the design of each year's questionnaire is not entirely consistent, the cases of specific survey years are dealt with separately when observing entrepreneurs' self-perceptions and political concerns.

The relative youth or generally short life-span of the private enterprises is immediately observable from the distribution of the respondents across surveys and in the merged data shown in Table 8.1. The proportion of the entrepreneur respondents who started their businesses before 1992 has gradually dropped from 26.8 per cent in the 1997 survey to 5.6 per cent in the 2008 survey. Accordingly, the proportion of entrepreneur respondents who started their business from 1998 onward has steadily increased from 15.3 per cent in 2000 to 72.5 per cent in 2008.

Table 8.1   *Distribution of Chinese domestic private entrepreneurs registered before 1992, 1992–1997 and from 1998 onward in SPEEC (row %)*

	Before 1992	1992–97	1998 onward	Total N
1997	26.8	67.0	–	1946
2000	22.4	51.9	15.3	3073
2002	17.9	47.4	31.7	3258
2004	8.7	33.6	53.2	3593
2006	7.7	27.0	60.9	4315
2008	5.6	21.9	72.5	4098
Merged 97–08	13.1	38.0	44.4	20283

Note: Row percentages may not equal 100% due to rounding and missing cases.

Backgrounds of Entrepreneurs

The personal characteristics and background information of the entrepreneur respondents and their businesses are summarized in Table 8.2.
First, this is a male preserve. Although the number of male entrepreneurs
shows a considerable decrease of 8 per cent between 1997 and 2008
(from 92 per cent among the enterprises registered before 1992 to 84 per
cent among the enterprises registered from 1998 onward), there is no
doubt that the private sector in China has always been dominated by men.

Second, entrepreneurs have become younger and better educated,
particularly in businesses registered from 1992 onward. Eighty per cent
of the respondents were 40 years or younger at the time of inquiry and
almost half of them held qualifications of higher education or equivalent.

In general, educational qualifications are an important factor for
individual career success (Hannum and Buchmann, 2005), and the
majority of the entrepreneur respondents had at least completed high
school (from about 62 per cent in 1997 to about 91 per cent in 2008).
Likewise, the proportion of entrepreneur respondents with high educational qualifications (including vocational school, college and graduate
school) increased from 20 per cent in 1997 to 62 per cent in 2006.

Regarding political identity, about a 12 per cent increase is found in
the proportion of Party members from 23 per cent in the group registered
before 1992 to 35 per cent among the most recent group. The increasing
proportion of Party members among private entrepreneurs indicates not
only their political status and expanding networks with local bureaucrats,
but also the evolving strategy of the CCP central government as it adapts
to the expanding private sector.

Characteristics of Business

The last section of background information on the business in Table 8.3
indicates that the proportion of the previous S/COEs that were transformed into privately owned businesses also increased from 15 per cent
to 24 per cent, which partially explains the increasing proportion of
former managers from the S/COEs among the respondents.

Approximately 80 per cent of the private enterprises operate in the
secondary and tertiary industries, although the proportion has been
increasing slightly in the latter and decreasing correspondingly in the
former.

Financial resources have been an essential factor for the successful
operation of businesses (Chen, GuangJin, 2005; Chen et al., 2006)
especially in light of the continuing privatization of capital-intensive

Table 8.2   General information: business establishment dates for SPEEC
respondents (1997–2008) (column %)

	Before 1992	1992–97	1998 onward
Age			
–30	1.5	4.3	5.0
31–40	24.7	32.4	33.3
41–50	43.5	41.5	40.7
51–60	24.6	18.0	18.0
60+	5.0	2.8	2.3
Male	92.0	88.6	84.4
Higher education	29.6	44.1	52.7
Political identities (multiple choice)			
CCP	22.8	26.0	34.7
DP	7.6	5.8	2.4
FIC	81.2	76.8	55.5
NPC	20.6	18.6	16.8
CPPCC	46.5	37.3	22.8
Work experience			
Cadre	7.4	9.9	8.5
Managers	34.4	40.4	36.7
Professional	16.0	20.4	18.2
Rural cadre	10.2	6.8	5.3
Getihu	29.0	24.6	17.7
Peasant	35.7	25.0	13.8
Total N	2666	7714	9012

Note: Column percentages may not equal 100% due to rounding and missing cases.
Key: CCP: Chinese Communist Party; DP: Democratic Party; FIC: Federation of Industry and
Commerce; NPC: National People's Congress; CPPCC: Chinese People's Political
Consultative Congress; *getihu*: self-employed.

Table 8.3   Background of the business: SPEEC 1997–2008 (column %)

	Before 1992	1992–97	1998 onward
Gaizhi (restructured S/COE)	14.8	19.4	23.8
Major business industry			
Primary	5.1	5.3	5.5
Secondary	50.5	48.0	41.0
Tertiary	30.6	32.4	37.3
Registered capital (10 000 RMB)			
50 or below	63.5	49.3	42.6
50–100	12.9	17.6	16.0
100–500	14.8	21.1	23.7
Above 500	8.7	12.0	17.7
Total annual turnover (million RMB)			
10 or lower	67.4	66.7	65.3
10–50	20.8	21.3	21.4
Above 50	11.8	12.0	13.2
Total N	2666	7714	9012

Note: Column percentages may not equal 100% due to rounding and missing cases.

sectors that the SOEs had monopolized throughout the 1990s. Table 8.3 demonstrates the distribution of registered capital at the founding of the business and the total annual turnover of the business in the year before the survey. The total proportion of businesses with registered capital between 0.5 and 5 million RMB has increased by about 13 per cent across three periods, and large-scale businesses with start-up investment over 5 million RMB also show a considerable increase of 9 per cent. The distribution of the total annual turnover, however, has been relatively constant.

As the SPEEC project included only private entrepreneurs, financial achievement has been used as the measurement of success of private entrepreneurs. However, in the SPEEC, as in ordinary business proced-ures in daily life, it is a common phenomenon that most entrepreneur respondents lie about their personal income and the profit of the business to avoid the relevant tax charges, or perhaps do not care since they regard the business as an extension of their personal household (Dai, 2004; Zheng and Li, 2004). The statistical analysis in this chapter uses a log of the annual turnover of the business instead of personal income.

The measurement of scale and performance of the business and success of the entrepreneur needs to take more than economic factors into account. (Gong et al., 2009, pp. 266–8). At its early stage of development, the pursuit and accumulation of maximum profit is still the main goal of the majority of entrepreneurs; thus the amount of financial return is an efficient and direct indicator of the success of entrepreneurs at this stage. However, given the relative youth of firms in the private economy, in addition to the financial returns, the years in business, number of employees, organizational efficiency and development of the enterprise's culture, social reputation, its contribution to society and so on, cannot be properly accounted for in this analysis.

Results

The effects of respondents' personal attributes and the characteristics of business on annual turnover (log) are shown in Table 8.4.

In terms of demographic background, the statistically positive effect of age stabilized across three periods. Being male increases the turnover of businesses registered between 1992 and 1997 by 42 per cent (= $e^{0.345}$ −1), and by 18 per cent (= $e^{0.164}$ −1) for businesses registered in 1998 or later.

Considering the expansion of higher education at present in China, it is not surprising to see that the positive and significant effect of having higher education decreases from 1.114 (SE = 0.077) in the earlier period to 0.344 (SE = 0.063) in the later period.

Being a CCP member is found not to be helpful in improving the annual turnover of the business for the entrepreneurs registered before 1998. In contrast, although its positive effect decreases as the variables of working experience and business background are included in the model, it appears slightly helpful for increasing the log of annual turnover by 20 per cent (= $e^{0.180}$ −1) for enterprises registered from 1998 onward.

Being a former manager in a S/COE significantly increases the log of annual turnover of the business by around 43 per cent (= $e^{0.357}$ −1) for enterprises registered before 1992, and it remains effective, but at a lower level of 15 per cent for enterprises registered between 1992 and 1997 (= $e^{0.139}$ −1), and returns to a higher level of 34 per cent for enterprises registered after 1997 (= $e^{0.295}$ −1).

*Table 8.4   OLS estimates of regression of annual turnover (log) of the
company registered before 1992, 1992–97 and 1998 onward
(merged data: SPEEC 1997–2008)*

	Before 1992	1992–97	1998 onward
Survey year	0.359(0.042)***	0.466(0.023)***	0.158(0.030)***
Age	0.114(0.046)**	0.116(0.025)***	0.119(0.028)***
Age^2	–0.001(0.000)**	–0.001(0.000)***	–0.001(0.000)***
Sex (male)	0.243(0.197)	0.345(0.094)***	0.164(0.085)*
Higher education	1.144(0.116)***	0.873(0.063)***	0.344(0.063)***
CCP (党员)	–0.014(0.118)	0.008(0.067)	0.180(0.067)**
Work experience			
Cadre	0.031(0.195)	0.274(0.102)**	0.394(0.127)**
Managers (S/COEs)	0.357(0.108)***	0.139(0.060)*	0.295(0.065)***
Professional	–0.155(0.129)	–0.165(0.071)*	0.024(0.074)
Rural cadre	0.098(0.156)	0.229(0.109)*	–0.043(0.123)
Getihu	–0.351(0.104)***	–0.162(0.064)*	0.046(0.070)
Peasant	–0.112(0.106)	–0.086(0.065)	0.125(0.081)
Business background			
Gaizhi (restructured SOE)	0.396(0.133)**	0.523(0.071)***	0.460(0.070)***
Registered capital (log)	0.015(0.013)	0.016(0.008)*	0.664(0.019)***
Primary industry	0.283(0.287)	0.128(0.158)	0.517(0.177)**
Secondary industry	0.351(0.199)	0.104(0.112)	0.566(0.142)***
Tertiary industry	–0.190(0.206)	–0.427(0.116)***	0.061(0.142)
Constant	2.491(1.126)*	1.993(0.569)***	–1.218(0.631)*
Adjust R^2	0.198	0.246	0.421

Note: *$p < 0.05$; **$p < 0.01$; ***$p < 0.001$.

Likewise, previous work experience as a cadre is also found to have an increasingly positive effect across the three periods, particularly from 1992 onward; but for the less competitive background of having been a rural cadre, the positive effect on company performance is only observed in those who started their enterprises during 1992–97.

Not surprisingly, the data suggest that having professional job experience was, in general, negatively associated with the annual turnover of the business during 1992 and 1997, and was insignificant for the other periods of business establishment.

Similarly, the negative effect of *getihu* experience found in the pre-1992 group gradually disappears in the later periods. The annual turnover is found to have decreased by about 30 per cent ($= 1 - e^{-0.351}$) among the owners who were self-employed before 1992, decreased 15 per cent for those first active during 1992–97, and is not significant (at the 0.05 level) for those starting private businesses since 1997.

Work experience in elite positions, for instance as professionals or rural cadres, or in a related sector, such as self-employment, or in a relatively more flexible sector, such as agricultural labour, do not affect the annual turnover or the business performance of the enterprise. Only already-privileged positions, such as cadres and managers in S/COEs could make use of the advantages accumulated from previous positions to access the scarce opportunities and resources, and of their established networks in the promotion and development of their businesses.

Nonetheless, the characteristics of the business itself and especially its finances are found to be more influential than the personal background of the entrepreneurs. First of all, the privileges of taking over the former S/COEs sustained statistical significance across the three periods and especially since the 1990s when the state started the strategic policy of 'grasping the big (state-owned enterprises) and releasing the small (state-owned enterprises)' to individual contractors. If the enterprise had been reformed in this way the effect increases from 0.396 (SE = 0.019) to 0.523 (SE = 0.012) with a slight drop to 0.460 (SE = 0.07) for the most recently established businesses. Accordingly, the financial capacity at the beginning of the business also becomes distinctively important for those businesses first registered as private enterprises after 1997.

State constraints on most sectors within the tertiary sector have been relatively loose (Yang, 2007, pp. 100–107). Therefore, entry requirements are comparatively lower than for other industries and the intensity of the competition varies across sectors and regions. It is possible to say that, due to the relatively loose legislation and lower requirements for start-up investment, doing business in the service sector has become more and more attractive to new individual investors and self-employed persons who are hoping to expand their businesses. Most small-scale businesses are more likely to be established within the service sector. As a result it is clear that doing business in the tertiary sector is common but it does not provide a competitive condition for raising the annual turnover of the enterprise.

Despite the ambiguous classification of occupation and variations between the survey years, these findings are consistent with previous research on several crucial points. First, as reforms have progressed, private entrepreneurs have become somewhat younger, exhibit a generally higher level of education, and have had relatively more privileged work experience, rather than being from the working class. Second, experience running self-employed businesses or residing in rural areas did facilitate respondents' entry into the private sector. However, these factors did not contribute to the annual income of the business, particularly during the period of expanding privatization. In contrast, the initial advantages provided by the resources and capabilities that the respondents had at the founding of their businesses – basically the registered capital, type of the business and location in a specific industry sector (mainly primary and secondary industries) – are shown to be positively associated with the operation of the business. As a result, one may argue that the reproduction of former administrative elites has been more profoundly embedded in the developing private sector since the early 1990s, when compared with the activities of those not from the elite in the period before that.

Further Discussion

For a short period in the early stage of market reform, the major inflow of people to private entrepreneurship originated from the non-elite class. However, their actual proportion has been decreasing since the market reform has become more embedded and the circumstances of the private economy have matured. People from other elite positions were either 'pushed' by the force of the market economy or 'pulled' by the lure of wealth the market provided. A particular question in the SPEEC about the motivation(s) for the respondents' entry to the private sector was raised in the 1997 and 2002 surveys, in which the respondents were asked to either select one from a list of motivations (in 1997) or choose as many as applied (in 2002).[2] Two motivations stand out in both surveys: first of all, for both years, approximately one-third of the respondents entered the private sector seeking money. Second, 48 per cent of the respondents in 1997 claimed that they were in search of 'the self-realization of the value of life', which is largely linked to the hope for the achievement of success on various fronts; in 2002, the proportion of the respondents who selected this statement increased to about 77 per cent. Moreover, for both years, money motivation decreased while the response 'achieving the value of life' increased. Twelve per cent of the respondents said they were motivated by the successful cases in the private sector around them. All three of these statements are considered 'pull' factors[3] for the respondents' entrance to the private sector.

Very few respondents claimed that 'push' factors, such as working circumstances and job insecurity, were the main motivations for their decisions to start their own businesses. Particularly, the importance of unemployment as a push factor decreased dramatically, from 22 per cent in 1993 (Chen et al., 2006, pp. 153–4) to about 5 per cent in 2002. This shift in motivation was consistent with the development of an entrepreneurship-friendly environment. It also reflected some new personal attributes of subsequent generations of private entrepreneurs: they were not satisfied with the status quo and were willing to take the risks in establishing their own businesses for personal development and achievement. The implications of this change are significant, as evidence elsewhere suggests, positive motivation or pull factors are far more likely to establish the business and keep it running successfully (Burns, 1999).

After successful entry to the private sector, most enterprises were at a significant disadvantage because they, unlike the S/COEs, did not have the important personal or administrative ties that could protect and channel scarce resources to them (Xin and Pearce, 1996). Starting with whatever initial complement of resources and capabilities they had at their founding, the enterprise operators had to acquire the additional resources and capabilities that enabled them to compete and survive, through a combination of manufacturing, sales and strong alliance strategies.

CONCLUSIONS

These findings suggest that private entrepreneurs as a newly rising class show a growing integration in terms of background and political concerns, but that they have not become a unified class. The formation of private entrepreneurs as a social category is continuously evolving and its boundaries are rapidly changing. The various backgrounds of newcomers to the private sector bring different advantages for their businesses.

From the mid-1990s, personal background was not as important as it had been in the 1980s. Similarly, the positive effect of CCP membership was also diminished immensely when variables more closely related to business attributes, such as work experience and characteristics of the business, were examined. Government connections, however, remained essential for access to resources and thus were a fact of life for the survival of private businesses. Among private entrepreneurs, the privileges of being a CCP member are not only reflected in their relatively higher level of education, but also in their working experiences as incumbent cadres, bureaucrats and managers in S/COEs. According to the survey data, around 27 per cent of CCP entrepreneurs are former cadres (including rural cadres), and more than half of them are former bureaucrats or managers in S/COEs. Meanwhile, only 7 per cent of non-CCP member entrepreneurs are former cadres. Forty-four per cent of co-opted entrepreneurs and 34 per cent of non-CCP member entrepreneurs were former administrative personnel from S/COEs. On the other hand, entrepreneurs with large-scale businesses who have been in business relatively longer than other entrepreneurs have always been the candidates for co-option by the CCP. The co-opted entrepreneurs themselves have also retained or sought closer contacts with local officials and have shown greater desire to participate in social activities and perform political duties. Given their divergent social and political backgrounds, entrepreneurs are still at the initial stage of developing a class consciousness; perhaps once the class is beyond its infancy, it may be a better advocate for democratization.

This chapter has examined the characteristics of the different types of private entrepreneurs and their growing political concerns. There are several constraints incumbent in the empirical analyses that must be acknowledged. First, since the empirical part of this chapter is based on data from surveys that mainly focused on the development of private enterprises and entrepreneurs, people from other social classes, who are supposed to be the reference groups for empirical analyses, are not included. This study has been restricted to the comparison of the attributes of private entrepreneurs' different political identities at different points in time. Second, since the SPEEC project has been implemented through a series of cross-sectional surveys, the sample was drawn from the pool of private enterprises extant at the time of inquiry. Thus, analysis is further restricted to those entrepreneurs who successfully 'survived' intensive market competition, while some entrepreneurs who left the private sector during the survey period were ignored. Third, the observation of entrepreneurs' current concerns is merely a preliminary exploration of their attitudes towards the prevailing policy. Future research should consider regional variations in the communication between private entrepreneurs and the local government at different administrative levels, and the impact on different industrial sectors, as well as the prominence of the local economic development plans.[4]

Along with the pace of political reform, private entrepreneurs have evolved from a marginalized and politically vague element to a much more defined and influential group. To some extent, they have gradually developed an awareness of their social status and reputation, and this is mainly reflected in their comparisons with other social groups outside the private sector, particularly with the more marginalized societal groups. However, some scholars have warned that there is no organization that represents the interests of the marginalized, such as peasants, laid-off workers (Chen, A., 2003; Chen, F., 2003), and employees who are maltreated by business owners (Sun, 2004, pp. 27–51). The slogan of 'harmonious society' advocated by the CCP since 2005 might outline an ideal society to pursue in the future, however, the reality is more challenging. How can China handle labour–employer conflicts, especially in the private sector, between the wealthy entrepreneur echelon and the underclass – between the new rich and poor – and, in turn, how will these conflicts affect the cooperative relationship between the Party and entrepreneurs?

NOTES

1. The massive restructuring and takeover of the middle- and small-sized S/COEs (state and/or collective-owned enterprises) started in the early 1990s. One plank of China's reform programme has sought to transform SOEs into the leaders of highly regulated industries or those considered important for national security. In industries such as oil, steel, mining, telecommunications, shipping and banking, the state has actively pushed industry consolidation to establish a few giant SOEs. They are expanding globally to secure China's access to raw materials for the sustainable growth of the economy.
2. In the 1997 survey, the respondents were asked to select only one reason for starting their own businesses from a list of possible answers: (1) Not getting along well with the bosses; (2) No chance of using their professional skills at the position (lack of career prospects); (3) For higher income; (4) Unemployed or semi-employed (unstable employment status); (5) Self-realization of the value of life; (6) Leaving the farm (for peasants); (7) Others (please specify). In the 2002 survey, the respondents were asked to select from a similar list as many reasons as applied, including statements of a more general sense: (1) Difficulty in interpersonal relationships in the office; (2) Insufficient operation of the business of the old company; (3) Laid-off/unemployed; (4) For higher income; (5) Self-realization of the value of life; (6) Encouraged by the successful cases; (7) Others (please specify). The statements 'For higher income' and 'Self-realization of the value of life' are exactly the same in the 1997 and 2002 surveys. Therefore, the higher proportions found in the latter might partially be explained by the multiple-choice option that was provided in the 2002 survey.
3. Chen et al. (2006) applied Burns's (1999) 'push' and 'pull' concepts to the analyses of the motivations of respondents to become entrepreneurs. In the Chinese context, and based on the SPEEC project, the 'push' factors can be recognized as all the negative

effects from the working or even larger social circumstances that push the respondents to leave their original positions; the 'pull' factors are comprised of all the positive conditions that attracted the respondents to join the private sector.

4. To study the regional differences on the interaction between government and entre-preneurs, a thorough grasp of the history of governments' development strategies and the characteristics of the local private economy is essential. For example, if we only focused on the east coast area where the open-door policy first initiated, there are at least three famous models of economic development discussed by many scholars, which are commonly known as: (1) the 'Pearl River Delta model' centred on Shenzhen, Guangzhou, Zhuhai and expanding to surrounding areas, which is charac-terized as an export-oriented economy with much foreign investment; (2) the 'South-ern Su (*Sunan*) model' centred on Shanghai and the Long River Delta including Suzhou, Hangzhou, Wuxi, Changzhou and Ningbo, which is characterized by a highly technical composite manufacturing industry mostly run by TVEs; (3) the 'Wenzhou model', an area in which most villages are famous for an industry of making small products rooted in family craft workshops. Therefore, discussion on regional variations of entrepreneurs' political status and attitudes has exceeded the initial purpose of this chapter.

Bibliography

Abercrombie, Nicholas and John Urry (1983), *Capital, Labour and the Middle Classes*, London: George Allen and Unwin.

Acker, Joan (1990), 'Hierarchies, jobs, and bodies: a theory of gendered organizations', *Gender and Society*, **4** (2), 139–58.

Acker, Joan (2000), 'Revisiting class: thinking from gender, race and organizations', *Social Politics*, **7** (2), 192–214.

Acker, Joan (2006), 'Inequality regimes: gender, class, and race in organizations', *Gender and Society*, **20** (4), 441–64.

Anagnost, Ann (2004), 'The corporeal politics of quality (*suzhi*)', *Public Culture*, **16** (2), 189–208.

Anagnost, Ann (2008), 'From "class" to "social strata": grasping the social totality in reform-era China', *Third World Quarterly*, **29** (3), 497–519.

Andreas, Joel (2009), *Rise of the Red Engineers: The Cultural Revolution and the Origins of China's New Class*, Stanford: Stanford University Press.

Ao, Daiya (2005), *Political Participation of Private Entrepreneurs*, Guangzhou: Zhong Shan University Press.

Atkinson, Rowland and Sarah Blandy (eds) (2006), *Gated Communities: An International Perspective*, London and New York: Routledge.

Bagguley, Paul (1992), 'Social change, the middle class, and the emergence of "new social movements": a critical analysis', *The Sociological Review*, **40** (1), 26–48.

Bai, Limin (2006), 'Graduate unemployment: dilemmas and challenges in China's move to mass higher education', *The China Quarterly*, **185**, 128–44.

Bayart, Jean-François (2008), *Global Subjects: A Political Critique of Globalization*, Cambridge: Polity.

'Beijing residents struggle to get on housing ladder' (2010), *China Daily*, accessed 19 July 2010 at www.chinadaily.com.cn/cndy/2010-07/19/content_10121252.htm.

'Beijing xingui: yezhudahui chengliqian yezhu bujiao wuyefei' [New regulations in Beijing: before the funding of homeowners' associations, homeowners do not have to pay management fees] (2010) *Zhongguo jianshe bao*, 2 June, accessed 10 September 2012 at www.chinajsb.cn/gb/content/2010-06/02/content_311733.htm.

'Beijing xinjian xiaoqu qianqi wuyefei jiang you kaifa shang tao' [In
  Beijing, from now on, before the completion of the building of a
  housing estate the management fees will be fished out from the
  developer's pocket] (2010), *Zhongguo qingnianbao* [*Journal of Chi-
  nese Youth*], 28 February.
Bell, Daniel (1973), *The Coming of Post-industrial Society: A Venture of
  Social Forecasting*, New York: Basic Books.
Bergère, Marie-Claire (1983), 'The Chinese bourgeoisie, 1911–37', in
  John K. Fairbank (ed.), *Republican China 1912–1949*, *Part 1*, Cam-
  bridge: Cambridge University Press, pp. 721–825.
Bergère, Marie-Claire (1989), *The Golden Age of the Chinese Bour-
  geoisie 1911–1937*, Cambridge: Cambridge University Press.
Boltanski, Luc (1987), *The Making of a Class: Cadres in French Society*,
  Cambridge and Paris: Cambridge University Press and the Maison des
  Sciences de l'Homme.
Bourdieu, Pierre (1984), *Distinction: A Social Critique of the Judgement
  of Taste*, R. Nice (trans.), London: Routledge & Kegan Paul.
Bourdieu, Pierre and Jean-Claude Passeron (1977), *Reproduction in
  Education, Society and Culture*, Beverly Hills: Sage.
Bray, David (2005), *Social Space and Governance in Urban China: The
  Danwei System from Origins to Reform*, Stanford: Stanford University
  Press.
Broudehoux, Anne-Marie (2004), *The Making and Selling of Post-Mao
  Beijing*, London: Routledge.
Burnham, James (1941), *The Managerial Revolution: What is Happening
  in the World*, New York: Norton.
Burns, Pearson (1999), *Entrepreneurship and Small Business*, Basing-
  stoke: Palgrave Macmillan.
Cartier, Carolyn (2002), 'Transnational urbanism in the reform-era Chi-
  nese city: landscapes from Shenzhen', *Urban Studies*, **39** (9), 1513–32.
Cartier, Carolyn (2008), 'The Shanghai-Hong Kong connection: fine
  jewelry consumption and the demand for diamonds', in David S.G.
  Goodman (ed.), *The New Rich in China*, London: Routledge,
  pp. 187–200.
Cartier, Carolyn (2009), 'Production/consumption and the Chinese city/
  region: cultural political economy and the feminist diamond ring',
  Urban Geography, **30** (4), 368–90.
Chan, Anita and Jonathan Unger (2009), 'A Chinese state enterprise
  under the reforms: what model of capitalism?', *The China Journal*, **62**,
  1–26.
Chao, Linda and Ramon H. Meyers (1998), *The First Chinese Democ-
  racy: Political Life in the Republic of China on Taiwan*, Baltimore:
  Johns Hopkins University Press.

Chen, An (2003), 'Rising-class politics and its impact on China's path to democracy', *Democratization*, **10** (2), 141–62.

Chen, Feng (2003), 'Between the state and labour: the conflict of Chinese trade unions' double identity in market reform', *The China Quarterly*, **176**, 1006–28.

Chen, GuangJin (2004), 'The formation of the stratum of private entrepreneur', in Lu X.Y. (ed.), *Social Mobility in Contemporary China*, Beijing: Social Science Documentation Publishing House, pp. 241–65.

Chen, GuangJin (2005), 'From elite circulation to elite reproduction: the changing mechanism for the formation of Chinese private entrepreneurs' class', *Study and Exploration*, **1**, 44–51.

Chen, GuangJin, Jun Li and Harry Matlay (2006), 'Who are the Chinese private entrepreneurs? A study of entrepreneurial attributes and business governance', *Journal of Small Business and Enterprise Development*, **13** (2), 148–60.

Chen, Guangxi (2005), 'Five waves of social mobility in contemporary China' [Dangdai zhongguo de wuci shehui liudong], in X. Lu (ed.), *Social Mobility in Contemporary China* [*Dangdai Zhongguo shehui liudong*], Beijing: Social Sciences Documentation Publishing House, pp. 33–97.

Chen, Jie (2004), *Popular Political Support in Urban China*, Washington, DC: Woodrow Wilson Center Press.

Chen, Jie (2010), 'Attitudes toward democracy and the political behavior of China's middle class', in Cheng Li (ed.), *China's Emerging Middle Class*, Washington, DC: Brookings Institution, pp. 334–58.

Chen, Jie and Bruce J. Dickson (2010), *Allies of the State: China's Private Entrepreneurs and Democratic Change*, Cambridge, MA: Harvard University Press.

Chen, Jie and Chunlong Lu (2006), 'Does China's middle class think and act democratically attitudinal and behavioral orientations toward urban self-government?, *Journal of Chinese Political Science*, **11** (2), 1–20.

Chen, Peng (2009), 'Cong "chanquan" zouxiang "gongminquan". Dangqian zhongguo chengshi yezhu weiquan yanjiu' [From property rights to citizens' rights. a study on homeowners' rights defence in contemporary urban China], *Kaifang shidai* [*Open Times*], 4, 126–39.

Cheng, Tun-jen (1989), 'Democratizing the quasi-Leninist regime in Taiwan', *World Politics*, **41** (4), 471–99.

China Consumers' Association (1997), 'Jiang chengxin, fan qizha' [Good faith, no fraud], 1 January, accessed 12 September 2012 at www.cca. org.cn/web/nzt/newsShow.jsp?id=22922&cid=507.

China Consumers' Association (2008), 'Shenzhenshi xiaoweihui: quanshi zhongxuesheng banbao sheji dasai lakai weimu' [Shenzhen Consumer Association: opening the curtain on the all-city high school blackboard design contest], 4 August, accessed 7 September 2012 at www.cca.org.cn/web/gddt/newsShow.jsp?id=40925.

China Consumers' Association (2010), 'Ningboshi gaoxinqu xiaobaowei: zhongxiao xuesheng xiaofei zhuangkuang wenjuan diaochao baogao' [*Ningbo High Technology Zone Consumer Protection Committee: survey report on consumption activity of primary and high school students*], 25 January, accessed 7 September 2012 at www.cca.org.cn/web/dcjd/newsShow.jsp?id=45879.

China Real Estate Statistics Yearbook (1999, 2001, 2004, 2007, 2009), Beijing: China Statistics Press.

China Statistical Yearbook (2010), Beijing: China Statistics Press.

Chou, Yangsun and Andrew J. Nathan (1987), 'Democratizing transition in Taiwan', *Asian Survey*, **27** (3), 277–99.

Chua, Beng-Huat (2000), *Consumption in Asia: Lifestyles and Identities*, London: Routledge.

Chuan, Chunhui (2009), 'Juzhu gaibian zhongguo: zuowei gongminquan shengchande yezhu weiquan yundong' [Residence changes China: the movement of homeowners rights' defence as giving birth to citizens' rights], Master of Sociology, thesis, Tsinghua Daxue.

Chung, Jae Ho (2011), 'Central-local dynamics: historical continuities and institutional resilience', in Sebastian Heilmann and Elizabeth Perry (eds), *Mao's Invisible Hand: The Political Foundations of Adaptive Governance in China*, Cambridge, MA: Harvard University Asia Center, pp. 297–320.

Clark, W.A.V. and Youqin Huang (2003), 'The life course and residential mobility in British housing markets', *Environment and Planning A*, **35** (2), 323–39.

Cleveland, John W. (2003), 'Does the new middle class lead today's social movements?', *Critical Sociology*, **29** (2), 163–88.

Credit Suisse (2010), *Analysing Chinese Grey Income*, 6 August 2010, Asia Pacific/China Equity Research, accessed 7 September 2012 at http://www.institutionalinvestorchina.com/arfy/uploads/soft/100925/1_1732139941.pdf.

Croll, Elisabeth (1985), *Women and Rural Development in China: Production and Reproduction*, Geneva: International Labour Office.

Croll, Elisabeth (2006), *China's New Consumers: Social Development and Domestic Demand*, London: Routledge.

Crompton, Rosemary (2010), 'Class and employment', *Work Employment Society*, **24** (1), 9–26.

'Curtain call today for Shanghai Xiangyang Market' (2006) [Shanghai Xiangyang lu shichang jinri xiemu], *Xinhua*, 1 July, accessed 7 September 2012 at http://news.xinhuanet.com/photo/2006-07/01/content_4776041.htm.

Dai, Jianzhong (2004), 'The study of owners of private enterprises in China today', in P.L. Li, Q. Li and L.P. Sun (eds), *Social Stratification in China Today*, Beijing: Social Sciences Documentation Publishing House, pp. 316–38.

Dalton, Russell and Manfred Kuechler (1990), *Challenging the Political Order: New Social Movements in Western Democracies*, Oxford: Polity.

Davis, Deborah S. (1992), 'Job mobility in post-Mao cities: increases on the margins', *The China Quarterly*, **132** (132), 1062–85.

Davis, Deborah S. (ed.) (2000), *The Consumer Revolution in Urban China*, Berkeley: University of California Press.

Delphy, Christine and Diane Leonard (1992), *Familiar Exploitation*, Oxford: Polity.

Demographia (2011), *7th Annual Demographia International Housing Affordability Survey: 2011*, accessed 7 September 2012 at www.demographia.com.

Devan, Janamitra, Micah Rowland and Jonathan Woetzel (2009), 'A consumer paradigm for China', *McKinsey Quarterly*, **4**, 36–49.

Diamond, Larry, Marc F. Plattner, Yung-Han Chu and Hung-Mao Tien (eds) (1997), *Consolidating the Third Wave Democracies: Regional Challenges*, Baltimore: Johns Hopkins University Press.

Dickson, Bruce J. (2003a), *Red Capitalists in China: The Party, Private Entrepreneurs, and Prospects for Political Change*, New York: Cambridge University Press.

Dickson, Bruce J. (2003b), 'Threats to party supremacy', *Journal of Democracy*, **14** (1), 27–35.

Dickson, Bruce J. (2004), 'Dilemmas of party adaptation: the CCP's strategies for survival', in Peter Hays Gries and Stanley Rozen (ed.), *State and Society in 21st Century China: Crisis, Contention, and Legitimation*, New York and London: RoutledgeCurzon, pp. 141–58.

Dickson, Bruce J. (2007), 'Integrating wealth and power in China: the Communist Party's embrace of the private sector', *The China Quarterly*, **192**, 827–54.

Dickson, Bruce J. (2008), *Wealth into Power: The Communist Party's Embrace of China's Private Sector*, New York: Cambridge University Press.

Dickson, Bruce J. (2010), 'China's cooperative capitalists: the business end of the middle class', in Cheng Li (ed.), *China's Emerging Middle Class*, Washington, DC Brookings Institution Press, pp. 291–306.

DiMaggio, Paul (1994), 'Social stratification, life-style, and social cognition', in D.B. Grusky (ed.), *Social Stratification: Class, Race, and Gender in Sociological Perspective*, Boulder: Westview Press, pp. 458–65.

Dong, Won Mo (1993), 'The democratization of South Korea: what role does the middle class play?', in James Cotton (ed.), *Korea under Roh Tae Woo: Democratization, Northern Policy and Inter-Korea Relations*, Sydney: Allen and Unwin, pp. 154–67.

Dong, Xiang (2011), 'Change in political values of Chinese youth since the beginning of the reform', Master's thesis, Tianjin University of Commerce.

Dou, H.M. (2010), 'State Administration of Industry and Commerce: non-state sector absorbed 90 per cent new employees', *Beijing Daily*, 12 June.

Duckett, Jane (1998), *The Entrepreneurial State in China*, London: Routledge.

Duyvendak, Jan (1995), *The Power of Politics: New Social Movements in France*, Boulder: Westview.

Eccleshall, Robert (1994), *Political Ideologies: An Introduction*, London: Routledge.

Edin, Maria (2003), 'State capacity and local agent control in China: CCP cadre management from a township perspective', *The China Quarterly*, **173**, 35–52.

Edwards, Louise (2008), 'Issue-based politics: feminism with Chinese characteristics or the return of bourgeois feminism?', in David S.G. Goodman (ed.), *The New Rich in China*, Abingdon: Routledge, pp. 201–12.

Englehart, Neil (2003), 'Democracy and the Thai middle class. Globalization, modernization, and constitutional change', *Asian Survey*, **43** (2), 253–79.

Eyal, Gil, Ivan Szelenyi and Eleanor Townsley (1998), *Making Capitalism without Capitalists: Class Formation and Elite Struggles in Post-communist Central Europe*, London: Verso.

Fang, Yiping (2006), 'Residential satisfaction, moving intention and moving behaviours: a study of redeveloped neighbourhoods in inner-city Beijing', *Housing Studies*, **21** (5), 671–94.

Farrell, Diana, Ulrich A. Gersch and Elizabeth Stephenson (2006a), 'The value of China's emerging middle class', *McKinsey Quarterly*, Special Issue, 2 June, 60–9.

Farrell, Diana, Eric Beinhocker, Ulrich A. Gersch, Ezra Greenberg, Elizabeth Stephenson, Jonathan Ablett, Mingyu Guan and Janamitra Devan (2006b), *From 'Made in China' to 'Sold in China': The Rise of the Chinese Urban Consumer*, McKinsey Global Institute, accessed 11 September 2012 at http://www.mckinsey.com/insights/mgi/research/urbanization/from_made_in_china_to_sold_in_china.

Fehér, Ferenc (ed.) (1990), *The French Revolution and the Birth of Modernity*, Berkeley: University of California Press.

Fu, Jianquan (2010), *'1980s-Birth' Generation Being 30 Years Old: A Description of Culture and Status of '1980s-Birth' Generation*, Beijing: China Yanshi Press.

Fussell, Paul (1992), *Class*, New York: Touchstone.

Gaetano, Arianne M. and Tamara Jacka (eds) (2004), *On the Move: Women in Rural-to-urban Migration in Contemporary China*, New York: Columbia University Press.

Galbraith, J.K. (1968), *The New Industrial Revolution*, London: Allen Lane.

Gao, Kaixiang (2007), 'Wuye gongsi zai goujian hexie shehui zhong gai ruhe fahui zuoyong', *Beijing fangdichan*, February, accessed 10 September 2012 at www.chinarec.com.cn/bbsxp/ShowPost.asp?action=next&id=5302.

Gerth, Karl (2003), *China Made: Consumer Culture and the Creation of the Nation*, Cambridge, MA: Harvard University Asia Center.

Gilley, Bruce (2004), *China's Democratic Future: How it Will Happen and Where it Will Lead*, New York: Columbia University Press.

Glassman, Ronald M. (1991), *China in Transition: Communism, Capitalism and Democracy*, New York: Praeger.

Glassman, Ronald M. (1995), *The Middle Class and Democracy in Socio-historical Perspective*, Leiden: E.J. Brill.

Glassman, Ronald M. (1997), *The New Middle Class and Democracy in Global Perspective*, London: Macmillan Press.

Goldthorpe, John H. (1987), *Social Mobility and Class Structure in Modern Britain*, Oxford: Clarendon Press.

Gong, Sen and Bingqin Li (2003), 'Social inequalities and wage, housing and pension reforms in urban China', Asia Programme Working Paper No. 3, The Royal Institute of International Affairs, London: Chatham House.

Gong, Yaping, Kenneth S. Law, Song Chang and Katherine R. Xin (2009), 'Human resources management and firm performance: the differential role of managerial affective and continuance commitment', *Journal of Applied Psychology*, **94** (1), 263–75.

Goodman, David S.G. (1996), 'The People's Republic of China: the party-state, capitalist revolution and new entrepreneurs', in R. Robison and David S.G. Goodman (eds), *The New Rich in Asia: Mobile Phones, McDonalds and Middle-class Revolution*, London and New York: Routledge, pp. 225–42.

Goodman, David S.G. (1999), 'The new middle class', in M. Goldman and R. MacFarquhar (eds), *The Paradox of China's Post-Mao Reforms*, Cambridge, MA: Harvard University Press.

Goodman, David S.G. (2000) 'The localism of local leadership: cadres in reform Shanxi', *Journal of Contemporary China*, **9** (24), 159–83.

Goodman, David S.G. (2001), 'The interdependence of state and society: the political sociology of local leadership', in Chien-min Chao and Bruce J. Dickson (eds), *Remaking the Chinese State: Strategies, Society and Security*, London: Routledge, pp. 132–56.

Goodman, David S.G. (ed.) (2008a), *The New Rich in China: Future Rulers, Present Lives*, Abingdon and New York: Routledge.

Goodman, David S.G. (2008b), 'Why China has no new middle class: cadres, managers and entrepreneurs', in David S.G. Goodman (ed.), *The New Rich in China*, Abingdon: Routledge, pp. 23–37.

'Government cramps space of existence for fake brands by closing Xiangyang Road Market' (2006) [Zhengfu bizi jia mingpai shengcun kongjian Shanghai Xiangyang lu shichang guanzhang], *International Business Daily*, 5 July, accessed 7 September 2012 at www.china assn.com/720.html.

Gramsci, Antonio (1975), *Letters from Prison: Antonio Gramsci*, Lynne Lawner (ed.), New York: Harper Colophon.

Gries, Peter Hays (2001), 'Tears of rage: Chinese nationalist reactions to the Belgrade Embassy bombing', *The China Journal*, **46**, 25–43.

Guo Yingjie (2008a), 'Class, stratum and group: the politics of description and prescription', in David S.G. Goodman (ed.), *The New Rich in China*, Abingdon: Routledge, pp. 38–52.

Guo Yingjie (2008b), *Middle Classes, Middle Strata, and Intermediate Groups: The Politics of Description and Classification*, London: RoutledgeCurzon.

Guo Yingjie (2009), 'Farewell to class, except the middle class: the politics of class analysis in contemporary China', *The Asia-Pacific Journal*, **26** (2), accessed 7 September 2012 at http://japanfocus.org/Yingjie-Guo/3181.

Guo Yingjie (2012), 'Political power and social inequality', in Yingjie Guo and Wanning Sun (eds), *Unequal China*, Abingdon: Routledge.

Hakim, Catherine (1998), 'Developing a sociology for the twenty-first century: preference theory', *The British Journal of Sociology*, **49** (1), 137–43.

Han, Hulong (1989), 'Middle class and China's democratization', *Theory and Exploration*, **2**, 27–9.

Han, Sung-Joo (1989), 'South Korean politics in transition', in Larry Diamond, Juan J. Linz and Seymour M. Lipset (eds), *Democracy in Developing Countries Vol. 3*, Boulder: Lynne Rienner.

Hannum, Emily and Claudia Buchmann (2005), 'Global educational expansion and socio-economic development: an assessment of finds from the social sciences', *World Development*, **33** (3), 333–54.

Hanser, Amy (2008), *Service Encounters: Class, Gender, and the Market for Social Distinction in Urban China*, Stanford, CA: Stanford University Press.

Hartmann, Heidi I. (1979), 'The unhappy marriage of Marxism and feminism: towards a more progressive union', *Capital and Class*, No. 8, 1–34.

Havighurst, Robert J. and Kenneth Feigenbaum (1959), 'Leisure and life-style', *American Journal of Sociology*, **64** (4), 396–404.

He, Jianzhang (1987), 'Adjustment of ownership system and change of class structure in the country', *Sociological Research*, **3**, 1–8.

He, Jianzhang (1988), 'Class structure of China in the present period', *Sociological Research*, **5**, 1–12.

He, Jianzhang (1990), 'A comment on middle class', *Sociological Research*, **2**, 1–9.

He, Li (2006), 'Emergence of the Chinese middle class and its implications', *Asian Affairs*, **33** (2), 67–83.

Heilmann, Sebastian and Elizabeth Perry (2011), 'Embracing uncertainty: guerilla policy style and adaptive governance in China', in Sebastian Heilmann and Elizabeth Perry (eds), *Mao's Invisible Hand: The Political Foundations of Adaptive Governance in China*, Cambridge, MA: Harvard University Asia Center, pp. 1–29.

Hendrischke, Hans (2007), 'Networks as business networks', in Barbara Krug and Hans Hendrischke (eds) *China in the 21st Century: Economic and Business Behaviour*, Cheltenham, UK and Northampton, MA, USA: Edward Elgar, pp. 227–48.

Hendrischke, Hans (2011), 'Changing legislative and institutional arrangements facing China's workplace', in Peter Sheldon, Sunghoon Kim, Yiqiong Li and Malcolm Warner (eds), *China's Changing Workplace: Dynamism, Diversity and Disparity*, London: Routledge, pp. 51–67.

Higonnet, Patrice (1990), 'Cultural upheaval and class formation during the French Revolution', in Ferenc Fehér (ed.), *The French Revolution and the Birth of Modernity*, Berkeley: University of California Press, pp. 69–101.

Hillman, Ben (2004), 'Chinese nationalism and the Belgrade Embassy bombing', in L.H. Liew and S. Wang (eds), *Nationalism, Democracy and National Integration in China*, London: Routledge Curzon, pp. 65–84.

Holbig, Heike (2002), 'The party and private entrepreneurs in the PRC', *Copenhagen Journal of Asian Studies*, **16**, 30–56.

Hood, Johanna (2012), 'Between entitlement and stigmatization: HIV/AIDS and the politics of suffering', in Yingjie Guo and Wanning Sun (eds), *Unequal China*, Abingdon: Routledge.

Hou, X.M. (2005), *The Development of Real Estate Market and Individual Housing Loan Guarantee in China*, People's Republic of China: Ministry of Construction.

Hsiao, Hsin-huang M. (1993), *Discovery of the Middle Classes in East Asia*, Taipei: Institute of Ethnology, Academia Sinica.

Hsiao, Hsin-huang M. (1999), *East Asian Middle Classes in Comparative Perspective*, Taipei: Academia Sinica.

Hsiao, Hsin-huang M. (2001), *Exploration of the Middle Classes in Southeast Asia*, Taipei: Academia Sinica.

Hsiao, Hsin-huang M. (2006), *The Changing Faces of the Middle Classes in Asia-Pacific*, Taipei: Academia Sinica.

Hsing, You-tien (2009), *The Great Urban Transformation: Politics of Land and Property in China*, Oxford: Oxford University Press.

Hsu, Carolyn L. (2007), *Creating Market Socialism: How Ordinary People are Shaping Class and Status in China*, Durham, NC: Duke University Press.

Hu, Haiyan and Wei Ma (2012), 'The private connection', *China Daily*, 27 April, accessed 10 September 2012 at http://europe. chinadaily.com.cn/epaper/2012-04/27/content_15161030.htm.

Hu, Xiuhong and David H. Kaplan (2001), 'The emergence of affluence in Beijing: residential social stratification in China's capital city', *Urban Geography*, **22** (1), 54–77.

Huang, Yasheng (2008), *Capitalism with Chinese Characteristics: Entrepreneurship and the State*, New York: Cambridge University Press.

Huang, Youqin (2005), 'From work-unit compounds to gated communities: housing inequality and residential segregation in transitional Beijing', in L.J.C. Ma and F. Wu (eds), *Restructuring the Chinese City: Changing Society, Economy and Space*, New York: Routledge, pp. 192–221.

Huang, Zeng (2005), 'Yezhu jiti weiquan shehui zuzhi kunjing yanjiu' [Study on the social and organizational deadlock of the homeowners' rights defence collective action], Master of Sociology thesis, Tsinghua Daxue.

Hull, Gloria T., Patricia Bell Scott and Barbara Smith (1982), *All the Women are White, all the Blacks are Men, but Some of Us are Brave*, Westbury, NY: Feminist Press.

Huntington, Samuel (1991), *The Third Wave: Democratization in the Late Twentieth Century*, Norman: University of Oklahoma Press.

Huntington, Samuel (2006), *Political Order in Changing Societies*, New Haven and London: Yale University Press.

Inglehart, Ronald (1977), *The Silent Revolution. Changing Values and Political Styles Among Western Democracies*, Princeton: Princeton University Press.

Inglehart, Ronald (1997), *Modernization and Post-modernization: Cultural, Economic, and Political Change in 43 Societies*, Princeton: Princeton University Press.

Inkeles, Alex (1971), *Social Change in Soviet Russia*, New York: Simon and Schuster.

Inkeles, Alex and David H. Smith (1975), *Becoming Modern: Individual Change in Six Developing Countries*, London: Heinemann Educational.

Jacka, Tamara (1997), *Women's Work in Rural China: Change and Continuity in an Era of Reform*, Cambridge: Cambridge University Press.

Jankowiak, William R. (2004), 'Market reforms, nationalism and the expansion of urban China's market moral horizon', *Urban Anthropology and Studies of Cultural Systems and World Economic Development*, **33** (2/4), 167–210.

Jiang, Wei (2011), '"Best employers" voted by university students' [2011 nian daxuesheng zuijia guzhubang fabu], *Beijing Morning Post*, 27 June.

Johnston, Alastair I. (2004), 'Chinese middle class attitudes towards international affairs: nascent liberalization?', *The China Quarterly*, **179**, 603–28.

Jones, David M. (1995), 'Democratization and the myth of the liberalizing middle class', in Daniel Bell et al. (eds), *Towards Illiberal Democracy in Pacific Asia*, Basingstoke: Palgrave Macmillan, pp. 78–106.

Jones, David M. (1998), 'Democratization, civil society and illiberal middle class culture in Pacific Asia', *Comparative Politics*, **30** (2), 147–69.

Jones, David M. and D. Brown (1994), 'Singapore and the myth of the liberalizing middle class', *Pacific Review*, **7** (1), 79–87.

Kennedy, Scott (ed.) (2011), *Beyond the Middle Kingdom: Comparative Perspectives on China's Capitalist Transformation*, Stanford: Stanford University Press.

Kim, Sungsoo (2008), *The Role of the Middle Class in Korea's Democratization*, Seoul and Edison, NJ: Jimoondang.

Kipnis, Andrew (2007), 'Neoliberalism reified: *suzhi* discourse and tropes of neoliberalism in the People's Republic of China', *Journal of the Royal Anthropological Institute*, **13** (2), 383–400.

Koo, Hagen (1991), 'Middle classes, democratization, and class formation: the case of South Korea', *Theory and Society*, **20** (4), 485–509.

Kraus, Richard (1981), *Class Conflict in Chinese Socialism*, New York: Columbia University Press.

Kriesi, Hanspeter (1995), *New Social Movements in Western Europe*, London: UCL Press.

Krug, Barbara (2004), *China's Rational Entrepreneurs: The Development of the New Private Business Sector*, London: Routledge.

Krug, Barbara and Hans Hendrischke (2010a), 'Market design in Chinese market places', *Asia Pacific Journal of Management* (online first: 25 August), 1–22.

Krug, Barbara and Hans Hendrischke (2010b), 'China's institutional architecture: interpreting the links between local governance and local enterprises', in U. Vollmer (ed.), *Institutionelle Ursachen des Wohlstands der Nationen*, Berlin: Duncker & Humblot, pp. 211–30.

Kurth, James (1979), 'Industrial change and political change', in David Collier (ed.), *The New Authoritarianism in Latin America*, Princeton: Princeton University Press.

Kurz, Karin and Hans-Peter Blossfeld (2004), 'Introduction: social stratification, welfare regimes, and access to home ownership', in K. Kurz and H.-P. Blossfeld (eds), *Home Ownership and Social Inequality in Comparative Perspective*, Stanford: Stanford University Press, pp. 1–20.

Lan, Xinzhen (2003), 'Housing policy falls short', *Beijing Review*, 8 May, 24–5.

Lan, Yahong (2011), 'Land enclosure by Beijing University in in-city village' [Beida 'Quandi' Chengzhongcun], *China Real Estate Business*, 18 July.

Leach, Robert (2002), *Political Ideology in Britain*, London: Palgrave.

Lee, Ching Kwan (1998), *Gender and the South China Miracle: Two Worlds of Factory Women*, Berkeley and Los Angeles: University of California Press.

Lee, Ching Kwan (2005), 'Livelihood struggles and market reform: (un)marking Chinese labour after state socialism', United Nations Research Institute for Social Development Paper, accessed 8 September 2012 at www.unrisd.org/publications/opgp2.

Leggett, Dave (2011), 'Vehicle market forecasts: positive outlook seen for 2011', accessed 7 September 2012 at www.just-auto.com/analysis/positive-global-outlook-seen-for-2011_id10921.

Li, Cheng (2010a), *China's Emerging Middle Class: Beyond Economic Transformation*, Washington, DC: Brookings Institution Press.

Li, Cheng (2010b), 'Chinese scholarship on the middle class: from social stratification to political potential', in Cheng Li (ed.), *China's Emerging Middle Class*, Washington, DC: Brookings Institution Press, pp. 55–83.

Li, Chunling (2010), 'Characterizing China's middle class: heterogeneous composition and multiple identities', in Cheng Li (ed.), *China's Emerging Middle Class*, Washington, DC: Brookings Institution Press.

Li, He (2006), 'Emergence of the Chinese middle class and its implications', *Asian Affairs*, **33** (2), 67–83.

Li, Hongbin and Scott Rozelle (2003), 'Privatizing rural China: insider privatization, innovative contracts and the performance of township enterprises', *The China Quarterly*, **176**, 981–1005.

Li, Jian and Xiaohan Niu (2003), 'The new middle class(es) in Peking: a case study', *China Perspectives*, **45**, 4–20.

Li, Linda Chelan (2012), *Rural Tax Reform in China: Policy Process and Institutional Change*, London: Routledge.

Li, Lulu (2008), 'Social function of middle class: a new perspective and multi-dimensional framework', *Transactions of Renmin University*, No. 4, pp. 96–105.

Li, Qiang (1999), 'Shichang zhuanxing yu Zhongguo zhongjian jieceng de daiji gengti' [Market transition and generational replacement of China's social intermediate stratum], *Zhanlue yu guanli* [*Strategy and Management*], **3**, 35–44.

Li, Qiang (2001), 'Guanyu zhongchan jieji he zhongjian jieceng' [On the middle class and the middle stratum], *Zhongguo remin daxue xuebao* [*Academic Journal of People's University*], **2**, 17–20.

Li, Si-Ming (2005), 'Residential mobility and urban change in China: what have we learned so far?', in L.J.C. Ma and F. Wu (eds), *Restructuring the Chinese City: Changing Society, Economy and Space*, New York: Routledge, pp. 175–91.

Li, Si-Ming and Youqin Huang (2006), 'Urban housing in China: market transition, housing mobility and neighbourhood change', *Housing Studies*, **21** (5) 613–23.

Li, Yang (2005), 'Zhongchan yu "chengdong" de miyue [The honeymoon between the 'middle class' and the 'eastern districts'], *Ju Zhoukan* [*Housing Weekly*], **11** (19 August).

Liang, Shaosheng (2011), *Zhongguo shehui ge jieceng fenxi* [*The Analysis of China's Social Classes*], Beijing: Wenhua meishu chubanshe.

Lin, N. (1999), 'Social networks and status attainment', *Annual Review of Sociology*, **25** (1), 467–87.

Lipset, Seymour M. (1959), 'Some social requisites of democracy: economic development and political legitimacy', *American Political Sciences Review*, **53** (1), 59–105.

Lipset, Seymour M. (1960), *Political Man: The Social Bases of Politics*, New York: Anchor Books.

Lipset, Seymour M. (1981), *Political Man: The Social Bases of Politics* (expanded edition), Baltimore: Johns Hopkins University Press.

Liu, Changjiang (2006), '"Zhongchan jieji" yanjiu: yiwen yu tanyuan' [Studies of the "middle class": questions and origins] *Shehui* [*Society*] **4**, 43–56.

Liu, Debin (1988), 'Middle class: a driving force of Western democratization', *Free Views*, **2**, 62–3.

Liu, Jieyu (2007), *Gender and Work in Urban China: Women Workers of the Unlucky Generation*, London and New York: Routledge.

Liu, Yuewen (2010), 'Shehui de shanbian: yi B shi yige yezhu lianhe zuzhi weili' [Social transmutation: an example of a joint organization of homeowners in the City of B], Master of Sociology thesis, Tsinghua Daxue.

Liu, Ziyi (2010), 'Jili yu kuozhan: fa yu shehui shijiaoxia de B shi yezhuweiquan' [Stimulate and expand: the B city homeowners' rights defence movement from a legal and social point of view], Bachelor of Sociology thesis, Tsinghua Daxue.

Logan, John R. and Yanjie Bian (1993), 'Inequality in access to community resources in a Chinese city', *Social Forces*, **72** (2), 555–76.

Logan, John R., Yanjie Bian and Fuqin Bian (1999), 'Housing inequality in urban China in the 1990s', *International Journal of Urban and Regional Research*, **23** (1), 7–25.

Low, Setha (2001), 'The edge and the centre: gated communities and the discourse of urban fear', *American Anthropologist*, **103** (1), 45–58.

Low, Setha (2003), *Behind the Gates: Life, Security, and the Pursuit of Happiness in Fortress America*, New York: Routledge.

Lu, Pierre Xiao (2008), *Elite China: Luxury Consumer Behaviour in China*, New York: Wiley.

Lü, Xiaobo and Elizabeth J. Perry (1997), *Danwei: The Changing Chinese Workplace in Historical and Comparative Perspectives*, Armonk, NY: M.E. Sharpe.

Lu, Xueyi (2001), *2002 Report on Social Classes of the Contemporary China*, Beijing: Social Science Academic Press.

Lu, Xueyi (2004), *Social Mobility in Contemporary China* [*Dangdai Zhongguo Shehui Liudong*], Beijing: Shehui kexue wenxian chubanshe.

Lu, Xueyi, Guokai Song, Jianguo Hu and Xiaozhuang Li (2009), 'Xin jieduan shehui jianshe de hexin renwu: tiaozheng shehui jiegou' [The core tasks of social construction in the new stage: adjustment of the social structure], in X. Ru, X. Lu and P. Li (eds), *2010 nian Zhongguo shehui xingshi fenxi yu yuce* [*Society of China: Analysis and Forecast 2010*], pp. 191–206.

Lukacs, Georg ([1922] 1968), *History and Class Consciousness*, Cambridge, MA: MIT Press.

Luo, Xiaowei and Yongjie Sha (eds) (2002), *Shanghai Xintiandi*, Nanjing: Nanjing daxue chubanshe.

Martin, Patricia Y. (2001), 'Mobilizing masculinities: women's experiences of men at work', *Organization*, **8** (4), 587–618.

McCall, Phil (2008), '"We had to stick together": individual preferences, collective struggle, and the formation of social consciousness', *Science & Society*, **72** (2), 147–81.

McNally, Christopher A. (2008), 'The institutional contours of China's emergent capitalism', in C.A. McNally (ed.), *China's Emergent Political Economy: Capitalism in the Dragon's Lair*, Abingdon, Oxford and New York: Routledge, pp. 102–25.

Melucci, Alberto (1982), *L'Invenzione del Presente. Movimenti Sociali Nelle Società Comesse*, Bologna: Il Mulino.

Mengin, Françoise (2000), 'Taiwan: la question nationale et la démocratisation' [Taiwan: the national question and democratization], in Christophe Jaffrelot (ed.), *Démocraties d'ailleurs*, Paris: Karthala, pp. 587–616.

Mertha, Andrew C. (2011), *China's Water Warriors: Citizen Action and Policy Change*, Ithaca, NY: Cornell University Press.

Metraux, Daniel (1991), *Taiwan's Political and Economic Growth in the Late Twentieth Century*, Lampeter: Edwin Mellen Press.

Mills, C. Wright ([1951] 2002), *White Collar: The American Middle Classes*, New York: Oxford University Press.

Mooers, Colin (1991), *The Making of Bourgeois Europe: Absolutism, Revolution, and the Rise of Capitalism in England, France and Germany*, London: Verso.

Moore, Barrington (1966), *Social Origins of Dictatorship and Democracy: Lord and Peasant in the Making of the Modern World*, Boston: Beacon Press.

Munro, Anne (2001), 'A feminist trade union agenda? The continued significance of class, gender and race', *Gender Work and Organization*, **8** (4), 454–73.

Murphey, Rhoads (1980), *The Fading of the Maoist Vision: City and Country in China's Development*, London and Toronto: Methuen.

Nathan, Andrew J. and Helena V.S. Ho (1997), 'The decision for reform in Taiwan', in Andrew J. Nathan et al., *China's Transition*, New York: Columbia University Press, pp. 90–111.

Naughton, Barry (2010), 'China's distinctive system: can it be a model for others?', *Journal of Contemporary China*, **19** (65), 437–60.

Nee, Victor and Sonja Opper (2010), 'Endogenous institutional change and dynamic capitalism', *Sociologia del lavoro*, **118**, 1110–35, accessed 10 September 2012 at http://www.soc.cornell.edu/faculty/nee/pubs/EndogenousInstitutionalChange%20Nee_Opper.pdf.

Nee, Victor and Sonja Opper (2012), *Capitalism from Below: Markets and Institutional Change in China*, Cambridge, MA: Harvard University Press.

'Netizens hone in on housing vacancy rate' (2010), *People's Daily Online*, 17 August, accessed 7 September 2012 at http://english.peopledaily.com.cn/90001/90776/90882/7106629.html.

'New Shanghai ICC: green, elegant and efficient' (2010), *The China Daily*, 8 December, accessed 7 September 2012 at www.chinadaily.com.cn/cndy/2010-12/08/content_11667304.htm.

Nisbet, Robert (1986), *Conservatism*, Buckingham: Open University Press.

Nyiri, Pal, Juan Zhang and Merriden Varrall (2010), 'China's cosmopolitan nationalists: "heroes" and "traitors" of the 2008 Olympics', *The China Journal*, **63**, 25–55.

Ockey, Jim (1999), 'Creating the Thai middle class', in Michael Pinches (ed.), *Culture and Privilege in Capitalist Asia*, New York and London: Routledge, pp. 231–51.

O'Donnell, Guillermo and Phillipe Schmitter (1986), *Transitions from Authoritarian Rule: Tentative Conclusions and Uncertain Democracies*, Baltimore: Johns Hopkins University Press.

Oi, Jean C. (1995), 'The role of the local state in China's transitional economy', *China Quarterly Special Issue: China's Transitional Economy*, **144**, 1132–49.

Oi, Jean C. and Andrew Walder (1999), 'Property rights in the Chinese economy: contours of process of change', in Jean C. Oi and Andrew Walder (eds), *Property Rights and Economic Reform in China*, Stanford: Stanford University Press, pp. 1–26.

Oppenheimer, M. (1985), *White Collar Politics*, New York: Monthly Review Press.

Pearson, Margaret M. (1997), *China's New Business Elite: The Political Consequences of Economic Reform*, Berkeley: University of California Press.

Pilbeam, Pamela (1990), *The Middle Classes in Europe, 1789–1914: France, Germany, Italy, and Russia*, London: Lyceum Books.

Pinches, Michael (1999), *Culture and Privilege in Capitalist Asia*, New York/London: Routledge.

Pizzigati, Samuel (2010), 'Long live the statistical middle class!', *Labour Studies Journal*, **35**(3), 386–97.

Pollert, Anne (1981), *Girls, Wives, Factory Lives*, Basingstoke: Macmillan.

Pollert, Anne (1996), 'Gender and class revisited; or, the poverty of "patriarchy"', *Sociology*, **30** (4), 639–59.

Pow, Choon-Piew (2009), *Gated Communities in China: Class, Privilege and the Moral Politics of the Good Life*, London and New York: Routledge.

Pun, Ngan (2005), *Made in China: Women Factory Workers in a Global Workplace*, Durham, NC: Duke University Press.

Qian, Yingyi (2000), 'The process of China's market transition 1978–98: the evolutionary, historical, and comparative perspectives', *Journal of Institutional and Theoretical Economics*, **156**, 151–71.

Ravallion, Martin (2009), 'The developing world's bulging (but vulnerable) "middle class"', Policy Research Working Paper No. 4816, The World Bank Development Research Group.

Read, Benjamin (2003), 'Democratizing the neighbourhood? New private housing and home-owner self-organization in urban China', *The China Journal*, **49**, 31–59.

Read, Benjamin (2008), 'Assessing variation in civil society organizations: China's homeowner associations in comparative perspective', *Comparative Political Studies*, **41** (9), 1240–65.

Rex, John and R. Moore (1967), *Race, Community and Conflict: A Study of Sparkbrook*, Oxford: Oxford University Press.

Robison, Richard and David S.G. Goodman (1992), 'The new rich in Asia: affluence, mobility and power', *The Pacific Review*, **5** (4), 321–7.

Robison, Richard and David S.G. Goodman (1996), 'The new rich in Asia: economic development, social status and political consciousness', in R. Robison and David S.G. Goodman (eds), *The New Rich in Asia: Mobile Phones, McDonalds and Middle-Class Revolution*, London and New York: Routledge, pp. 1–18.

Rocca, Jean-Louis (2008), 'Power of knowledge: the imaginary formation of the Chinese middle class stratum in an era of growth and stability', in Christophe Jaffrelot and Peter van der Veer (eds), *Patterns of Middle Class Consumption in India and China*, Los Angeles, London, New Delhi and Singapore: Sage, pp. 127–39.

Rocca, Jean-Louis (2009), 'Zhengzhi jiaocha, shehui biaozheng yu xueshu ganyu : zhongchan jiejie zai zhongguo de xingcheng' [Political crossroads, social representations and academic intervention: the formation of a middle class in China], in Li Chunling (ed.), *Bijiao shiyexia zhongguo zhongchan jieji xingcheng* [*The Formation of the Chinese Middle Class from a Comparative Point of View*], Beijing: Shehui kexue chunbanshe, pp. 122–38.

Rofel, Lisa (1999), *Other Modernities: Gendered Yearnings in China After Socialism*, Berkeley and Los Angeles: University of California Press.

Rofel, Lisa (2012), 'Grassroots activism: non-normative sexual politics in post-socialist China', in Yingjie Guo and Wanning Sun (eds), *Unequal China*, Abingdon: Routledge, pp. 231–52.

Rosen, Kenneth T. and Madelyn C. Ross (2000), 'Increasing home ownership in urban China: notes on the problem of affordability', *Housing Studies*, **15** (1), 77–88.

Rosen, Stanley (2004a), 'The state of youth/youth and the state in early 21st century China: the triumph of the urban rich?', in P.H. Gries and S. Rosen (eds), *State and Society in 21st Century China*, New York and London: Routledge Curzon, pp. 159–79.

Rosen, Stanley (2004b), 'The victory of materialism: aspirations to join China's urban moneyed classes and the commercialization of education', *The China Journal*, **51**, 27–51.

Rossi, P.H. (1980), *Why Families Move*, Beverly Hills: Sage Publications.

Rostow, Walt (1960), *The Stages of Economic Growth*, Cambridge: Cambridge University Press.

Santoro, Michael (2009), *China 2020: How Western Business Can – and Should – Influence Social and Political Change in the Coming Decade*, Ithaca, NY: Cornell University Press.

Saunders, P. (1990), *A Nation of Home Owners*, London: Unwin Hyman.

Sautman, Barry (1992), 'Sirens of the strongman: neo-authoritarianism in recent Chinese political theory', *The China Quarterly*, **129**, 72–102.

Savage, Mike, James Barlow, Peter Dickens and Tony Fielding (1995), *Property, Bureaucracy and Culture: Middle Class Formation in Contemporary Britain*, London: Routledge.

'Shanghai suppresses counterfeit international brands: Carrefour is sentenced to pay compensation, Xiangyang Road closes' [Shanghai weijiao jiamao guoji mingpai: jialefu panpei Xiangyang lu guanbi] (2006), *China Youth Daily*, 21 April, accessed 7 September at http://news.xinhuanet.com/fortune/2006-04/21/content_4455183.htm.

Shi, Yuntong (2008), 'Youchanzhe de kangzheng yu shehui de shengchan: B shi yezhu weiquan de leixing yanjiu' [The resistance against the wealthy and the birth of society: a study on homeowners' rights defence movement], Master of Sociology thesis, Tsinghua Daxue.

Shin, Doh Chull (1994), 'On the third wave of democratization: a synthesis and evaluation of recent theory and research', *World Politics*, **47** (1), 135–70.

SHKP (Sun Hung Kai Properties) (2007), 'Re-branded Beijing apm to redefine shopping in the capital', press release, accessed 7 September at www.shkp.com/en-US/Pages/press-release-detail/1018.

'SHKP lands Nike in race to reprise mall success' (2007), *The Standard* [Hong Kong], 8 June, accessed 7 September at http://www.the

standard.com.hk/news_detail.asp?we_cat=2&art_id=46332&sid=1396 9203&con_type=1&d_str=20070608&fc=8.

Skeggs, Beverly (2005), 'The re-branding of class: propertizing culture', in F. Devine, M. Savage, J. Scott and R. Crompton (eds), *Rethinking Class: Culture, Identities and Lifestyles*, Basingstoke: Palgrave Macmillan, pp. 46–68.

Sklair, Leslie (2001), *The Transnational Capitalist Class*, Oxford: Blackwell.

So, Alvin Y. (2003), 'The changing pattern of classes and class conflict in China', *Journal of Contemporary Asia*, **33** (3), 363–76.

Spanou, Calliope (1991), *Militants et Fonctionnaires: l'Administration et les Nouveaux Milieux Sociaux*, [*Activists and Officials: Administration and the New Social Order*] Paris: L'Harmattan.

Stark, David (1991), 'Path dependence and privatization strategies in East Central Europe', *East European Politics & Societies*, **6**, 17–54.

State Administration for Industry and Commerce of the PRC (2010) 'Private and non-state enterprises absorbed over 90 per cent of new entrants to the labour market', 11 June.

Sun, Liping (2004), *Imbalance: The Logic of a Fractured Society*, Beijing: Social Sciences Academic Press (China).

Sun, Wanning (2008), 'Men, women and the maid: at home with the new rich', in David S.G. Goodman (ed.), *The New Rich in China*, Abingdon: Routledge, pp. 213–28.

Tan, Li (2008), 'Gongmin rentong-Yi yezhu weiquan yundong weili' [Citizens' identity. The example of homeowners' rights defence movement], Bachelor of Sociology thesis, Tsinghua Daxue.

Tang, Beibei (2009), 'The making of housing status groups in post reform urban China: social mobility and status attainment of gated community residents in Shenyang', PhD dissertation, Australian National University, Canberra.

Tarrow, Sydney (1989), *Democracy and Disorder: Protest and Politics in Italy, 1965–75*, Oxford: Clarendon Press.

Thompson, E.P. (1968), *The Making of the English Working Class*, Harmondsworth: Penguin.

Tien, Hung-mao (1996), *Taiwan's Electoral Politics and Democratic Transition: Riding the Third Wave*, Armonk, NY: M.E. Sharpe.

Tilly, Charles (1990), 'State and counterrevolution in France', in Ferenc Fehér (ed.), *The French Revolution and the Birth of Modernity*, Berkeley: University of California Press, pp. 49–69.

Tomba, Luigi (2004), 'Creating an urban middle class: social engineering in Beijing', *The China Journal*, **51**, 1–26.

Tomba, Luigi (2005), 'Residential space and collective interest formation in Beijing's housing disputes', *The China Quarterly*, **184** (1), 934–51.

Tomba, Luigi (2008), 'Making neighbourhoods: the government of social change in China's cities', *China Perspective*, **4**, 48–61.

Tomba, Luigi (2009a), 'Gating urban spaces: inclusion, exclusion and government', in S. Bagaeen and O. Uduku (eds), *Gated Communities: Social Sustainability in Contemporary and Historical Gated Developments*, London: Earthscan, pp. 27–38.

Tomba, Luigi (2009b), 'Of quality harmony and community. Civilization and the middle class in urban China', *Positions: East Asia Cultures Critique*, **17** (3), 592–616.

Tomba, Luigi and Beibei Tang (2008), 'The Forest City: homeownership and new wealth in Shenyang', in David S.G. Goodman (ed.), *The New Rich in China*, Abingdon: Routledge, pp. 171–86.

Touraine, Alain (1978), *La Voix et le Regard* [*The Voice and the Look*] Paris: Seuil.

Tsai, Kellee S. (2002), *Back-alley Banking: Private Entrepreneurs in China*, Ithaca, NY: Cornell University Press.

Tsai, Kellee S. (2005), 'Capitalists without a class: political diversity among private entrepreneurs in China', *Comparative Political Studies*, **38** (9), 1130–58.

Tsai, Kellee S. (2007), *Capitalism without Democracy: The Private Sector in Contemporary China*, Ithaca, NY: Cornell University Press.

Tsai, Kellee S. (2011), 'Comparing China's capitalists: neither democratic nor exceptional', in Scott Kennedy (ed.), *Beyond the Middle Kingdom*, Stanford: Stanford University Press, pp. 136–58.

Tsinghua daxue shehuixuexi shehui fazhan yanjiu kejizu [Tsinghua University Sociology Department Research Group on Social Development] (2010), 'Yiliyi biaoda zhiduhua shixian shehui de changzhijiuan' [Relying on an institutionalization of interest groups voicing to ensure a long period of order and stability], *Tsinghua shehui fazhan luntan* [*Tsinghua Forum of Social Development*], April.

Tsui, Anne S., Yanjie Bian and Leonard Cheng (eds) (2006), *China's Domestic Private Firms: Multidisciplinary Perspectives on Management and Performance*, New York: M.E. Sharpe, pp. 1–24.

Tsui, Ming and Lynne Rich (2002), 'The only child and educational opportunity for girls in urban China', *Gender and Society*, **16** (1), 74–92.

Unger, Jonathan (1982), *Education under Mao: Class and Competition in Canton Schools, 1960–1980*, New York: Columbia University Press.

Unger, Jonathan (1996), '"Bridges": private business, the Chinese government, and the rise of new associations', *The China Quarterly*, **147**, 795–819.

Unger, Jonathan (2002), *The Transformation of Rural China*, Armonk, NY: M.E. Sharpe.

Unger, Jonathan and Anita Chan (1999), 'Inheritors of the boom: private enterprise and the role of local government in a rural south China township', *The China Journal*, **42**, 45–74.

Veblen, Thorstein (1939), *The Theory of the Leisure Class*, New York: The Modern Library.

Wajcman, Judy (1991), *Feminism Confronts Technology*, Pennsylvania: Penn State University Press.

Walby, Sylvia (1986), *Patriarchy at Work*, Cambridge: Polity.

Walby, Sylvia (1990), 'Theorising patriarchy', *Sociology* **23** (2), 213–34.

Walder, Andrew G. (1986), *Communist Neo-traditionalism: Work and Authority in Chinese Industry*, Berkeley: University of California Press.

Walder, Andrew G. (2002), 'Markets and income inequality in rural China: political advantage in an expanding economy', *American Sociological Review*, **67** (2), 231–53.

Walder, Andrew G. (2003), 'Elite opportunity in transitional economies', *American Sociological Review*, **68** (6), 899–917.

Walder, Andrew G. (2006), 'China's private sector: a global perspective', in A.S. Tsui, Y.J. Bian and L. Cheng (eds), *China's Domestic Private Firms: Multidisciplinary Perspectives on Management and Performance*, New York: M.E. Sharpe, pp. 311–26.

Walder, Andrew G. and Songhua Hu (2009), 'Revolution, reform, and status inheritance: urban China, 1949–1996', *American Journal of Sociology*, **114** (5), 1395–427.

Wang, Jianying and Deborah Davis (2010), 'China's new upper middle classes: the importance of occupational disaggregation', in Cheng Li (ed.), *China's Emerging Middle Class*, Washington, DC: Brookings Institution, pp. 157–76.

Wang, Le (2010), 'Evaluation on research funding applications should not be formatted' [Xueshu pingshen buneng liuyu xingshi], *Wenhui Bao*, 9 July.

Wang, Yalin (2003), *Chengshi xiuxian: Shanghai, Tianjin, Haerbin chengshi jumin shijian fenpei de kaocha* [*Report on the Distribution of Time among Urban Residents in Shanghai, Tianjin and Haerbin*], Shehui kexue wenxian chubanshe.

Wang, Yaping and Alan Murie (1996), 'The process of commercialisation of urban housing in China', *Urban Studies*, **33** (6), 971–89.

Wang, Yaping and Alan Murie (2000), 'Social and spatial implications of housing reform in China', *International Journal of Urban and Regional Research*, **24** (2), 397–417.

Wang, Yijun (2011), 'The number of CCP members reaches 80,269,000' [Zhongguo Gongchandang dangyuan zongshu 8026.9 wan ming], *Xinmin Evening Post*, 24 June.

Wang, Zheng (2000), 'Gender, employment and women's resistance', in Elisabeth Perry and Mark Selden (eds), *Chinese Society: Change, Conflict and Resistance* (1st edition), London and New York: Routledge, pp. 62–82.

Wank, David L. (1995a), 'Bureaucratic patronage and private business: changing networks of power in urban China', in A.G. Walder (ed.), *The Waning of the Communist State: Economic Origins of Political Decline in China and Hungary*, London: University of California Press, pp. 153–83.

Wank, David L. (1995b), 'Private business, bureaucracy, and political alliance in a Chinese city', *The Australian Journal of Chinese Affairs*, **33**, 55–71.

Wank, David L. (1996), 'The institutional process of market clientelism: *guanxi* and private business in a south China city', *China Quarterly*, **147**, 820–38.

Weber, Max, G. Roth and C. Wittich (eds) (1978), *Economy and Society: An Outline of Interpretive Sociology*, Berkeley: University of California Press.

Webster, Chris J. (2001), 'Gated cities of tomorrow', *Town Planning Review*, **72** (2), 149–70.

Whyte, Martin King (2010), *Myth of the Social Volcano: Perceptions of Inequality and Distributive Injustice in Contemporary China*, Stanford: Stanford University Press.

Wolf, Margaret (1985), *Revolution Postponed: Women in Contemporary China*, Stanford: Stanford University Press.

Wright, Erik Olin (1997), *Class Counts: Comparative Studies in Class Analysis*, New York: Cambridge University Press.

Wright, Erik Olin (2005), *Approaches to Class Analysis*, Cambridge: Cambridge University Press.

Wu, Fulong (2002), 'Sociospatial differentiation in urban China: evidence from Shanghai's real estate markets', *Environment and Planning A*, **34** (9), 1591–615.

Wu, Fulong (2004), 'Urban poverty and marginalization under market transition', *International Journal of Urban and Regional Research*, **28** (2), 401–23.

Wu, Fulong (2005), 'Rediscovering the "gate" under market transition: from work-unit compounds to commodity housing enclaves', *Housing Studies*, **20** (2), 235–54.

Wu, Xiaogang (2002), 'Work units and income inequality: the effect of market transition in urban China', *Social Forces*, **80** (3), 1069–99.

Wu, Xiaoyin (2006), 'Intergenerational conflict and the change of youth discourse', *Youth Studies*, **8**, 16–22.

'Wuquanfa shishi xianqi yezhu weiquan gaochao, peitao fagui jidai chutai' [The implementation of the law on the real estate law sets off an upsurge of homeowners' rights defence movements. Set of rules need prompt publishing] (2007), *Zhongguo qingnianbao* [*Journal of Chinese Youth*], 26 October, accessed 10 September 2012 at http://law.cctv.com/20071026/100614.shtml.

'Xiangyang Market also has originality' [Xiangyang lu shichang ye you yuanchuang] (2006), *Liberation Daily*, 4 January, accessed 7 September 2012 at http://jfdaily.eastday.com/eastday/node4/node101/node2993/userobject1ai44213.html.

Xie, Andy (2010), 'Fear empty flats in China's property bubble', *Caixin*, 3 August, accessed 7 September 2012 at http://english.caixin.cn/2010-08-03/100166589.html.

Xie, Yu and Xiaogang Wu (2008), 'Danwei profitability and earnings inequality in urban China', *The China Quarterly*, **195**, 558–81.

Xin, Katherine R. and Jone L. Pearce (1996), '*Guanxi*: connections as substitutes for formal institutional support', *Academy of Management Journal*, **39** (6), 1641–58.

Xinhua (2010), 'Five sins of university administrativization' [Daxue Xingzhenghua wu zong zui], accessed 9 Sepember 2012 at http://news.xinhuanet.com/comments/2010-02/11/content_12967503.htm.

Xu, Feng (2008), 'Gated communities and migrant enclaves: the conundrum for building "harmonious community/shequ"', *Journal of Contemporary China*, **17** (57), 633–51.

Xue, Charlie Q.L. (2006), *Building a Revolution: Chinese Architecture since 1980*, Hong Kong: Hong Kong University Press.

Xue, Charlie Q.L. (2008), *Building Practice in China*, Beijing: China Architecture and Building Press.

Xue, Charlie Q.L. (2010), *World Architecture in China*, Hong Kong: Joint Publishing.

Yang, Huayun (2009), 'National public servant admission rate sets record of 93:1' [Guokao zhaolubi 93:1 chuangxingao], *Beijing News*, 27 October.

Yang, Keming (2007), *Entrepreneurship in China*, Aldershot: Ashgate.

Yang, Shixing (2011), 'Price of Qinghua's self-built housing is lower than market price' [Qinghua Zijianfang jiage diyu shichangjia], *China Times*, 11 June.

Yueh, Linda (2011), *Enterprising China: Business, Economic and Legal Developments since 1979*, Oxford: Oxford University Press.

Zang, Xiaowei (2001), 'Educational credentials, elite dualism, and elite stratification in China', *Sociological Perspectives*, **44** (2), 189–205.

Zang, Xiaowei (2008), 'Market transition, wealth and status claims', in David S.G. Goodman (ed.), *The New Rich in China*, Abingdon: Routledge, pp. 53–70.

Zelin, Madeleine (2009), 'The firm in early Modern China', *Journal of Economic Behavior and Organization*, **71** (3), 623–37.

Zhang, Jianming (1998), 'Status quo and trend of middle class in urban China', *Transactions of Renmin University of China*, **5**, 62–7.

Zhang, Lei (2005), 'Yezhuweiquanyundong: chansheng yuanyin ji dongyuan jizhi- duibeijingshijige xiaoqu gean de kaocha' [Homeowners' rights defence movements: causes of emergence and mechanisms of mobilization. A research on ten cases], *Shehuiyanjiu* [*Social Studies*], **6**, 1–39.

Zhang, Li (2010), *In Search of Paradise: Middle-class Living in a Chinese Metropolis*, Ithaca, NY: Cornell University Press.

Zhang, Xing Quan (2000), 'The restructuring of the housing finance system in urban China', *Cities*, **17** (5), 339–48.

Zhang, Xing Quan (2002), 'Governing housing in China: state, market and work units', *Journal of Housing and the Built Environment*, **17** (1), 7–20.

Zhang, Xing Quan and Kioe Sheng Yap (2002), 'State and market: governing housing in Asia', *Journal of Housing and the Built Environment*, **17** (1), 1–6.

Zhang, Yi (2009), 'Is middle class a social stabilizer?', in Li Chunling (ed.), *Formation of Middle Class in Comparative Perspective: Process, Influence and Socioeconomic Consequences*, Beijing: Social Science Academic Press, pp. 231–51.

Zheng, Hangsheng and Lulu Li (2004), 'Private entrepreneurs and the change of social stratification', in H.S. Zheng and L.L. Li (eds), *Social Structure of the Cities in Contemporary China*, Beijing: People's University Press.

Zheng, Yongnian (2004), *Will China Become Democratic? Elite, Class and Regime Transition*, Singapore: Eastern Universities Press.

Zheng, Yongnian (2006), 'The party, class, and democracy in China', in Karl-Eric Brodsgaard and Yongnian Zheng (eds) *The Chinese Communist Party in Reform*, New York: Routledge, pp. 231–60.

'Zhongguo shehui diaochasuo de diaocha xianshi, jiucheng wuguangongsi zhuan "heixinqian"' [A survey of the Chinese Society Research Center reveals that 90% of management companies earn "black money"], (2006), *Beijing yule xinbao* [*Beijing Entertainment Economic Journal*], 3 September, accessed 10 September 2012 at www.beyoyo.net/x2q/bbs/viewthread.php?tid=2841&extra=page%3D1 59.

Zhou, Xiaohong (ed.) (2005), *Zhongguo zhongchanjieceng diaocha* [*Survey of the Chinese Middle Classes*], Beijing: Shehui kexue wenxian chubanshe [Social Science Academic Press].

Zhou, Xueguang (2004), *The State and Life Chances in Urban China*, Cambridge: Cambridge University Press.

Zhou, Xueguang, Nancy Brandon Tuma and Phyllis Moen (1997), 'Institutional change and job-shift patterns in urban China, 1949–1994', *American Sociological Review*, **62** (3), 339–65.

Zhu, Ronglin (2009), *Jiedu Tianzifang* [*Interpreting Tianzifang*], Shanghai: Wenhui chubanshe.

Zhu, Yaoqun (2005), *Zhongchan jieceng yu hexie shehui* [*Middle Strata and Harmonious Society*], Beijing: Zhongguo renmin gong'an daxue chubanshe.

Zou, Lixia (2009), 'Shehui zizhiguanli: boyi yu tuoxie' [Self-management by the society: game and compromise], *Fazhi yu shehui* [*Legal System and Society*], **12**, 265–66.

Index

production–consumption dynamic 45
production–consumption shift 50
production-led domestic economy 34
professionals 59, 64, 90–91
    and class 68, 69
    intellectuals 92–109
    and *suzhi* 71–2, 72, 73, 103
profits 81, 150, 161
property 38–9
    development 43–6, 50
    disputes 73, 118–21
    recognition 152
    redevelopment 52
Property Law, 2007 130
property rights 17, 73, 111, 117, 139,
    145, 154
protests 91, 104, 106, 114, 115, 119–32
public–private enterprises 6
public sector
    and contracts 102
    desirability of posts 102–3
    as good employers 101
public sector employees 55, 60, 64, 68,
    69, 91, 100
    and housing 96–9
    and *suzhi* 70, 71–2
public social status 139
Pudong 46, 47
'pull' factors 165
'push' factors 165
Puxi 46 '

'Q' 130
Qing 84–5
qipao 46
quality 69–73

real estate 38–9
    see also property
real estate companies 44–5, 48, 50, 118,
    119, 121
real estate interest group 128
red capitalists 152
'red hat' enterprises 139
'red hat' entrepreneurs 144
'reds' 92, 94

'Regulations on Estate Management',
    March 2007 117
remuneration 80–82
    see also salaries
research market 95–6
residents' committees 72, 118
resistance strategy 83–4, 89
retail space development 43–6
revenues of private enterprises 150
rewards 56, 57, 95, 101, 154
rights of homeowners 127
risks 11, 154, 165
rural collectives 6
rural population 105, 164
Russia 106

salaries 68–9, 81–2, 102
    professionals 92, 93–6
    public sector employees 91
sales assistants
    attitude to female senior managers
        86–7
    attitude to junior male staff 88
    pay 81–2
    role 78, 83–5, 88, 89
sales department of state-owned foreign
    trade company 77–80
sales managers
    pay 81, 82
    role 78, 79–80, 84–5, 88
satisfaction 17, 18
schools 63–4
S/COEs 158, 160, 161, 162, 166
secondary industries 158, 160
sector sales manager, role 78
security
    economic 14
    for homes 58–9, 120–21
    jobs 100, 101
'self-built' apartments 97
self-employed 90, 164
    see also private entrepreneurs
self-made entrepreneurs 152
self-regulation 142
senior managers 86–7
    see also sales managers
service sector 163–4